THE LIFE, STYLE AND MUSIC OF

SABRINA CARPENTER

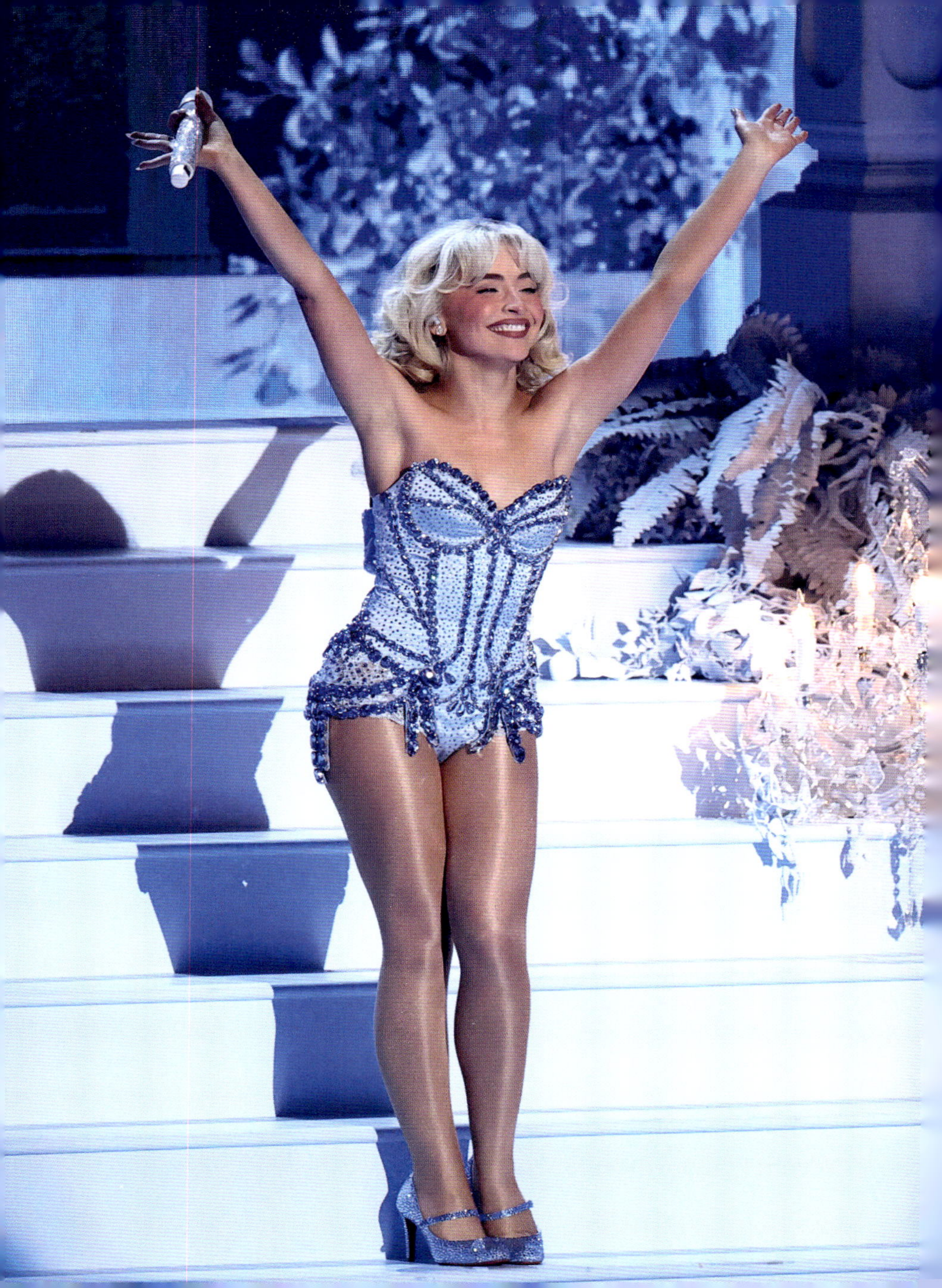

THE LIFE, STYLE AND MUSIC OF SABRINA CARPENTER

UNOFFICIAL AND UNAUTHORIZED

BY ERICA CAMPBELL

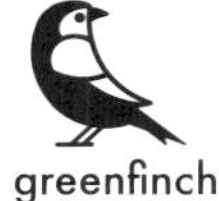

greenfinch

CONTENTS

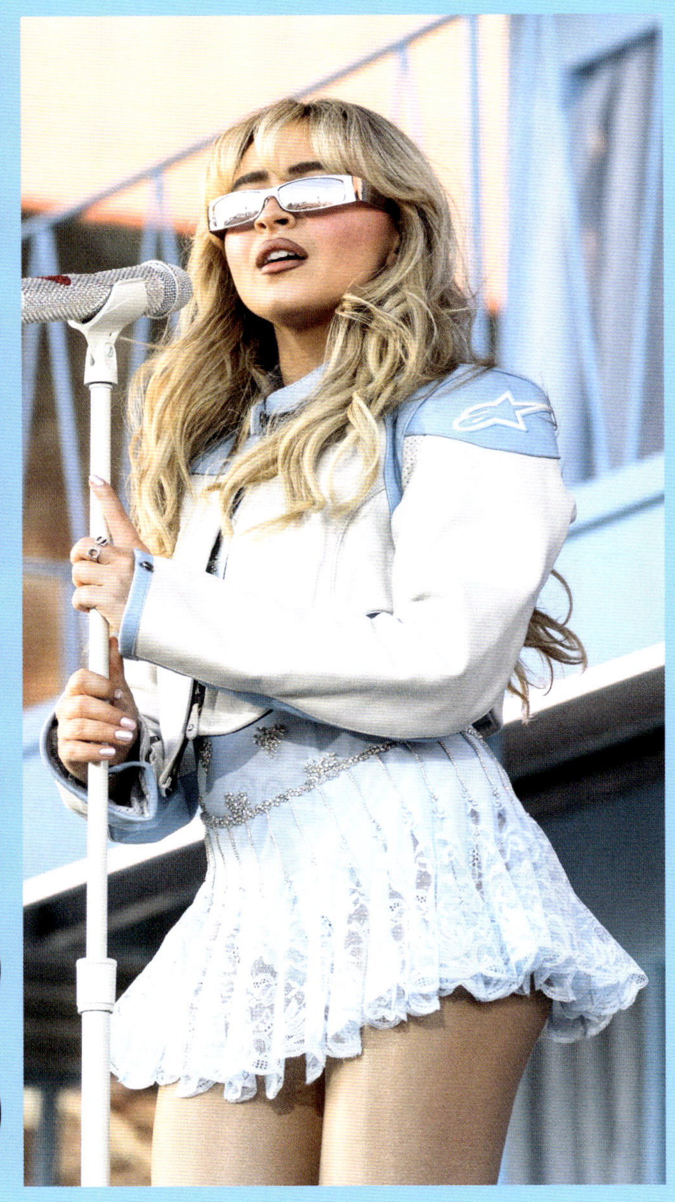

FROM DISNEY DARLING TO POP *Princess*

Introducing Sabrina Annlynn Carpenter

In the early spring of 2024, a soon-to-be pop-music juggernaut, standing at just five feet tall and wearing a pink, heart-ornamented minidress, and with bright blonde ringlets framing her face, spoke three words that would ultimately push her from the corners of pop-culture consciousness to its beating centre.

'This is "Espresso",' Sabrina Carpenter purred at the throng of fans dancing beneath her in the California desert heat, adding a flirty, 'We hope you love it, Coachella!' They did.

That performance – promoted by billboards lining the road to the festival grounds that showed a larger-than-life Sabrina in a vintage, light-blue Victoria's Secret babydoll nightgown the same colour as her eyes, and the words 'She's gonna make you come ... to her Coachella set!' beneath her – was the world's first live taste of 'Espresso'.

From the moment the lo-fi funky opening beat hit the ears of Carpenter's fans, they were insatiable for the caffeinated hit, pushing the track to Song of the Summer status (based on its millions of Spotify streams and Billboard chart data) and making the absurd yet infectious line 'that's that me espresso' a viral catchphrase. Less than a year after that desert showcase, Carpenter would perform the cheeky disco track at the 67th Annual Grammy Awards. That same night, 'Espresso' won the Grammy for Best Pop Solo Performance.

For many watching her quickly rise up the charts, it seemed like the pint-sized singer had appeared overnight. But, for Carpenter, the song's success was a goal she'd been working towards for more than a decade – the result of five albums released between 2015 and 2022, a fruitful acting career, the support of family, friends and fans, and a massive amount of self-belief. 'I always knew deep down that this was something I would do with my life,' she told *PAPER* magazine a few months after her Coachella debut. 'I didn't ever really doubt that.'

p.2: Performing at the 67th Annual Grammy Awards, Los Angeles, February 2025
p.4: Performing at Coachella Valley Music and Arts Festival, Indio, April 2024

POP PROPHECY

Sabrina Annlynn Carpenter was born on 11 May 1999 in Quakertown, Pennsylvania, and grew up outside of Philadelphia in East Greenville, Pennsylvania. Her parents, David Carpenter and Elizabeth Carpenter, a former dancer, have consistently supported her career. (Sabrina says David once said he was in a band, but that it was a garage band and she doesn't really know if that's true.) The youngest of four daughters, she was home-schooled with her siblings, who also happen to have pursued creative careers: Cayla is a hairstylist, Shannon is a dancer and Sarah is also a singer. Sabrina's tight-knit family includes her aunt Nancy Cartwright, the voice actress known for her portrayal of Bart Simpson in *The Simpsons*, so it's safe to say that extraordinary vocal talent was always in her blood. At only two years old, she enrolled in ballet and practised jazz, hip-hop, lyrical and modern dance, following in her mother's footsteps. She'd turn a night out with family into a chance to show off her chops, singing for patrons at her hometown's Irish pub at the request of a friendly waitress, who got her to sing 'Happy Birthday'. Customers would try to tip the small singer, but her mum would make her give the cash back. Sabrina recalls the customers of the Limeport Inn as her first real audience.

The first official hint that Sabrina's pop prophecy would come to fruition happened when she was just nine years old. Ambitious and precocious, she started posting covers of her favourite songs on YouTube, emulating the delivery of her idols: Taylor Swift's 'Picture to Burn', Adele's 'Set Fire to the Rain' and Christina Aguilera's 'Beautiful'. She even taught herself how to play piano, and then guitar, to upgrade her performances. She used those same videos in her submission to a contest run by one of her heroes – a singing competition called *The Next Miley Cyrus Project*. As a big Cyrus stan, Carpenter found the competition through fansite mileyworld.com and was the youngest contestant to enter. The judges were

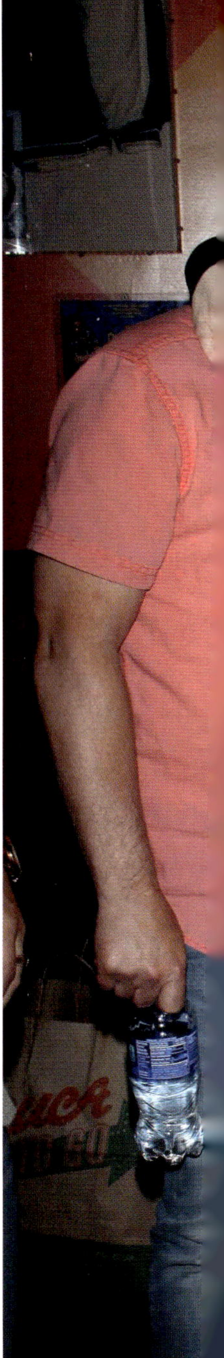

Promoting Eyes Wide Open *with her father, mother and sister Shannon, New York, June 2015*

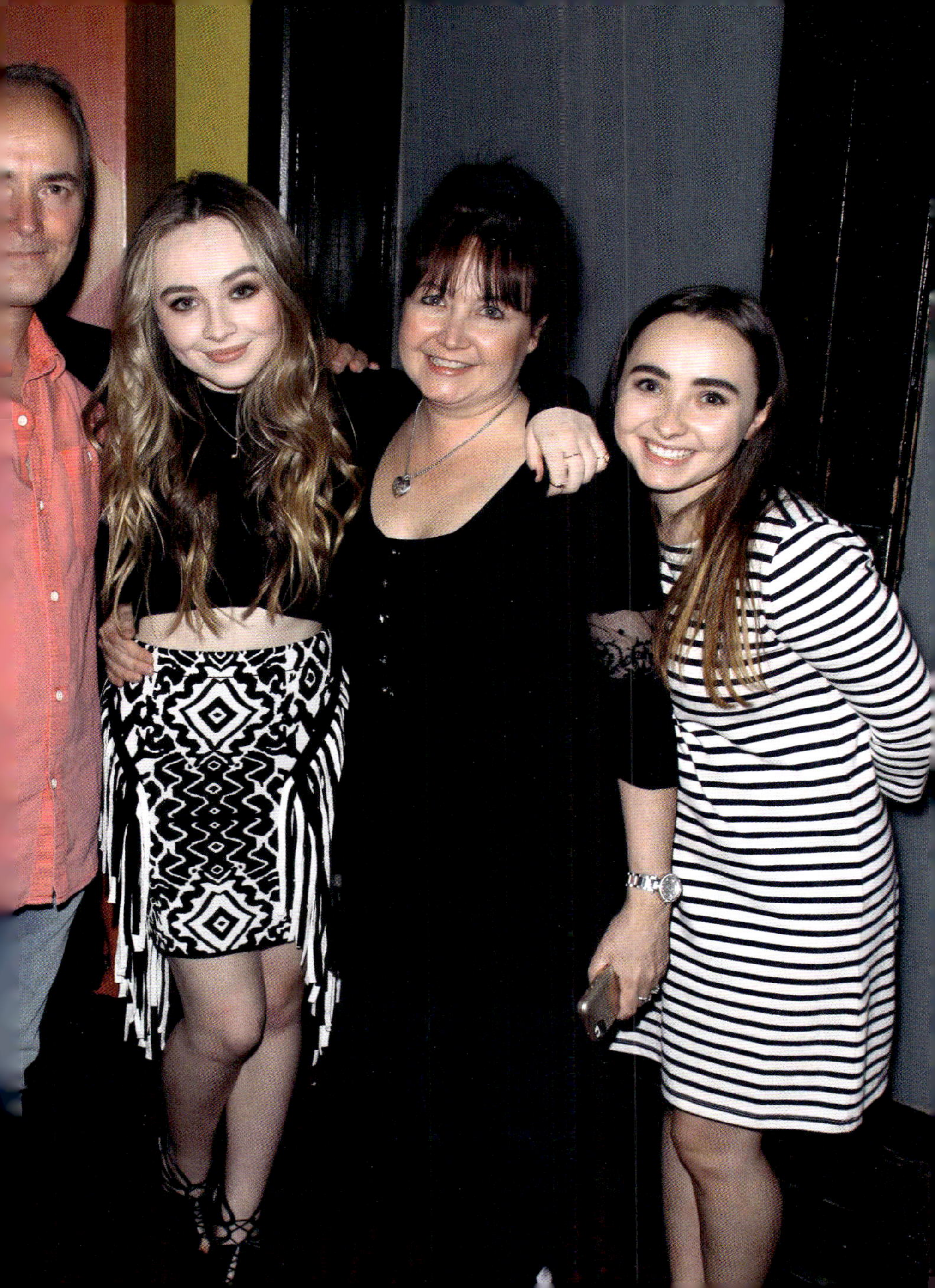

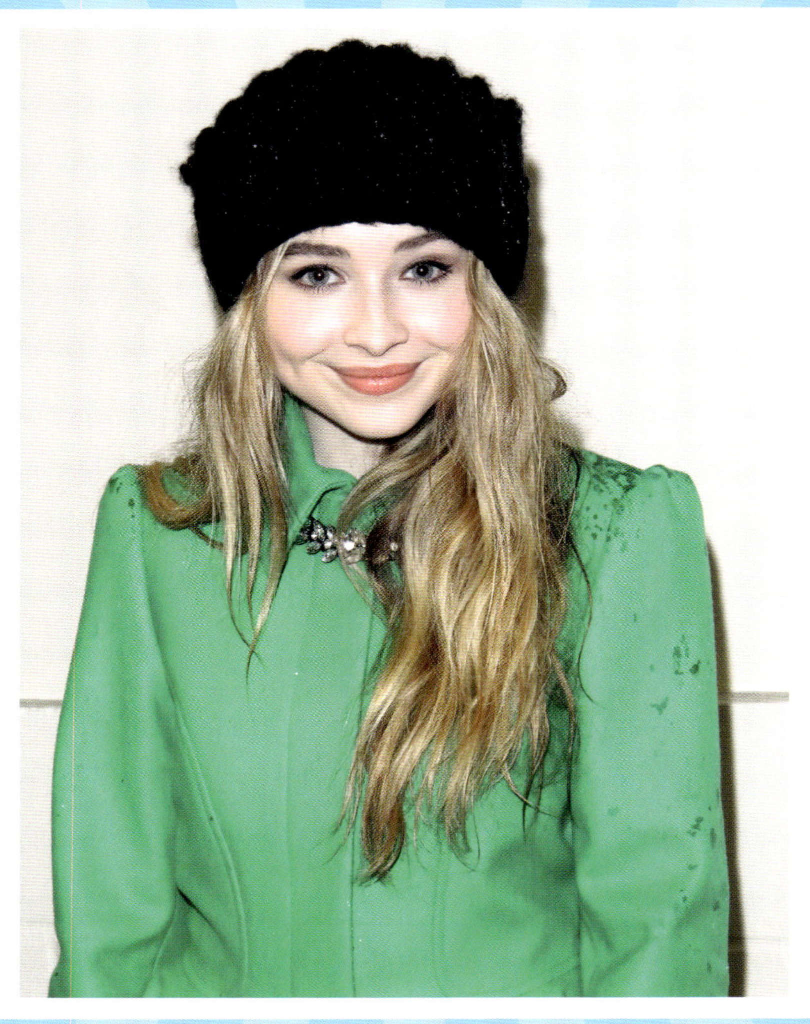

awed by her videos, including a choreographed rendition of Cyrus's 'Hoedown Throwdown'. In recent interviews, as Carpenter cringes over the old footage of her miming the lyrics, she recalls that as a time when she was finally able to get out of her shell and really perform for the camera. She landed in third place (out of 10,000 entries ... a distinction Carpenter likes to wink at in interviews), further igniting her desire to pursue a pop career. 'After that contest ended – did not win, got to meet Miley, though, big perk – I kept doing it because I just loved it so much,' Carpenter told *Vogue* in 2025.

That love continued to blossom as she started taking her quest for success more seriously, her dad even transforming one of their family closets into a studio: putting up acoustic foam panels and painting the walls Sabrina's favourite purple hue. Her parents helped her edit her YouTube videos, some of which are still going viral to this day (like the one where a pre-teen Sabrina, showing off her quirky personality, claims she can speak to cats). Sabrina's mum also drove her to voice lessons – something Sabrina revealed and thanked her for during her Grammy acceptance speech. They would travel to Bala Cynwyd, a suburb outside of Philadelphia, where she would visit Rita Cavell Music Studio and work with her first vocal coach, the late Rita Cavell. In a 2018 post, around the time of Cavell's passing, Sabrina noted that Cavell was also her mum's vocal coach, and that her belief in the young artist's vocal ability at just six years old was the reason her parents invested in her singing career. She thanked Cavell for teaching her about the greats, like Patsy Cline, Judy Garland and Etta James. At 11 years old, she released her first single, a love song called 'Fall Apart' (she later joked to *Teen Vogue* that she doesn't recommend anyone listen to that song).

HOLLYWOOD RECORDS

At 12 years old, two years after being spotted on the Miley Cyrus competition, Sabrina signed a five-album deal with Disney-owned label Hollywood Records. But becoming a world-class pop act wasn't the only entertainment avenue Carpenter was interested in. Even before signing with Hollywood Records, Sabrina had begun developing her acting career. Her television debut took place in 2011, when she played the role of a victim called Paula on NBC's *Law & Order: Special Victims Unit*. The following year she became a regular on the short-lived Fox series *The Goodwin Games*, and in 2012, she featured in the made-for-TV movie *Gulliver Quinn*. She was also cast in the hit Netflix series *Orange Is the New Black*, where she played a high-school bully during flashback sequences. In 2013 she appeared in the dark fantasy film *Horns*, playing the younger version of the protagonist's

At the 83rd annual Hollywood Christmas Parade, California, December 2014

girlfriend. She also had multiple supporting and voice-over roles on Disney shows like *Austin & Ally*, *Phineas and Ferb*, *Milo Murphy's Law* and *Sofia the First*, as well as the Disney film *Adventures in Babysitting* (2016).

GIRL MEETS WORLD

Sabrina and her family made the move from Pennsylvania to Los Angeles when she was around 13 years old so that she could get serious about her acting career. That's when she took on her biggest television role: a main character in the Disney reboot of the popular '90s sitcom *Boy Meets World*. In the new version, aptly titled *Girl Meets World*, Sabrina played Maya Hart, the best friend of the series protagonist. She put her own quick-witted, rebellious and openly emotional spin on the role, playing the part for three seasons. 'The beauty of the show was that we really were at the age that we were playing,' Carpenter told *Teen Vogue* about playing Hart, 'and we were coming into ourselves as we were playing characters that were coming into themselves.' The show was a success, running for 72 episodes and ending in January 2017.

After her series ended, Sabrina continued to pursue acting roles. In 2019 she starred in *Tall Girl*, followed by the sequel, *Tall Girl 2*, in which she played Harper, the main character's smaller, more confident beauty-queen sister. In 2018 she starred in the film adaptation of the book *The Hate U Give*, playing Hailey Grant, one of the lead's friends from prep school. In 2019, she also played the character of Nola in *The Short History of the Long Road* – a young girl trying to find herself after travelling in an RV with her father across the country. In 2020, she got to show off all those years of dance lessons in the Netflix film *Work It*. In the critically acclaimed 2022 film *Emergency*, Sabrina played Maddy, the sister of a college student drugged at a frat party. She also took on the lead role of Cady Heron in the Broadway musical *Mean Girls* in March 2020, though, unfortunately, she was only able to perform in two shows before the Covid-19 lockdown cut the run short.

Despite Sabrina finding early success in acting and quickly building a lucrative career, music remained her first love. In 2023 she told *Glamour UK* that she had no preference between acting and singing, and made career decisions based on the feeling of effortlessness and ease that came when an opportunity called to her. But, as the coming years would prove, as she shifted from Disney darling to big-label pop princess, music's shouting would be a whole lot louder.

Opposite, clockwise from top left: With the Girl Meets World *cast at the Creative Arts Emmy Awards, Los Angeles, September 2015; promoting* Girl Meets World *with Rowan Blanchard, New York, June 2014;* Girl Meets World *production still*

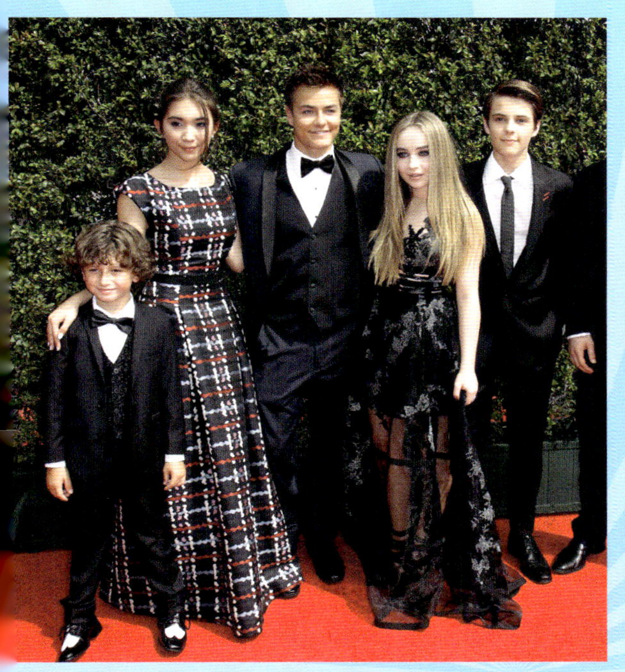

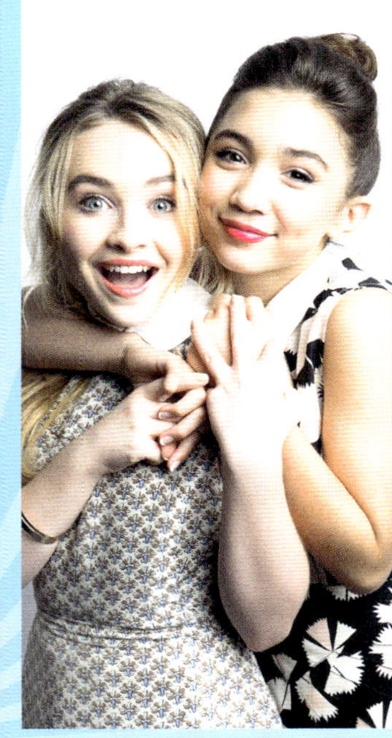

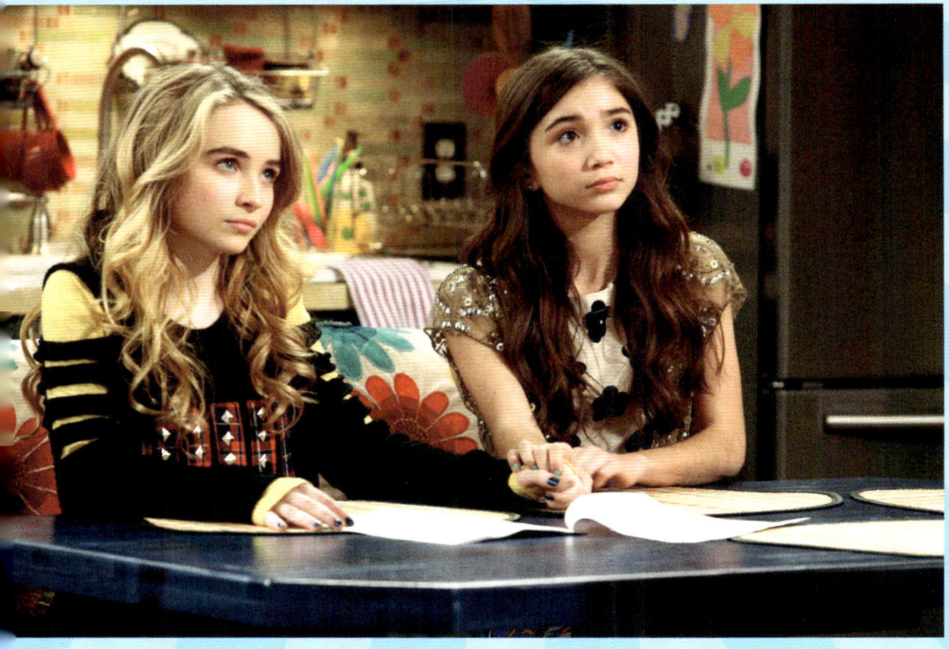

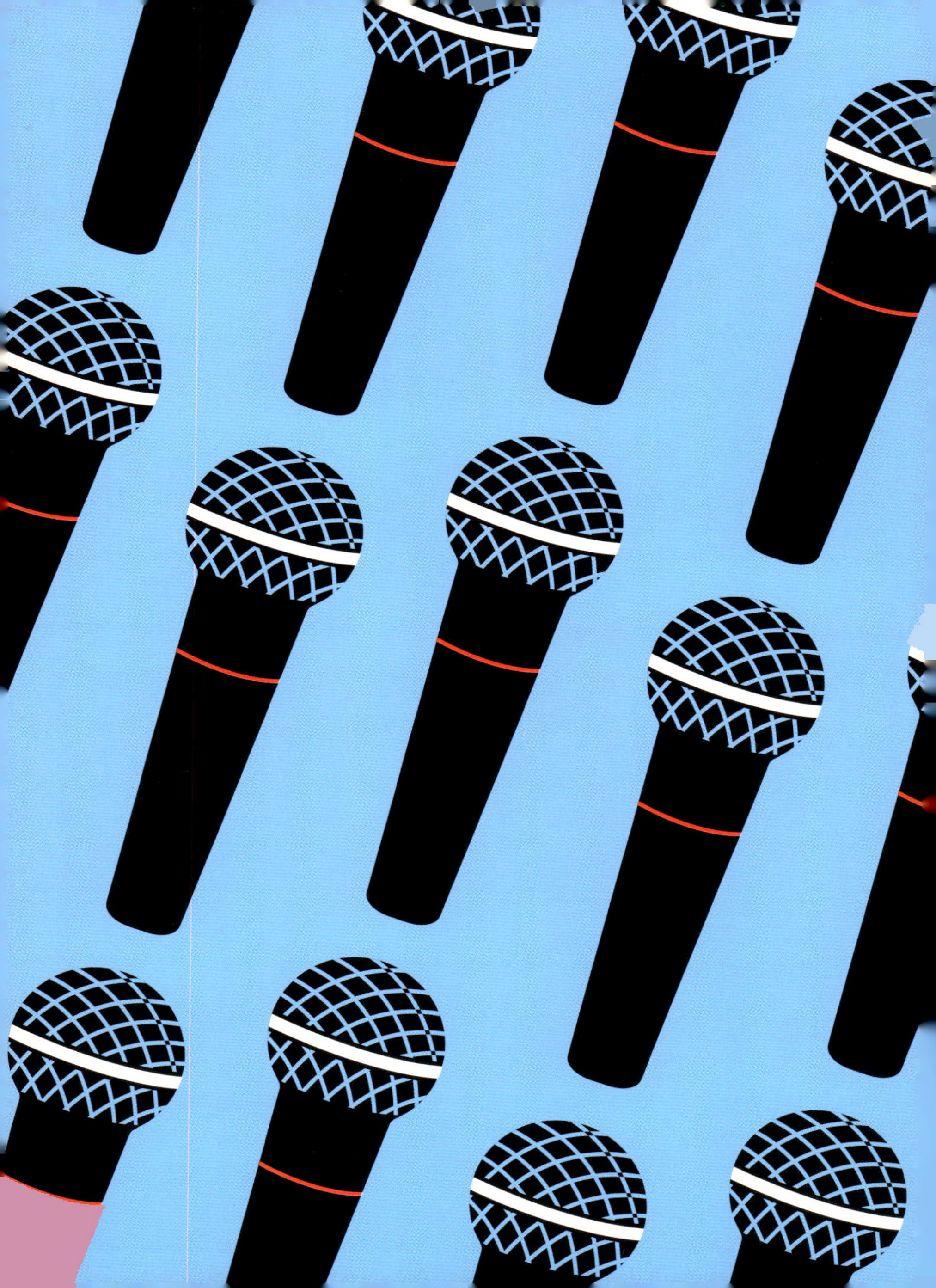

SABRINA THE SINGER

Setting the Stage for Stardom

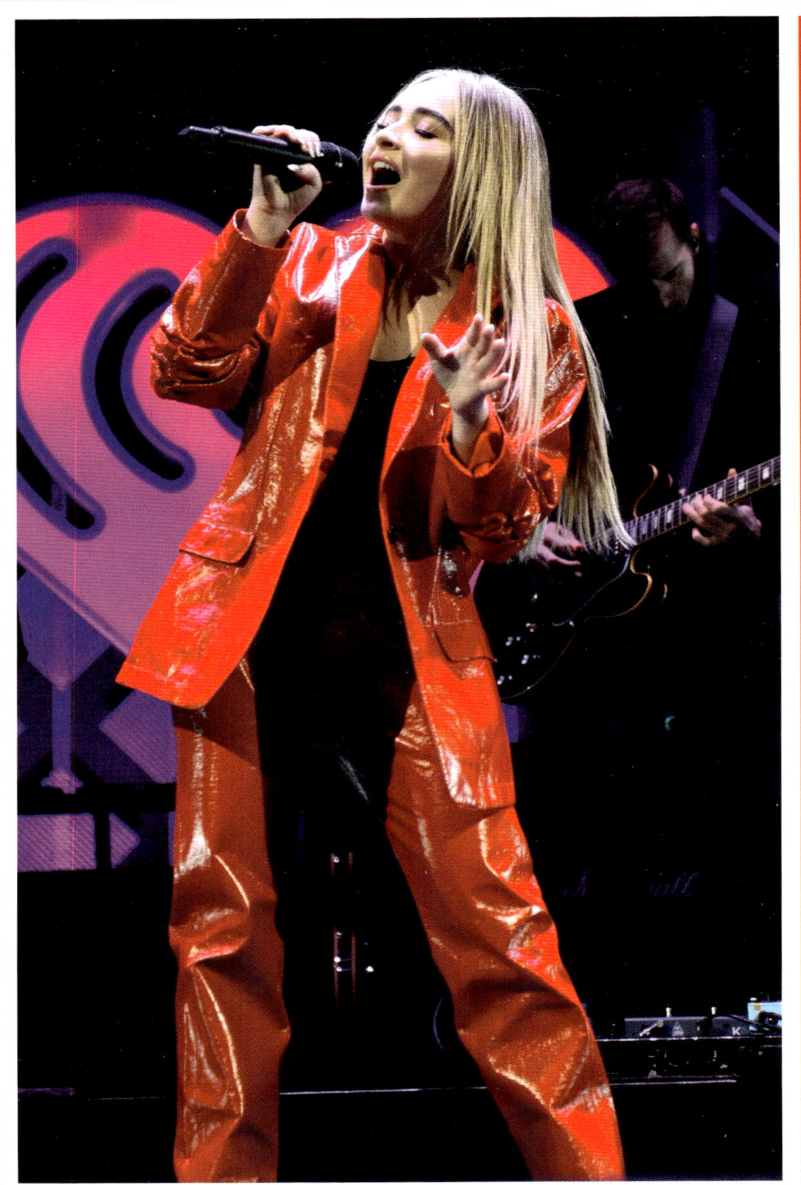

Although Sabrina Carpenter has never shied away from her past (her YouTube channel still proudly displays the early pop covers she recorded at just nine years old), she has expressed mixed feelings about her early discography – albums she released between 2015 and 2019 on Hollywood Records. 'For the people who love those early records and listen to them, I love you for that,' she told *Variety* in 2024. 'But I personally feel a sense of separation from them, largely due to the shift in who I am as a person and as an artist.'

The shift makes sense. Sabrina was only 12 years old when she signed her first artist contract, and in the years that followed, she recalls a lot of people in the industry leading her astray, either in the direction of her acting or music career. 'I had to fight off a lot of voices and opinions and people controlling me when I was younger,' she told *PAPER*. 'Whether that be in music or acting because I was a child coming into this.'

Always the optimist, however, she's also shared that she's grateful for those experiences – that they honed her intuition, making it easier for her to trust her creative and business instincts as her career continued to grow. And despite those earliest music moments not always reflecting Sabrina's true vision and ability, they did hint at who she would become as a global star – whether it be in terms of her worldview, vocal delivery or the lyricism that shines a light on emotional chaos and vulnerability.

Performing at Hot 99.5's Jingle Ball 2018, Washington D.C., December 2018

CAN'T BLAME A GIRL

In March 2014, after releasing multiple promotional songs for Disney – including the track 'Smile' for the album *Disney Fairies: Faith, Trust and Pixie Dust* (2012) and 'All You Need' for the *Sofia the First* soundtrack – Sabrina turned to self-focused pursuits and released her debut single, 'Can't Blame a Girl for Trying'. The bubblegum, Colbie Caillat-esque folk-pop song – written in part by singer-songwriter Meghan Trainor – was a stripped-back acoustic track with lyrics about being dumb, young and happy to take a leap of faith for love. The early story arc, though not written by Carpenter, was a precursor to the complicated emotions she'd one day feel compelled to write about from her own perspective.

In her first-ever music video, Sabrina strums a guitar, accidentally steps in glitter, uses a banana as a phone and fumbles around as she awkwardly attempts to make it through the day. In a Vevo behind-the-scenes look for the video, Carpenter shares the story of the song, saying it focuses on the idea that 'you can mess up a lot and you can fail a lot of times', but you should embrace who you are because there's nothing better than being yourself. The song picked up the Best Crush Song award at the 2015 Radio Disney Music Awards and, more importantly, introduced Sabrina Carpenter, the singer, to the world.

The next month, Sabrina released her first EP, also titled *Can't Blame a Girl for Trying*, with songs she recorded while simultaneously filming for *Girl Meets World*. The four-track compilation included her previously released title track and a second single called 'The Middle of Starting Over' – a stomp-and-clap guitar moment with an inspirational message about embracing life mistakes. In the video, tween Sabrina is surrounded by friends, pillow-fighting, dancing in front of bright graffitied walls and picking petals from a daisy. She performed the song at the Big Ticket Summer in Halifax, Nova Scotia, on the chat show *Fox & Friends* and at the Macy's Thanksgiving Day Parade.

The EP also featured 'White Flag', a country-pop track, with lyrics about surrendering to life and learning to always get back up again. In it, Carpenter's vocals shine through, as she dabbles in runs and showcases her vocal range. In a Popheads Reddit Q&A after the EP's release, Carpenter shared that if she had to choose three songs to describe her life at the time, one of them would be 'White Flag'. The EP closes with 'Best Thing I Got', a bubbly piano-focused love song with a climbing chorus.

At the 88th Annual Macy's Thanksgiving Day Parade, New York, November 2014

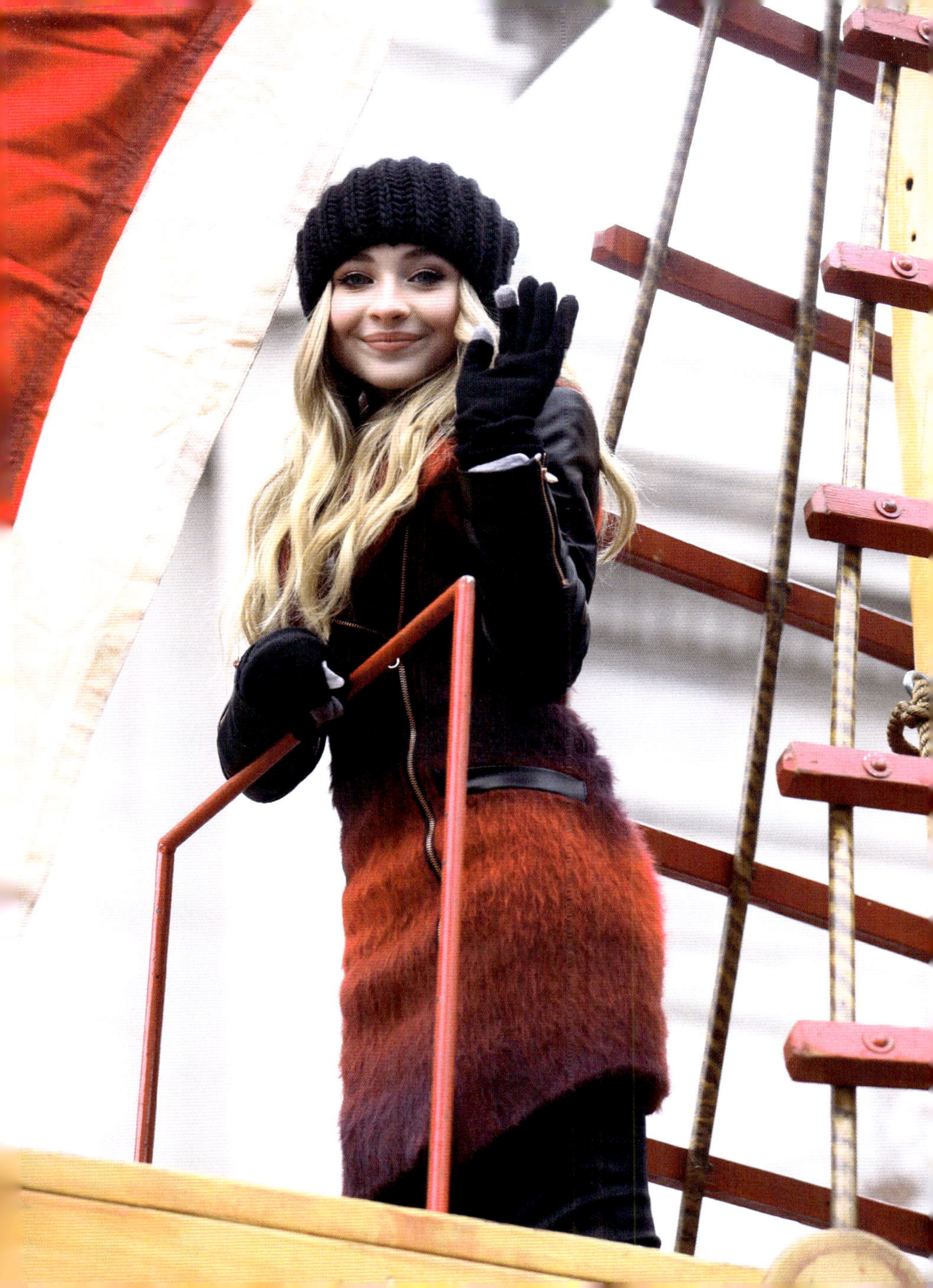

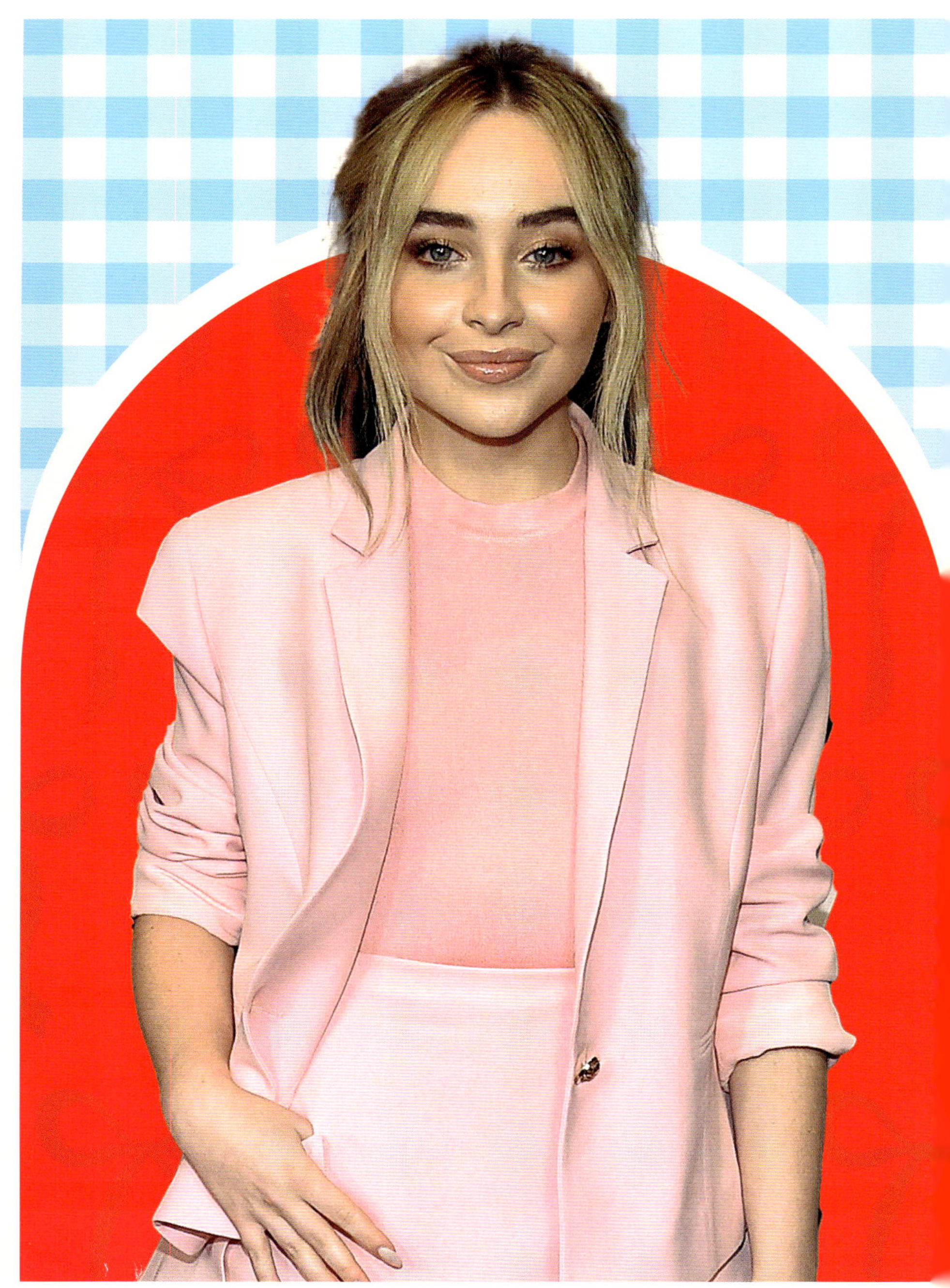

AN EVOLUTION

In 2015, those same songs featured on Sabrina's debut album, *Eyes Wide Open*. The album opens with the soulful title track and the phrase 'Everybody loves to tell me I was born an old soul', one that Sabrina says she heard often growing up. The slow-crawling 'Too Young' highlighted another saying, this time one she wanted to rally against in her personal and creative life, and the up-tempo 'Right Now' was a mantra for living in the moment. The album also featured 'Darling I'm a Mess', another Hawaiian-folk song written by Meghan Trainor, this time about being friend-zoned by an ex-love. Some critics remarked that Sabrina's debut was a bit derivative but they still gave it credit for being rich in personality, with a magnetic, approachable energy.

In October 2016, she followed her debut with *EVOLution*, a sway from folk-pop straight into dance territory. The album's lead single, 'On Purpose', showed off a bolder Sabrina, with echoing vocals and a spiralling electronic backing track, as she sang about falling for someone unexpectedly. The visuals also revealed a new version of the star, as she walked alone through London dressed in black – a stark contrast to the bright colours and teenybopper wardrobe that defined her *Eyes Wide Open* era.

EVOLution also saw one of Sabrina's first hits. The album's second single, 'Thumbs' – a jazzy bop with a menacing back beat, clashing percussion and scatting at the chorus – marked her first real chart impact, hitting number 1 on Billboard's Bubbling Under Hot 100. She also performed the song, which was certified Platinum in the US, Australia and Norway, on *The Late Late Show with James Corden*, *Today* and at the Radio Disney Music Awards. In the video, Carpenter, again in black, shifts around a New York City subway as passengers sing along to the song. The album was promoted through two additional singles: an anthemic dance track called 'All We Have Is Love', with a backing gospel choir and surging chorus, and 'Run and Hide', a bare R&B song that spotlighted Sabrina's soulful vocals.

In interviews, Carpenter explained the shift in her sound, noting that she had more writing credits on *EVOLution* than her previous release and pointing to the span of time between making music as a pre-teen and creating her second album as a young woman. She also mentioned wanting to have a bigger voice this time around, something more akin to that of vocalists like Adele and Christina Aguilera. Fans and critics appreciated this more mature, bolder version of Carpenter, and *EVOLution* debuted at number 28 on the US Billboard 200, giving Sabrina the opportunity to go on her first headline global tour. It sold out. There were early hints of what we now know as Sabrina's iconic look, as she wore black lace outfits on stage and performed in front of a bright pink neon sign of her signature.

Arriving at the 2018 Radio Disney Music Awards, Los Angeles, June 2018

A SINGULAR TALENT

Sabrina's third release, *Singular: Act I*, which came out in November 2018, was a pivotal moment for the star, as it was the first time she received co-writer credit for every song on the release. Originally, she planned to release one album under the title *Singular*. However, the songs she recorded over the two-year period after the release of *EVOLution* both thematically and musically felt like they belonged in two separate collections. The album led with the single 'Almost Love', a kinetic track that saw the 19-year-old singing with sultry R&B vocals about themes she hadn't hit on in previous releases, spinning out a story of romantic tensions rising and even showing off her witty, lyrical ability with the line 'I want you like a loner wants an empty room'. She told *Billboard* that when she first listened back to the song, she heard a confidence and personality in herself that she hadn't registered before. The music video, set at the Pasadena Museum of History, was full of firsts for Sabrina; it featured provocative choreography, backing dancers, and our first look at her now-iconic platinum-blonde hair. The video also features a love interest, played by actor Noam Sigler, whom she kisses and turns into a Greek statue.

The album's second single, 'Sue Me', was, according to Sabrina, who talked about the song with *Variety*, one of the first times she was super autobiographical in a song. The track, unfortunately, takes its inspiration from a lawsuit between Sabrina and her former music managers, Stan Rogow and Elliot Lurie, who argued that their termination by the star was without cause. Ultimately, Carpenter won the case and wrote the song about the feelings she experienced, likening it to a break-up and 'how it feels when they want what they can't have anymore'. She was back at it with her cheeky one-liners, too, remarking that her favourite line from the song was 'That's my name, don't wear it out though'. The music video, inspired by the plot of *Legally Blonde*, shows Sabrina in a fur-trimmed sheer robe and polka-dot two-piece bathing suit – an aesthetic similar to that she would show off during future album releases. Her friend, the actress Joey King, also features in romcom-inspired visuals. In 'Paris', she sings, over synths and a gyrating beat, about the romantic city while distracted by a love interest in Los Angeles. She told fans on Twitter that her track 'Bad Time' was one of the songs on the album she had the most fun writing, noting that she had an 'epiphany' afterwards. In the jittery, electro-pop song, she sings about a lover who gets bored easily, and how their behaviour turns even a good time into a bad one. Her song 'Why' considers the idea of opposites attracting and she told *Genius* the lyrics were inspired by star-crossed relationships and the movies *10 Things I Hate About You* (1999) and *When Harry Met Sally* (1989).

Performing at Y100's Jingle Ball, Sunrise, Florida, December 2018

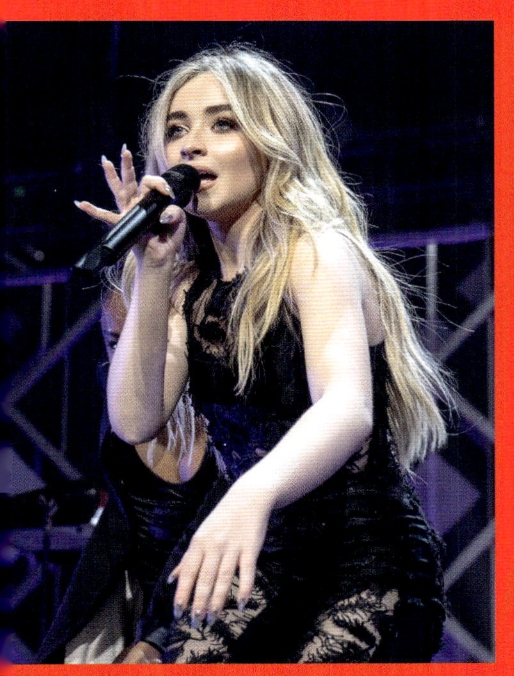

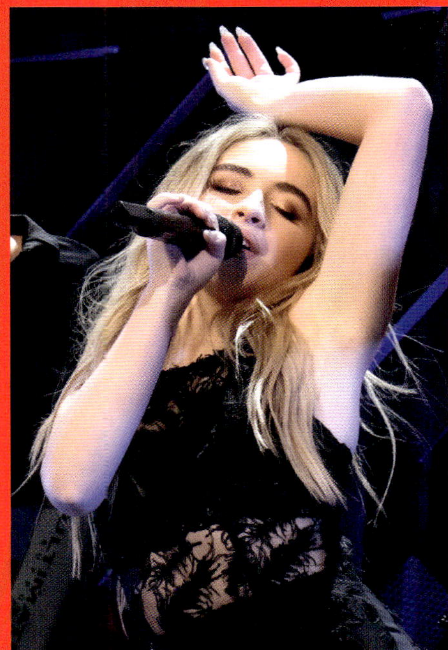

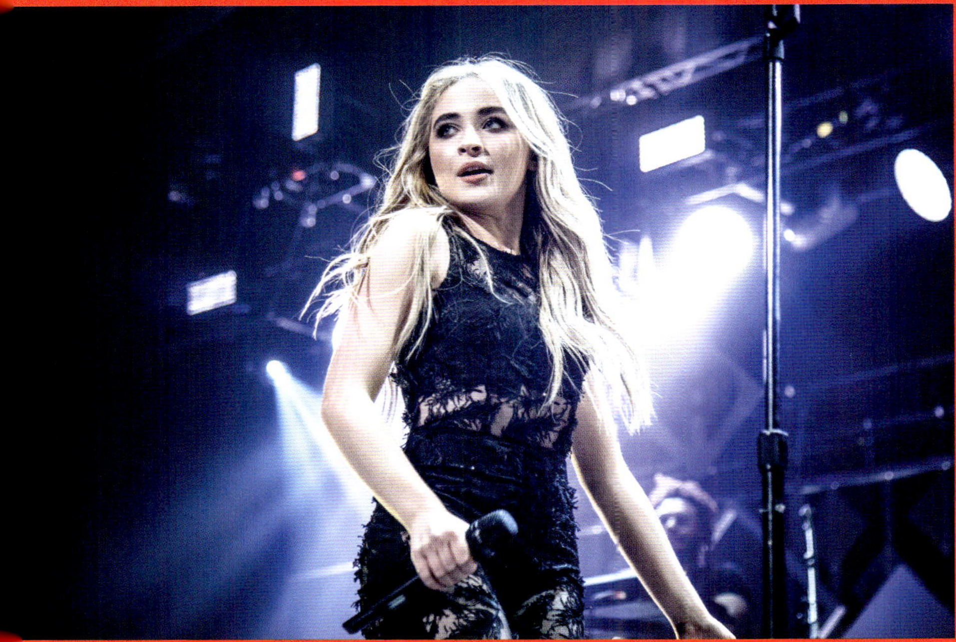

In the music video, she stars with Casey Cott as they spend time together in New York City; it was intentionally shot cinematically to capture the song's inspiration. The album also featured 'Alien', a collaboration with DJ and dance producer Jonas Blue, about feeling alienated and lost in your feelings. In an interview with *Billboard*, she shared that she initially reached out to Blue on Twitter, telling him she was a fan and wanted to work together. The result is a mix of vulnerable lyricism over hip-hop and electronic beats; it hit number 1 on the US Dance Club Songs chart. On 'Mona Lisa', the track Sabrina referred to as her favourite on the album, she sings about urging a crush to make the first move. The brisk synth track comes in at just over two minutes – something she joked about on social media with fans, offering a formal apology and performing an extended version during the *Singular* tour.

The album was a big step forward for Sabrina, with *PopCrush* calling out her 'playful psyche' and many pointing to her leap from Disney Channel darling to pop artist, saying that she was finally coming into her own as a star.

Sabrina released her fourth album, *Singular: Act II*, in July of 2019. There was a notable difference in her sound and she talked about the difference between this release and her previous album, saying that *Act I* makes you comfortable, but *Act II* makes you feel uncomfortable enough to grow; she told *Marie Claire* that it was her most personal album to date. The album's lead single, 'Pushing 20', came with heavy bass, R&B vocal delivery, and in-your-face lines about the autonomy she felt as she got closer to a new decade of life. In an interview with *PopCrush*, she recalls a producer asking her 'How old are you now, you pushing 20?' as being the initial lyrical inspiration, with the rest of the song being about the expectations that come with becoming an adult. Her next single, 'Exhale', was one of her most intimate releases, as she talked about her family, feeling overwhelmed with life and imposter syndrome. In the track, over lush strings, she sings about the struggle of listening to labels, 'the man', and outside voices. She continues with that streak of vulnerability on her third single, 'In My Bed', an electro-pop song about dealing with anxiety – the song title and lyrics a play on the idea of being in her head.

Her pop-meets-hip-hop track 'I Can't Stop Me' featured rapper Saweetie; Sabrina crooned about calling the shots in her relationships. Sabrina spoke to *PopCrush* about the track, saying that although she was hesitant about having a feature, she felt that Saweetie's contribution added to the confident, feminine dynamic of the song. She also mentioned that it was originally titled

Performing at the Good Morning America *show, New York, July 2019*

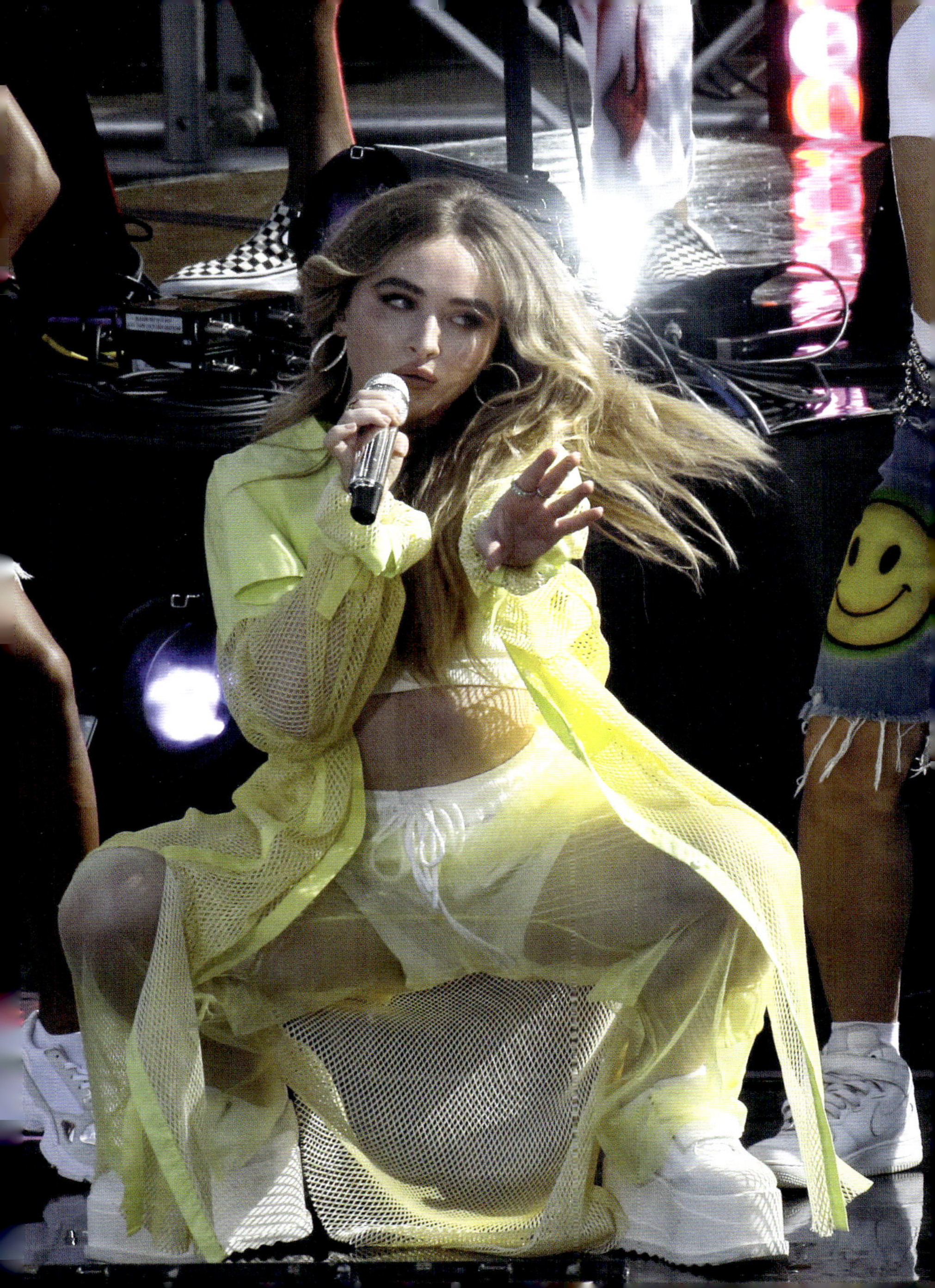

'You Can't Stop Me', but in an attempt to give the power back to the song's protagonist, she renamed the track. On 'I'm Fakin' Sabrina gets seductive, delivering smooth vocals and catchy hooks with the line 'Everytime I tell you that I'm done I'm fakin''. It's one of the album moments that feels most similar to her current discography. Her track 'Tell Em' was written on Valentine's Day, which she notes makes sense due to its sensuality – the soulful R&B track moves at a smouldering pace, with accentuating backing vocals as she sings about keeping a romantic relationship private; she repeats 'You can be my dirty little secret' as the song slides to a close. If there were any questions of whether Sabrina could successfully pivot from Disney child star to developed pop act, *Act II* answered with a resounding yes. The album was a critical success and debuted at number 138 on the US Billboard Charts.

Singular: Act I and *Act II*, showed what could happen when Sabrina took the reins creatively – whether that was through featuring other rising artists, like Saweetie and Jonas Blue, or showing off her quirky personality by teasing 'In My Bed' with an ASMR video, AirDropping album art to long-time fans, and continuing her tradition of sitting in a Target cart on album release day holding her album (a habit she started with *EVOLution*). It also marked the start of her taking on fewer acting roles, her musical trajectory taking over the majority of her creative output. It was also a time for Sabrina to show off her skills on stage as she took her first albums around the globe (one interviewer remarked on how her 'crotch grab' during the choreography for 'Pushing 20' made him cover his eyes, though that's nothing in comparison to the 'Juno' stage antics that we'll dig into later). With a cohesive vision, lyrics that reflected her sense of humour and cleaner production, many critics ordained Sabrina pop's next big hitmaker on the basis of these albums, acknowledging that each track felt like a warning of what was to come for the star. They were right.

Singular: Act II was Sabrina's fourth and last album on Hollywood Records. She released one more single with the label, 'Honeymoon Fades', surprising fans by teasing the track on 13 February 2024 and dropping it the next day as a Valentine's Day gift to fans. She called it a love letter to her fans who had stuck with her thus far, and her sister Sarah captured the photo for the album art. It felt like the perfect bookend for that chapter in her creativity; although Hollywood Records would forever represent her first foray into songwriting, touring and performance, Sabrina was happy to leave those early songs and moments behind. In 2021, a bigger label came calling.

Performing at 93.3 FLZ's iHeartRadio Jingle Ball, Tampa, Florida, December 2017

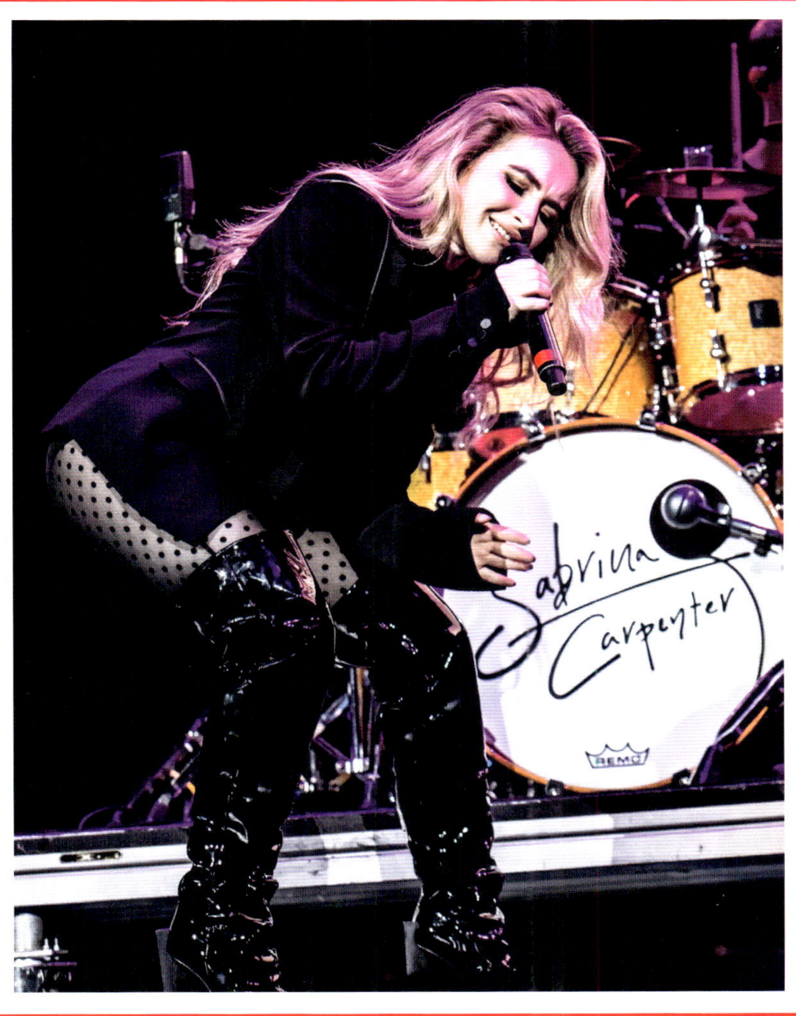
Sabrina
Carpenter
REMO

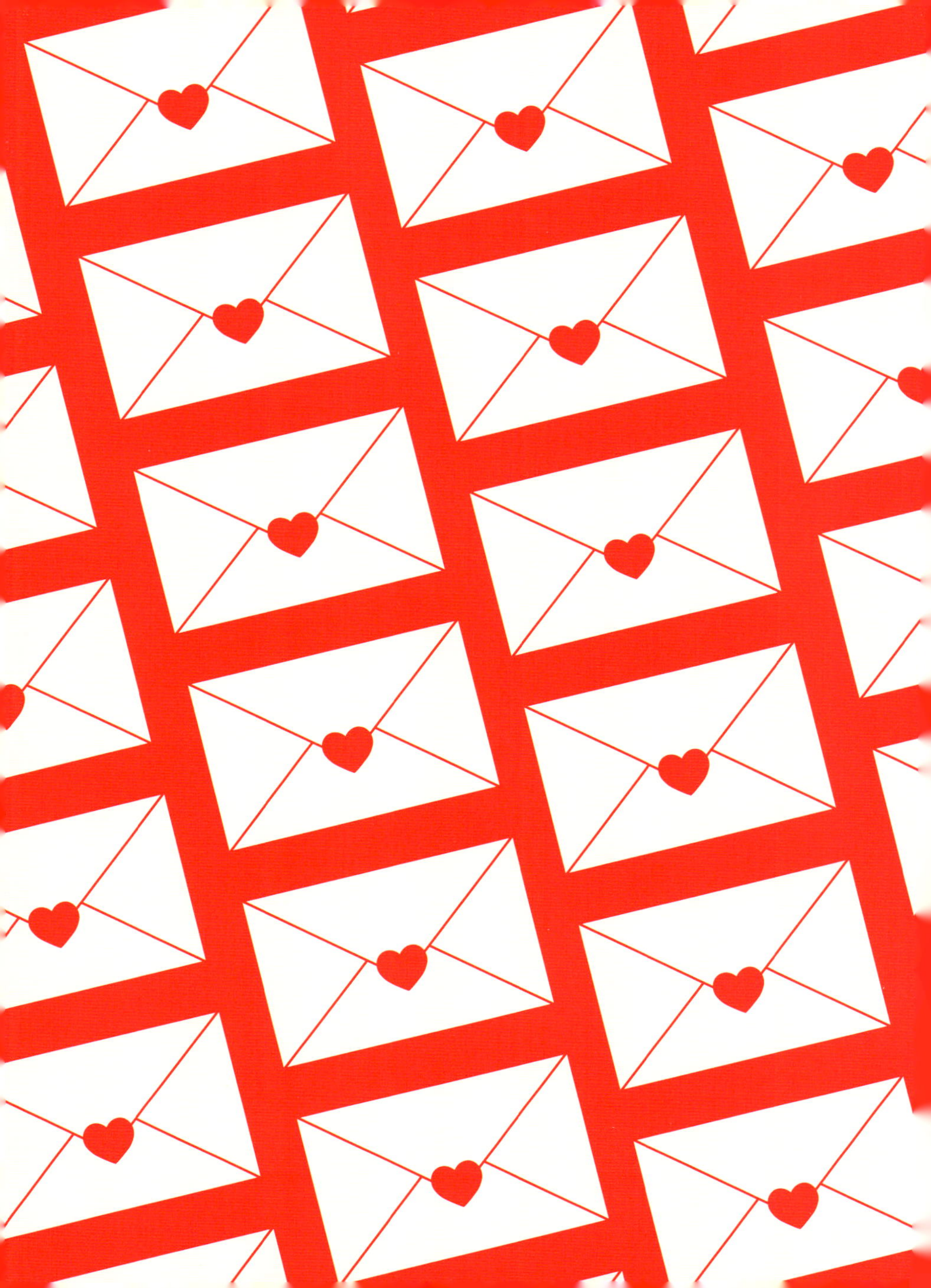

SABRINA'S INTERNET *Era*

Vent and Type

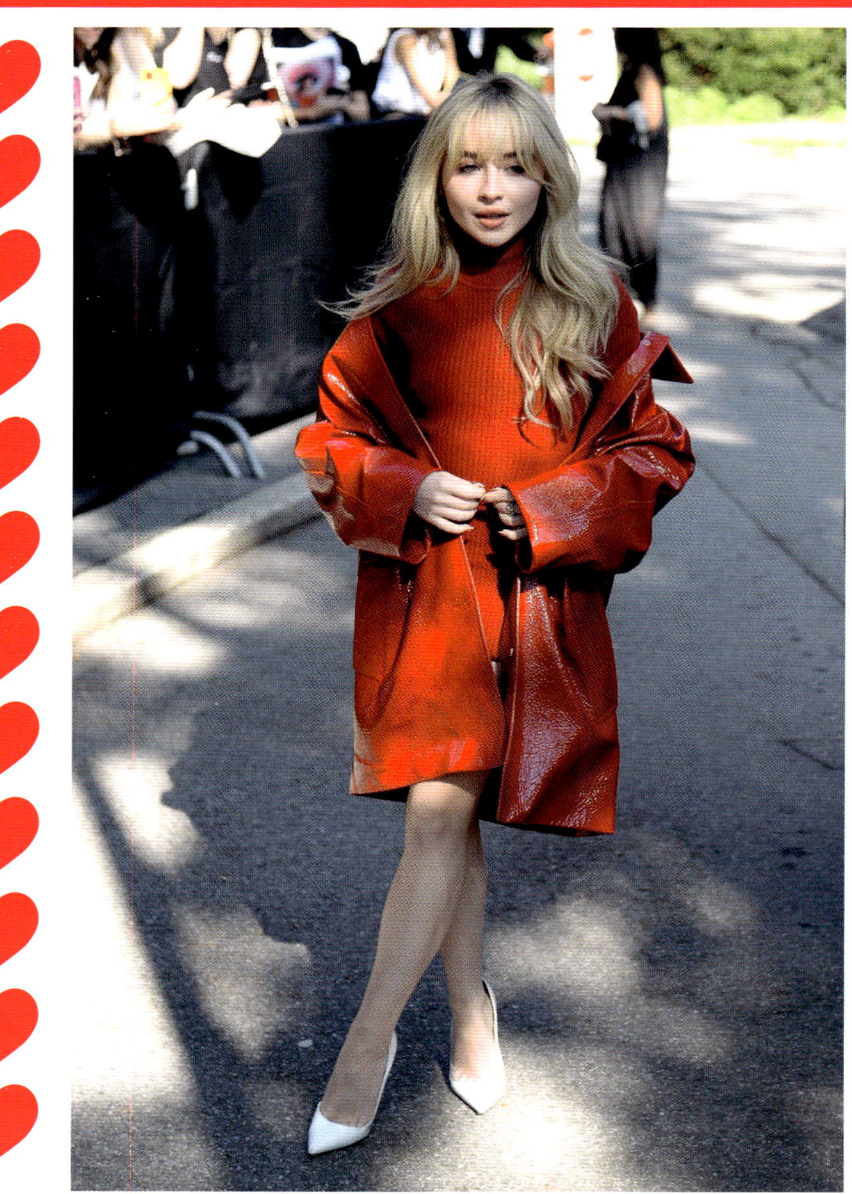

In January 2021, after releasing four albums in her five-album deal with Disney's Hollywood Records, Sabrina Carpenter made a pivot that would change the trajectory of her career, prematurely leaving her first deal behind and joining major label Island Records – she later told *Vogue*, 'Thank God I didn't finish my contract!'

At the time of her signing, she gave a shout-out to Darcus Beese, CEO and president of Island, sharing that he and the team really understood her vision, were supportive of her art, and that she felt the label was the right place to continue her evolution as an artist. For Island's part, they called out Sabrina's star quality, 'powerful vocals, infectious personality', and success thus far as the reasons they wanted to work with her.

Not long after the news broke of her new recording deal, Sabrina dropped her first single with the label, a synth-pop ballad called 'Skin'. The track debuted at number 48 on the Billboard Hot 100, making it her first top 100 entry. The song came with visuals showing a more mature Sabrina playing opposite actor Gavin Leatherwood, who was cast as her love interest. They lie on the couch, share a meal, and read and write together, experiencing small romantic moments, before an earthquake hits their home and shakes up the little world they've created. 'Skin''s success was an early indicator of the trajectory of Carpenter's pop career, but outside of it stirring up stellar reviews, it also pushed Sabrina down a rabbit hole of internet gossip and viral drama.

New York Fashion Week, September 2021

MUSICAL LOVE TRIANGLE?

'Skin' was released in the same month that fellow pop prodigy and Disney star Olivia Rodrigo released her hit 'drivers license'. Many speculated that Rodrigo's song about being heartbroken over her ex was based on the fallout of her romantic relationship with her *High School Musical: The Musical: The Series* co-star Joshua Bassett. In the ballad, Rodrigo sings, 'And you're probably with that blonde girl/Who always made me doubt/She's so much older than me/She's everything I'm insecure about.' Since there were whispers and sightings of Sabrina out to lunch with Bassett, fans assumed she was, in fact, the golden-haired homewrecker to whom the song referred.

It didn't help that the same month Bassett released a song called 'Lie Lie Lie' – a track about someone purporting to be innocent while throwing you under the bus with their stories about you. As each track hit the airwaves, rumours of a musical love triangle between Sabrina, Rodrigo and Bassett continued to make headlines. To be fair, 'Skin' did seem like a lyrical response to all those online assertions, as Sabrina poses, 'Maybe we could've been friends/If I met you in another life' and 'Maybe you didn't mean it/Maybe "blonde" was the only rhyme,' adding 'Don't drive yourself insane/It won't always be this way' as a kicker.

Arriving at the British Fashion Awards, London, December 2022

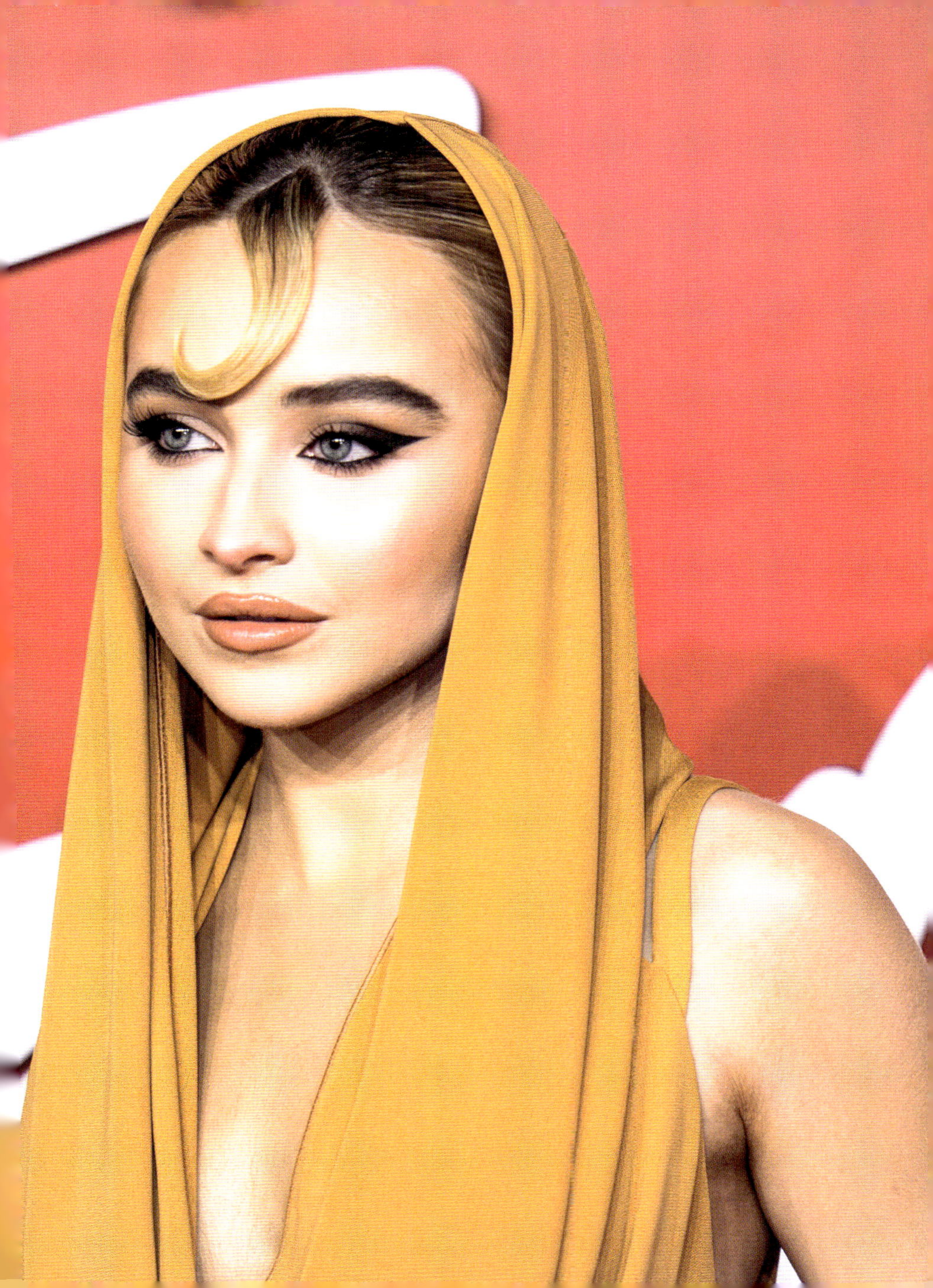

None of the singers ever confirmed the love triangle theory. Rodrigo told *Billboard* that, although she understood people's curiosity over who the song was about, she didn't feel like that information was an important aspect of the song. She also told *Variety* that she was surprised people had speculated so much over the song's content, before making it clear she wasn't interested in the drama, adding: 'I don't really subscribe to hating other women because of boys.'

Eventually, Sabrina spoke up as well. As the fan theories and internet assumptions hit tabloid-esque peak hysteria, Sabrina posted on Facebook, sharing that '["Skin"] isn't calling out one single person.' She also said that, while some parts of the song were about specific situations, most of the song was about learning not to give her power away to outside forces, particularly when those forces had got under her skin. She closed her statement by asking fans not to send any hate anyone's way. Five years later, she explained to *Vogue* that she'd written the song reactively and in a 'whirlwind', with no real intention of ever putting it out.

VENT AND TYPE

Her decision to write a song that pulled so much from her personal life and personal experience didn't come about without trials, tribulations and introspection. She's noted in multiple interviews that the pandemic shifted her perspective and that she came out of lockdown – much of which she spent quarantining with her family in Los Angeles – a different person. She'd lost her grandfather and a friend, actor Cameron Boyce, in a short span of time. Not to mention that, after the internet obsession and villainization of her could-be role in 'drivers license', she also felt a desire to speak her truth. It was around that same time that inspiration struck in the form of a spiralling email written by an ex.

She read his candid, unfiltered message and felt moved by the raw and open nature of it. She decided to write her own as a practice, jotting down admissions, questions and revelations into emails to people, without any thought of the outside world reading them or ever actually sending them. She's shared that she'd culled hundreds of drafts during that process and she'd 'vent, vent, vent' and 'type type type', with no regard to punctuation or what she was saying, just with the goal of getting what was bothering her out of her head. It was not only therapeutic but fertile ground for her next collection of songs.

At the MTV Video Music Awards, Newark, New Jersey, August 2022

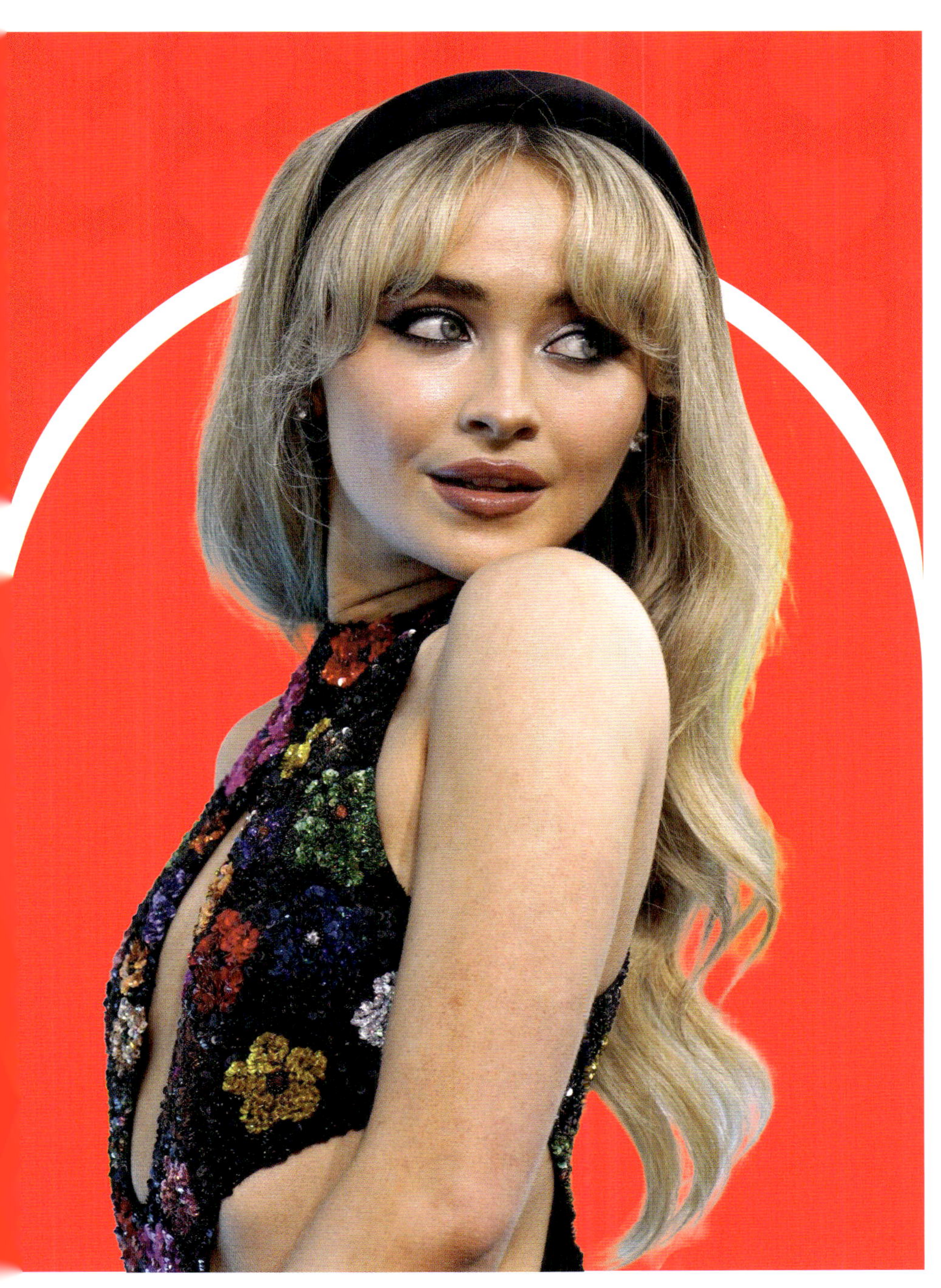

EMAILS I CAN'T SEND

In July 2022, Sabrina released *emails i can't send* and that practice was shared with the world. It was the first album with Island Records and despite it being her fifth release, for her it felt like a debut – not only because she was a fully realized adult with more experiences to pull from for her songwriting, but also because she was able to finally take the reins when it came to the overall direction of the project.

In an interview with *Vogue*, she called it her 'first big-girl album' and noted that it was written in the wake of her first actual heartbreak – one where she felt like she was grieving someone who was still alive. She told *Rolling Stone* that creating the album felt like experiencing 'growing pains', because after protecting herself with a shell of confidence in her early career (since that's what she thought fans wanted – a confident, positive, popstar), she felt like she could let her guard down and, at long last, actually *feel* her feelings.

She was finally 'entirely ***steering the ship'.***

She homed in on her writing process, making a pact with collaborators JP Saxe and Julia Michaels that they'd finish the album together during the summer in New York City. They'd order takeaways and drink champagne on the roof, looking towards the skyline when they hit a rut. She found inspiration from the greats: a soundtrack written by Stevie Nicks, The Beach Boys, Imogen Heap, Carole King, Taylor Swift, Joni Mitchell and Dolly Parton, who she acknowledged as a huge reference for the album. She wrote the way she spoke to her friends, infusing the songs with her own sense of humour, and even choosing album titles without correct capitalization because, as she told fans, she wanted song titles 'to feel like a random chaotic email'. She told *Teen Vogue* that she felt like she could be more imaginative, not take herself too seriously. She was finally 'entirely steering the ship'.

On the album's title track, Sabrina hits close to home, as she writes about love, not from the perspective of someone going through their own heartbreak, but as a daughter dealing with and learning from the infidelity in her parents' marriage. Being vulnerable with her pen was something she'd done before with tracks like 'Sue Me', but the writing on 'emails i can't send' proved that she was willing to sing things that were hard to say out loud. She sings about being disgusted, wanting to cuss her father out, asking why he let her down and ultimately rejects his apology before sharing that she feels that situation is why she can't 'love right'. At one point, holding nothing back, she sings, 'And God, I love you/but you're such a dipshit.'

Years later, reflecting on the song with *Vogue*, she said that that experience gave her more understanding of why and how she ended up in the romantic relationships she had in her life. When asked what her dad – who is still happily married to her mother and has a close relationship to Sabrina – felt after hearing the track, she quipped back: 'You birthed me so you kind of have to deal with the repercussions.'

The album's first single, 'skinny dipping', also takes its inspiration from Sabrina's personal life, with mentions of an unnamed former love and even a shout-out to her sister Shannon. In the jangly guitar track, she sings about running into her ex at a coffee shop, intermixing singing and talking as she plays out scenes where the pair are finally able to make peace with their past – going from swimming to skinny dipping in 'water under the bridge'. The track foreshadowed her now well-versed ability to unfurl metaphors and simplify complex relationship issues into witty lines. She told *Teen Vogue* that, at the time of writing the single, it was a manifestation of sorts, a wish that she and her co-writers conjured up together.

'because i liked a boy' revisits the 'drivers license' chaos – a time in Sabrina's life when she was labelled a 'rebound' and a 'homewrecker'. In the dark pop track, she sings evenly about falling in love innocently, before her delivery speeds up over a building beat and she spills out a litany of attacks she'd

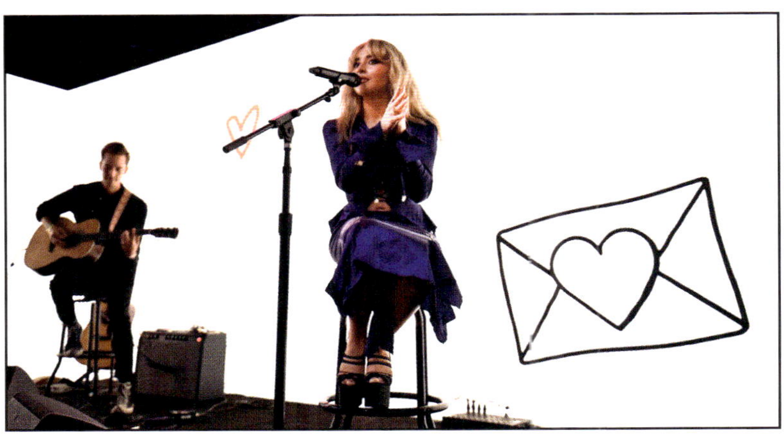

Performing at the Samsung 2022 Galaxy Creators Lounge, New York, August 2022

read about herself online, recalling everything from receiving death threats to being called a slut and rumours that she was stealing men from younger women. In the music video, she performs at a circus in choreographed scenes with backing dancers, wears multiple glamorous costumes and eventually ends up sitting on the floor in tears, defeated in the centre of the ring. She told *Rolling Stone* that the song resonated with fans and friends who had experienced being labelled something they're not. She also shared that her favourite line was 'tell me who I am, cause I don't have a choice', a reflection of her feeling that she is not able to convince people of who she really is, while dealing with the weight of their misconceptions. The lyrics linger between a feeling of defeat and confidence, and seem to reflect the realization that, moving forward, having her good intentions perceived in negative ways would just be part of her life in the limelight.

On 'Vicious', she shows off her knack for clever writing over a retro-rock beat, singing 'Oh, you're so vicious' sweetly at the chorus and over a climbing guitar solo at the bridge. On 'Fast Times', she travels into glittery, bossa-nova slow rock territory as she weaves a tale of impulsive love and the feeling of speeding into a relationship with no concern for the dangerous consequences. The music video is a perfect match to the sound, showing Carpenter disguised with dark locks in espionage-themed scenes inspired by *Charlie's Angels* (2000) and the *Kill Bill* movies. The visuals and song showed her ability to world-build and her penchant for reviving retro sounds. In 'Tornado Warnings', she sings about ignoring the signs of a toxic relationship. This was inspired by a real experience of hanging out with an ex-lover at a park on a seesaw as the sky opened up and it started to hail. Her phone lit up with a tornado warning, and she ignored it. The next day, during therapy, she decided not to divulge the story to her therapist. In the hypnotic synth track, she depicts the moments of that evening, spinning out a story in which she conceals the truth from herself and her therapist, reflecting on what it feels like when you're not quite ready to heal.

Sabrina opens the slow serenade 'how many things' with a line that fans latched on to: 'You used a fork once/It turns out forks are fucking everywhere.' As it turns out, there was more to the line than just Sabrina getting 'worked up over a fork,' as she told *Nylon*. Reminiscing on a past love, she mentioned to a friend 'he used to use a fork' and the joke made it into the song, pointing to how even the most mundane and simple things can set you off, and make you emotional when they remind you of the person you're heartbroken over. Fans picked up on her humour, turning the slightly silly lyric into memes, making artwork of her album with a fork on it, and even bringing forks to shows. When asked on Twitter what her favourite lyric of the album was, Sabrina met her fans where they were and responded with a fork emoji.

At Riccardo Tisci, Kate Moss and Naomi Campbell's Met Gala afterparty, New York, May 2022

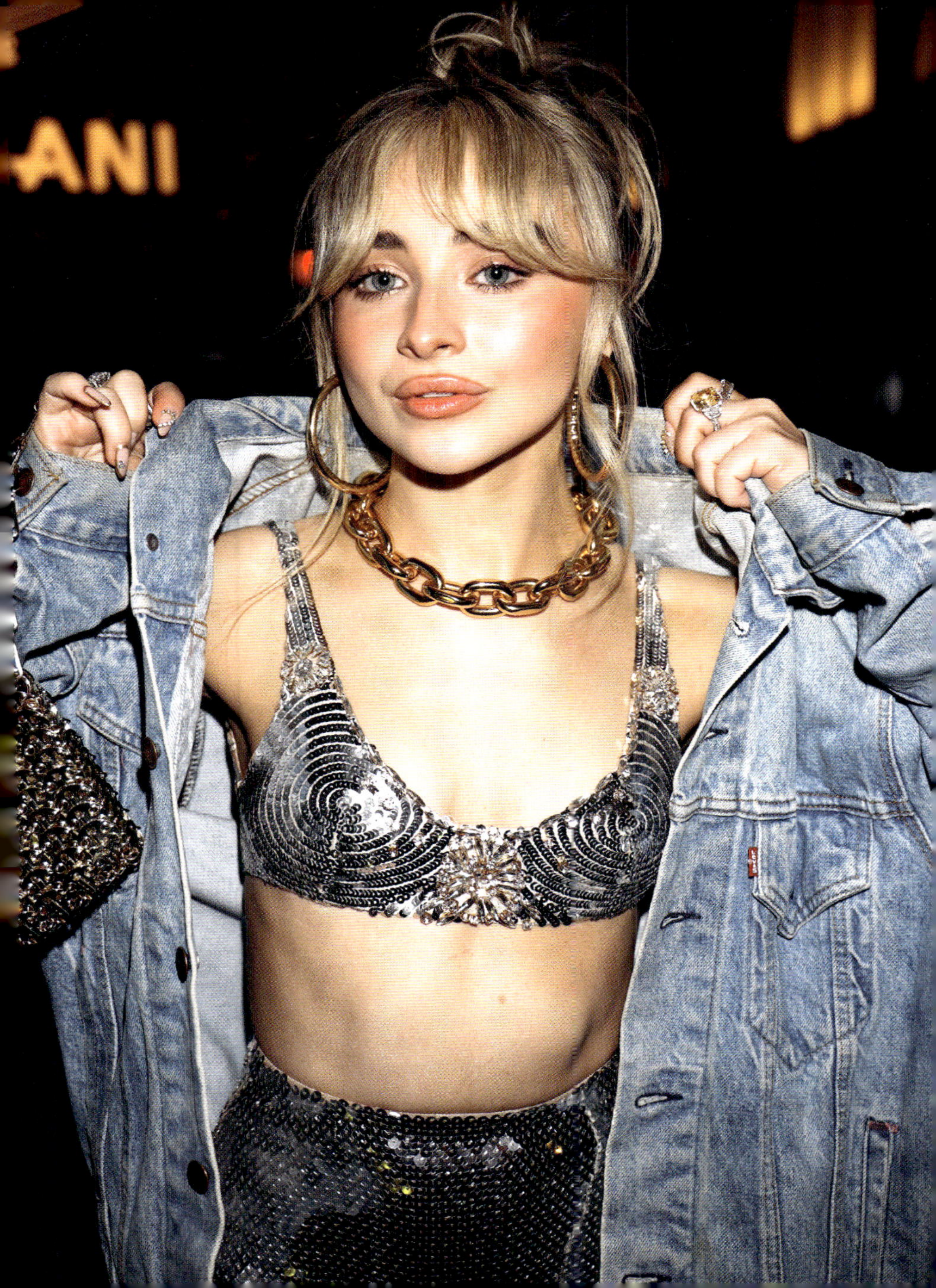

TONGUE-TIED

One of the biggest hits on *emails i can't send* came about accidentally. During one of her writing sessions, Sabrina felt like she'd hit a wall. Instead of pushing through it, she spent the next two hours with her co-writer Steph Jones, going off the beaten path and stringing together nonsensical phrases. Two hours later, they'd created a track about feeling so flustered, so taken by someone, that you become speechless, dumbfounded and tongue-tied around them. They called it 'Nonsense'. The track was brimming with one-liners, like the clever 'Treat me like a queen now you got me feelin' thrown' and, of course, the absurd 'Baby my tongue goes numb sounds like bleh, bleh, bleh.' The song took on another life on TikTok, where fans created short videos to a sped-up version of the track, pushing it to virality on the app. At the time of its release, it became Sabrina's best-performing pop radio hit thus far, spending four weeks in the top 20 of the Billboard Pop Airplay chart and 19 weeks on the Billboard Hot 100. More importantly, it showed that when her personality was on full display – a mix of sharp writing, innuendos and charisma – people ran to listen. In the music video, Sabrina's real-life close friends actress Whitney Peak and Paloma Idalia Sandoval dress up like guys at a party, embracing their inner swag and hilariously hitting on the real versions of themselves.

The song that took her the longest to write on the album was 'decode', a steady and lingering melodic meditation about accepting things you can't change. Speaking to *Rolling Stone* about the song, Sabrina began to well up, saying that she hoped for the rest of her life she could use the song as a compass.

The focus on songwriting, and hands-on approach to creating music and corresponding visuals was a success for Sabrina and *emails i can't send* peaked at number 12 on the Billboard Top Album Sales chart, sitting on the Billboard 200 for 42 weeks. Both the album and its artwork signify one of the most vulnerable and stripped-back versions of Carpenter she would ever share with fans. The album cover, tellingly, shows Sabrina with her back exposed, sitting on a bed in a bare room with a laptop. She told *Vogue* the image was inspired by a classic image of Kate Moss in a black slip dress. Her hair drapes naturally as she gazes back at the camera. Although she's remarked that, at times, she was nervous to put herself out there so fully, her open honesty on this album made way for an even bolder and more self-assured Sabrina as she moved towards the next chapter of her career. Her security in her art infused everything going forward, from her performance choices to her stage banter and, even, a fresh, iconic look.

At the 2022 Nickelodeon Kids' Choice Awards, Santa Monica, April 2022

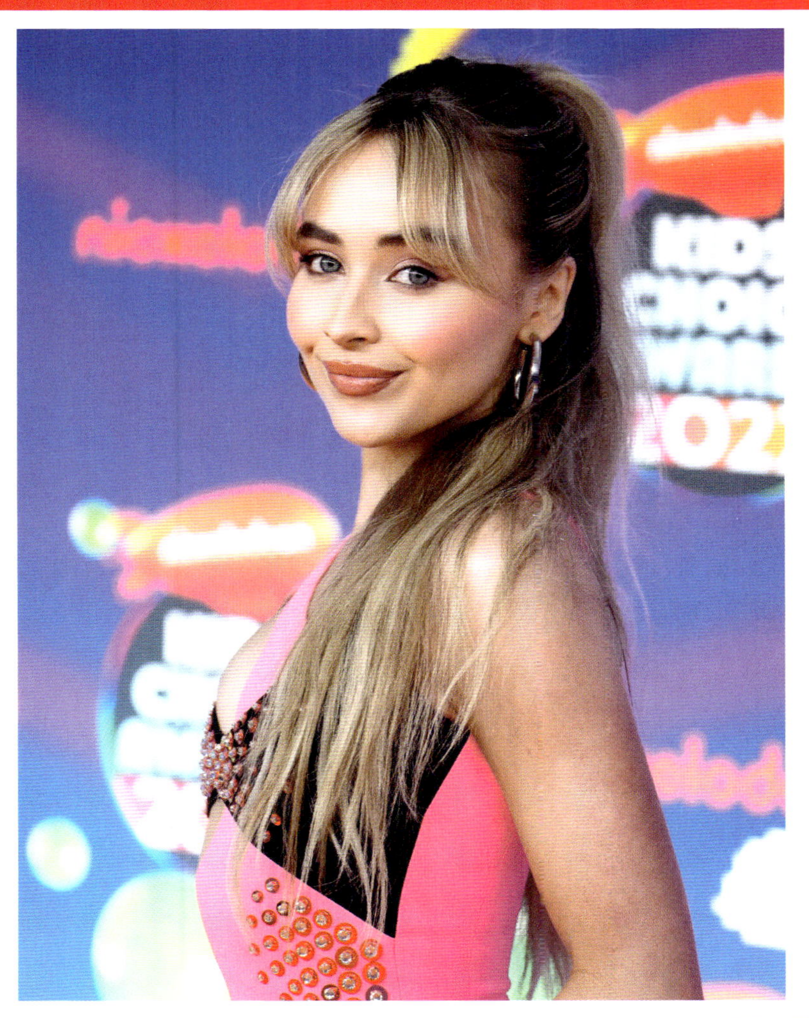

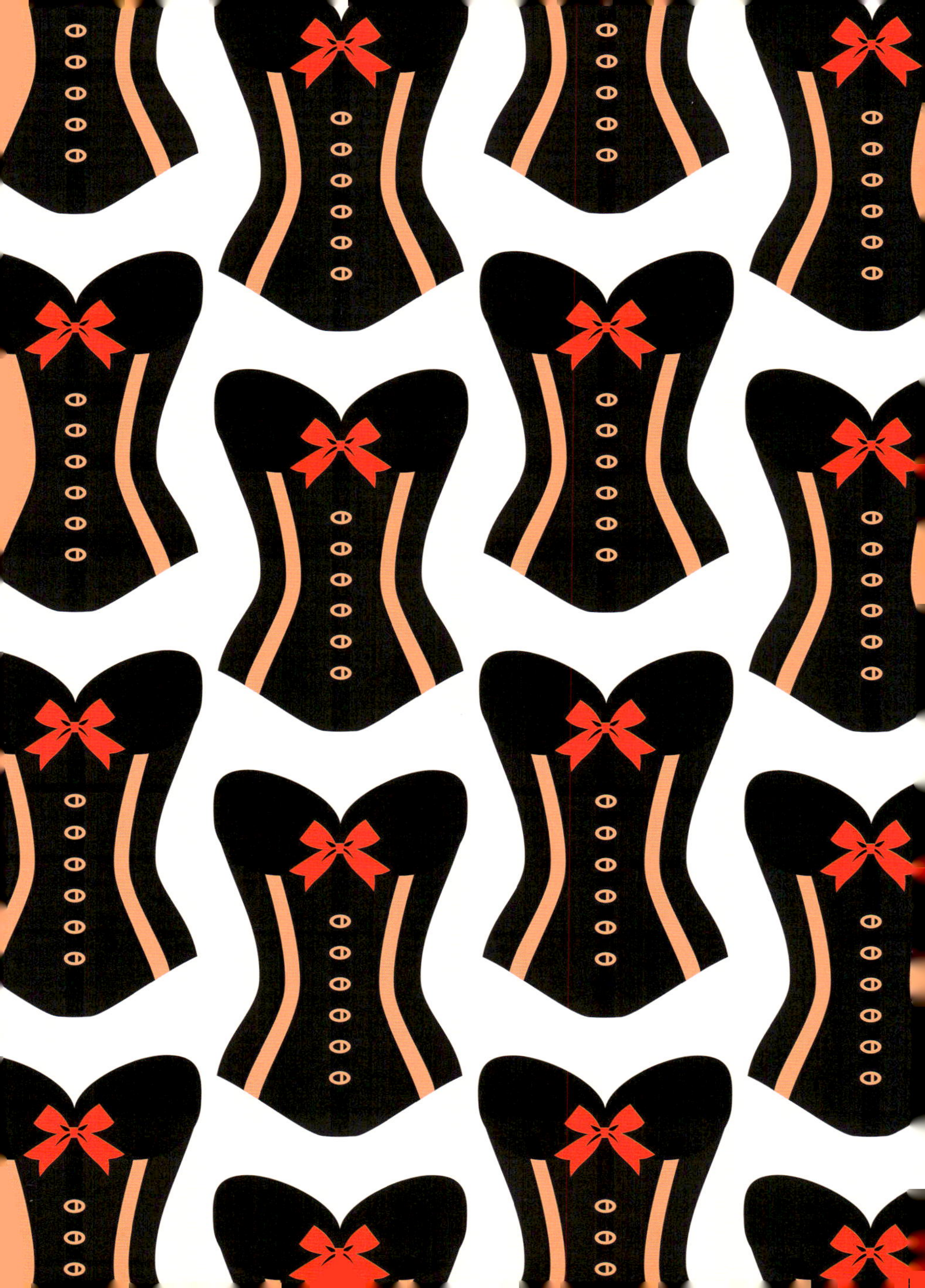

TALKIN'

'Nonsense'

Always Funny, Sometimes Filthy

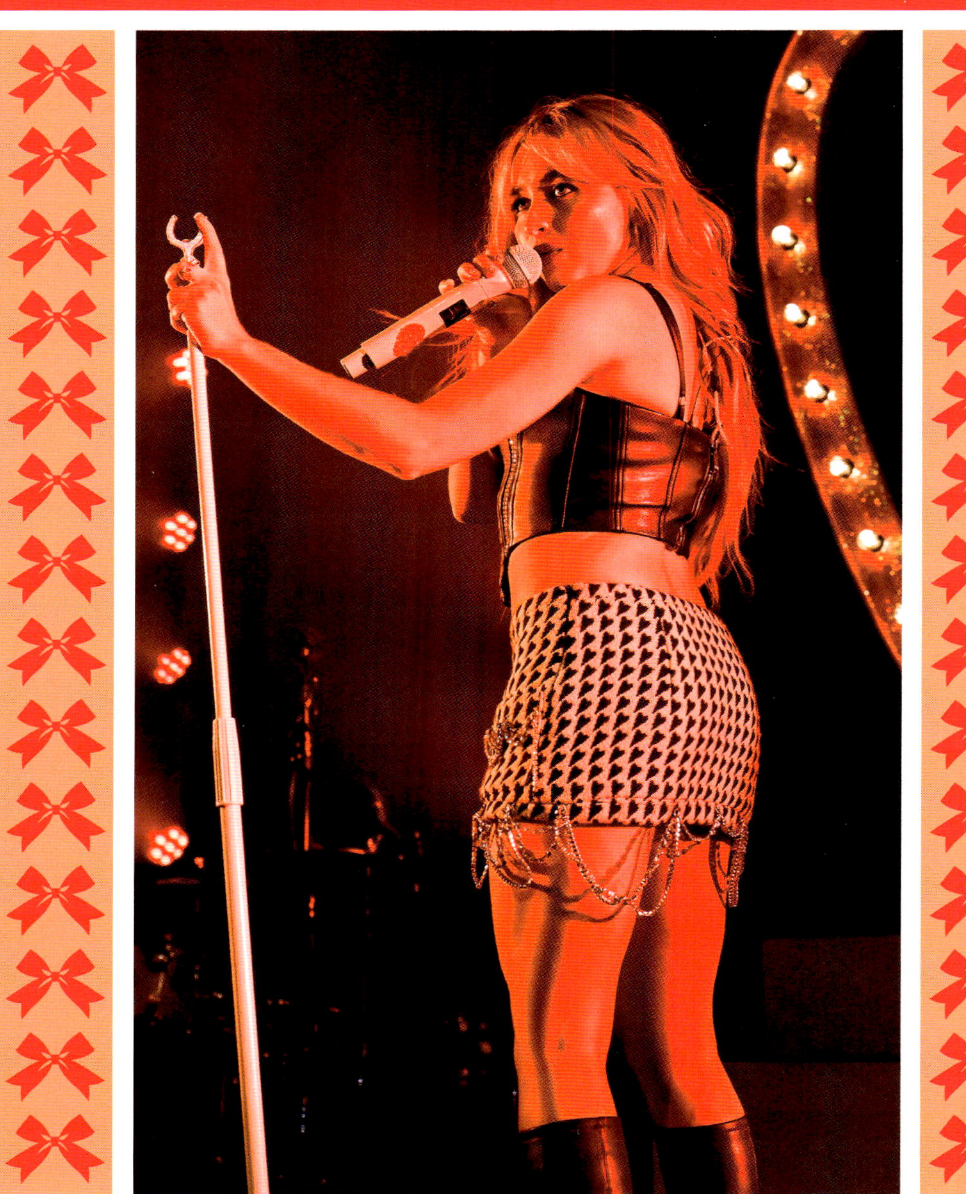

At the end of July 2022, shortly after the release of her fifth album, Sabrina Carpenter dropped a hint to fans via Instagram.

A throwback photo of herself as a child, wearing a white cowboy hat and pink tracksuit while holding a microphone, was captioned 'what songs would you guys wanna hear on tour ... asking for a friend.' She officially announced her *emails i can't send* tour on 22 August, with 12 shows spread out between September and October 2022, starting in Orlando, Florida, and ending in San Francisco, California. She then amended the first announcement with a second New York City stop to meet fan demand. Those shows, which marked Sabrina's first tour outing in three years, since she wrapped *Singular: Act II*'s live run, sold out in less than a day.

Then, in December of 2022, she shared another announcement on social media: 'i said i was done but i was just confused,' she wrote, adding that she couldn't wait to see her fans' faces and sing some new songs, before dropping another 36 dates of the tour. But she didn't stop there. In January 2023, Sabrina announced her first-ever headline UK and European tour, with 10 stops, including dates in London, Paris, Brussels and Amsterdam. She shared her excitement on Twitter, writing 'emails i can't send is finally coming to you and all your perfect accents!'

The tour was another marker in the upward trajectory of her career, as she played bigger venues and showed off a higher level of production. On her first run of dates, she performed in front of a massive bulb and neon-lit heart, filling each club with warm red light, and a backdrop draped with velvet curtains and tassels, giving the stage the look and feel of a cabaret. There was a moment in the set where crimson confetti and red balloons seemed to fall from the sky. It also marked the beginning of fans matching Sabrina's energy when it came to her stage costumes; they showed up covered in pink hearts, feathers and sequins, matching her aesthetic. The set was mostly made up of her current album tracks, with added surprises for fans like a cover of Jazmine Sullivan's soulful, vengeful track 'Bust Your Windows' and a throwback to one of her earliest songs, 'Can't Blame a Girl For Trying'. But one of the biggest surprises came as she performed her favourite from the album, 'Nonsense'.

Performing at the Regency Ballroom, San Francisco, October 2022

OUT-THERE OUTROS

On the album version, the sweltering song ends with the lines, 'This song catchier than chicken pox is/I bet your house is where my other sock is/ Woke up this morning thought I'd write a pop hit/How quickly can you take your clothes off? Pop quiz.' But when she performed it at her first tour stop in Georgia, she put a spin on the live version, ad-libbing and nodding to the city's nickname of 'Hotlanta' as she sang: 'Come over tonight, my room is spotless/I'm sorry this outro is so chaotic/Atlanta, it's official, you're the hottest.' That first switch up on the original phrasing would turn into online conversation-stirring, viral clip-making tour tradition.

She told *PAPER* that 'The "Nonsense" outros were a happy accident', adding that they came to her while sitting with her sister and thinking, 'I have all these extra lines from the song, let's shout out the city!' But then, as fans started to capture and anticipate each new ad lib, 'It took on a life of its own.' As the dates went on, so did the raunchy outros, with Sabrina pushing the limits further at each new stop. For example, when she got to Philadelphia, Pennsylvania, for her hometown show, she took her speech up a notch, saying 'This crowd is giving me all the endorphins/I wish someone would rearrange my organs/Philly is the city I was born in.' In response to her outros a fan tweeted, 'sabrina carpenter could write romeo and juliet but shakespeare could never and i mean NEVER write this'. At her headline set at San Francisco's Outside Lands music festival, she played into the joke, singing 'Soon cometh my album so exciting/My heart doth pound beneath my chest so mighty/Outside Lands, it's like thou art inside me.'

Though some called the 'Nonsense' outros vulgar, for Sabrina this was a natural way to share her sense of humour with fans. For many Disney stars, the transition to womanhood has come with risky music videos, provocative photo shoots (that seem to beg people to understand that they are officially no longer under the mouse ears), and even, sadly, public breakdowns. But for Sabrina it felt like a natural way to bridge from her younger persona to the person she was slowly becoming behind the microphone, holding the pen and on stage. This was no gimmick, it was just her being her, and fans appreciated it. She told *Cosmopolitan* that writing the outros gave her an opportunity to learn more about her sexuality, noting: 'I think people think I'm just obnoxiously horny when in reality, writing them comes from the ability to not be fearful of your sexuality as opposed to just not being able to put it down.' She told *Vogue* how much she appreciated the fan reaction to the (often NSFW), always ridiculous lyrical additions, sharing 'I was happy that people felt they got an unfiltered version of me, and they weren't running from it.'

Performing at Outside Lands festival, San Francisco, August 2024

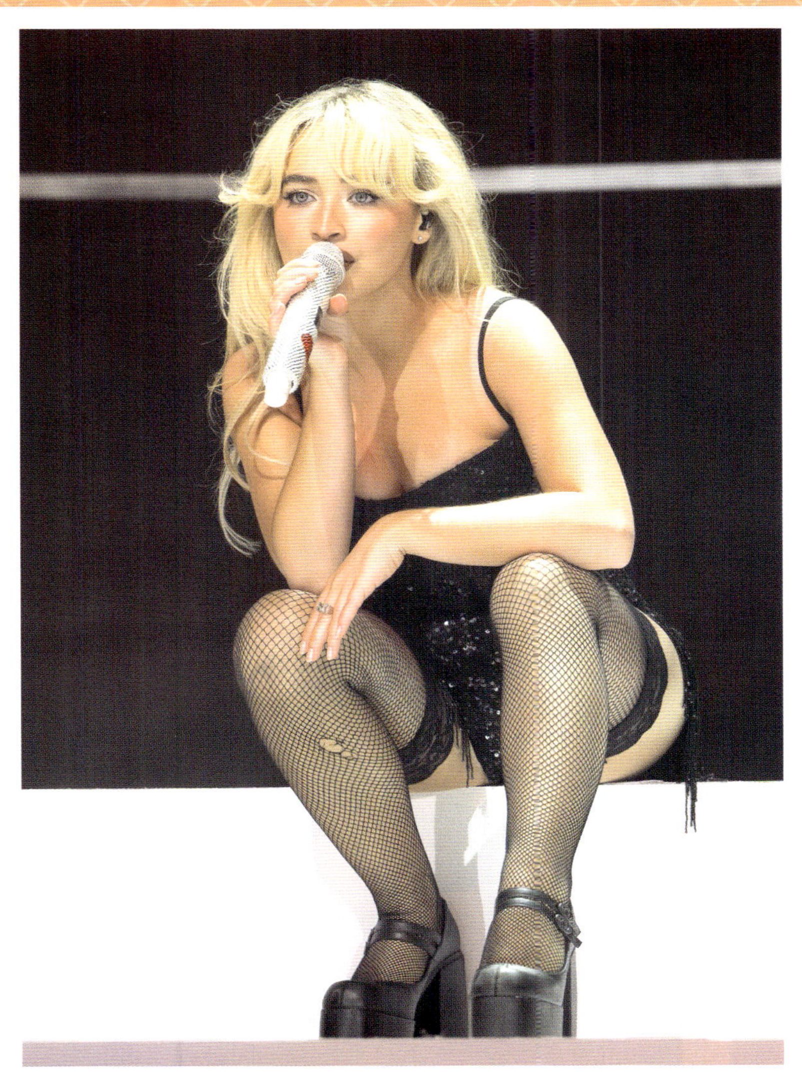

She also told *Billboard* why she felt unapologetic about her comfort with her own sexuality fused with humour. 'I'm not going to lie, I've made a lot of provocative jokes and I talk a big talk,' she told the mag, before adding, 'The outros are partially inspired by real-life and partially it's just [that] the more outrageous, sometimes the more fun it is.' And outrageous became the goal.

During a stop in California, she used her outro as an opportunity to call out the 'drivers license' controversy. She joked, 'I've got a great personality but no tits/This song is not about Joshua Bassett/Los Angeles your energy is big dick.' And during her Coachella set in 2024, she nodded to her then-partner, actor Barry Keoghan, by referencing a shocking scene in his film *Saltburn*, singing 'Man his knees so weak he had to spread mine/He's drinkin' my bath water like it's red wine/ Coachella, see you back here when I headline.'

The 'Nonsense' freestyle continued throughout her *emails i can't send* tour and on her global outings as she supported Taylor Swift's Eras dates. They even occurred on multiple live broadcasts. During the BBC's Radio 1 Live Lounge outro, she made a not-so-safe-for-TV play on the network's name. The network took down that version of the performance from YouTube, and even fellow popstar Charli xcx laughed about Sabrina's audacious lyricism, sharing 'sabrina carpenter explaining bbc on the bbc is so funny i can't.'

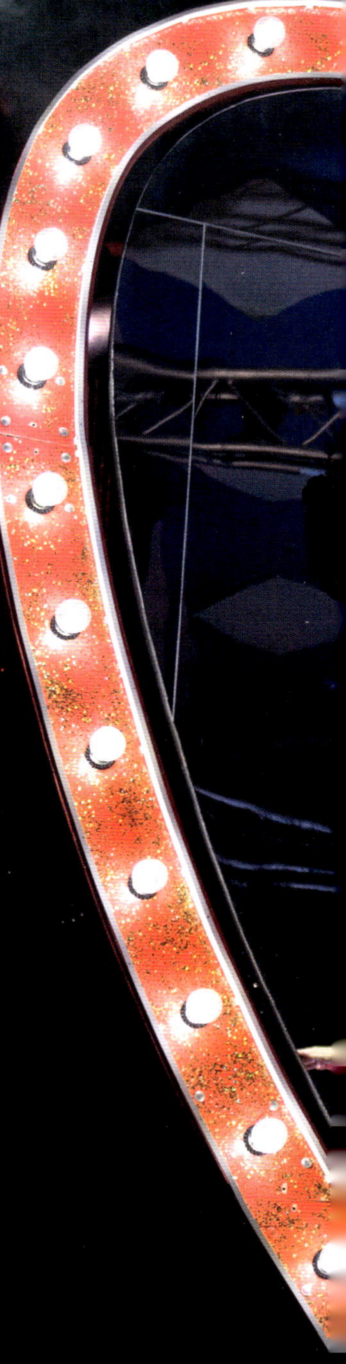

The Barrowland Ballroom, Glasgow, June 2023

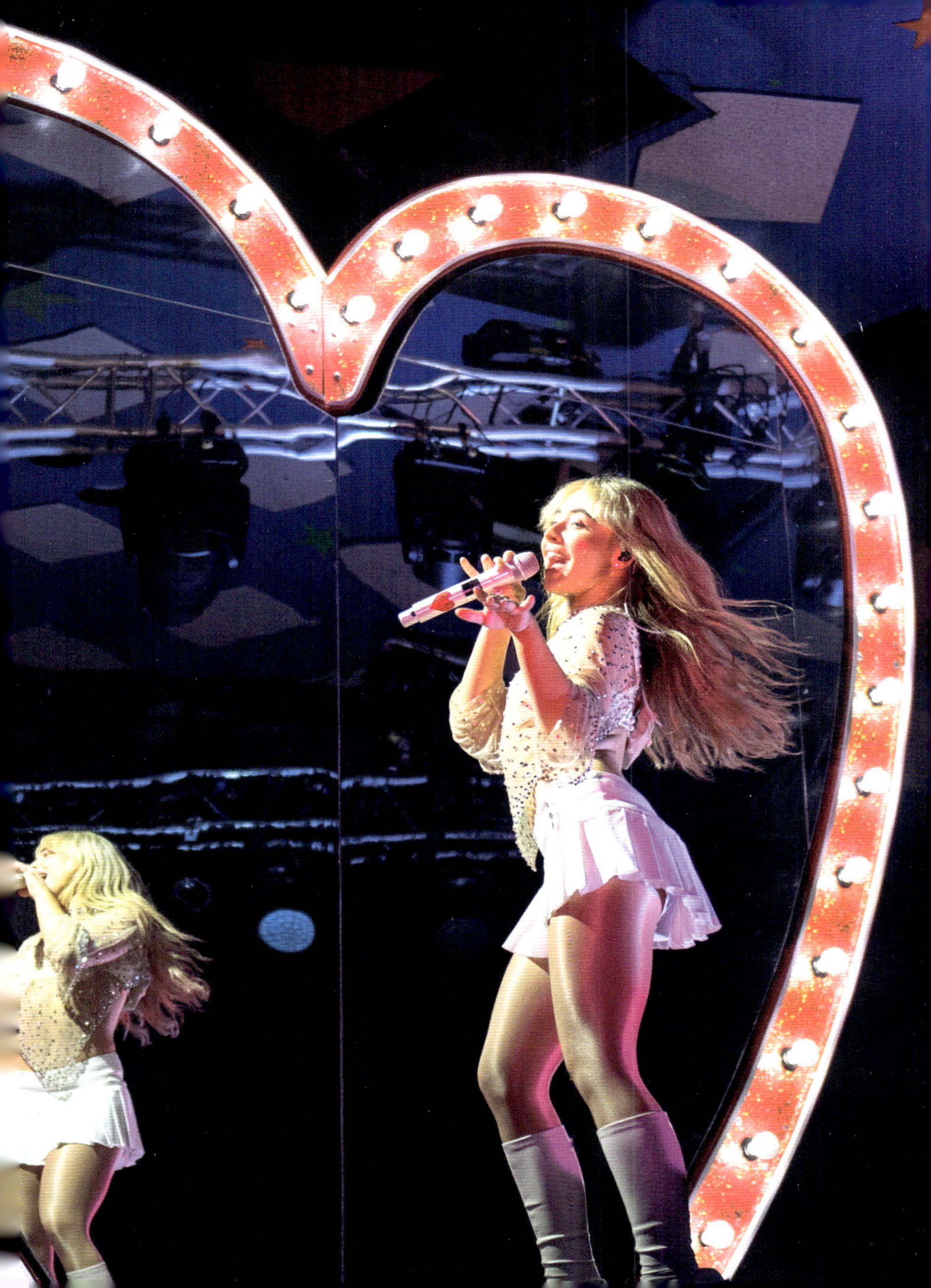

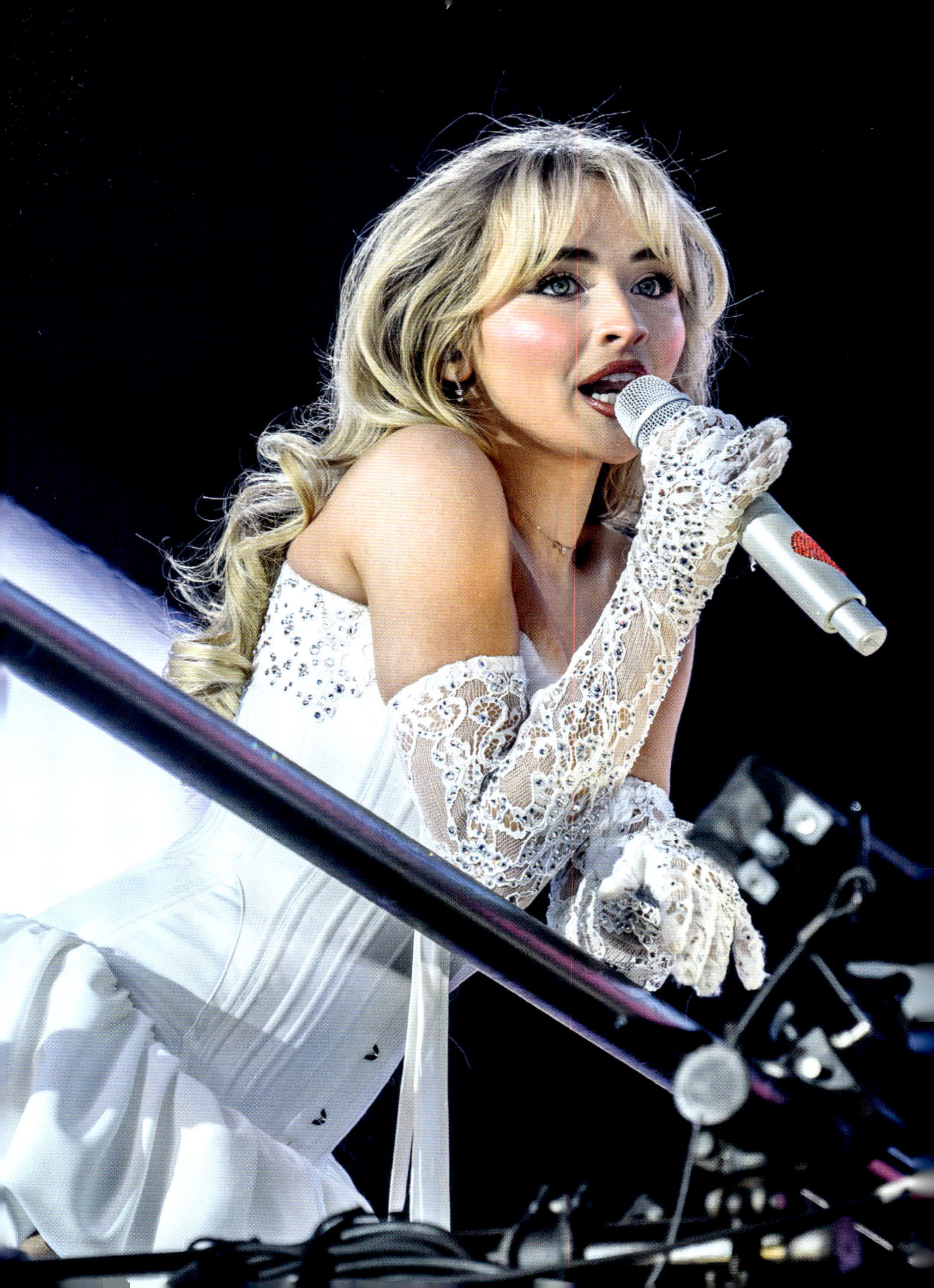

During her *Saturday Night Live* debut, she took the opportunity to show off her cheeky wit by pulling together a medley about the show's iconic location and her first visit, singing 'He is *30 Rock* hard cause I said hi./My sense of humour is, but I am not dry./SNL I just came for the first time.' When she performed on *Dick Clark's New Year's Rockin' Eve* she made viewers blush, closing out her 'Nonsense'/'Feather' medley with 'Clark is everybody's favourite dick type./Make a toast to everyone you dislike./Balls are dropping everywhere at midnight.' She just couldn't stop making quips, or headlines.

'Nonsense' will always be tied to a time when Sabrina was coming into her own as an artist – pushing her own boundaries, letting her guard down and bravely going where no lyrics had gone before. The song took on multiple forms, from 'A Nonsense Christmas', a holiday remix that saw the track re-written with festive nods to Charles Dickens, mistletoe and oversized packages. She also released a sped-up version, official, to match the one going viral on TikTok, as well as an official remix featuring rapper Coi Leray, with a new, collab outro: 'This song harder than keepin' a secret./He said my head's crazy, I'm a genius./What's better than one pop star? It's two, b*tch./ It's Coi Leray and 'Brina on the remix.'

'Maybe I'll feel ***random*** *one day and bring it back. [But] that was for that album,* ***for that era.****'*

Eventually, when she was heading out on tour in support of her sixth album, *Short n' Sweet*, she decided to put the outros to rest. At her first tour stop, in Columbus, Ohio, she pretended to start her off-the-cuff lyrics, but it appeared as though her microphone wasn't working. Then on a large screen, an apology for 'technical difficulties' appeared as Sabrina disappeared beneath the stage. She told *TIME* magazine that she felt it was time to move away from the bit: 'The extreme,"it's over forever" is just not in my repertoire,' she said, adding, 'Maybe I'll feel random one day and bring it back. [But] that was for that album, for that era.'

Chatting with the host of *Hot Ones* about the track, she called it a great lesson. She said that the song was so 'kindred' with her personality that she worried that it wouldn't be a good fit for the album. Its success showed her that 'whatever feels the most honest and connects with me the most will connect with other people.' Moving forward, that idea permeated each next, high-platformed step in her career.

Performing at the Times Square New Year's Eve 2024 Celebration, New York, December 2023

The REAL SABRINA

Sabrina the Popstar

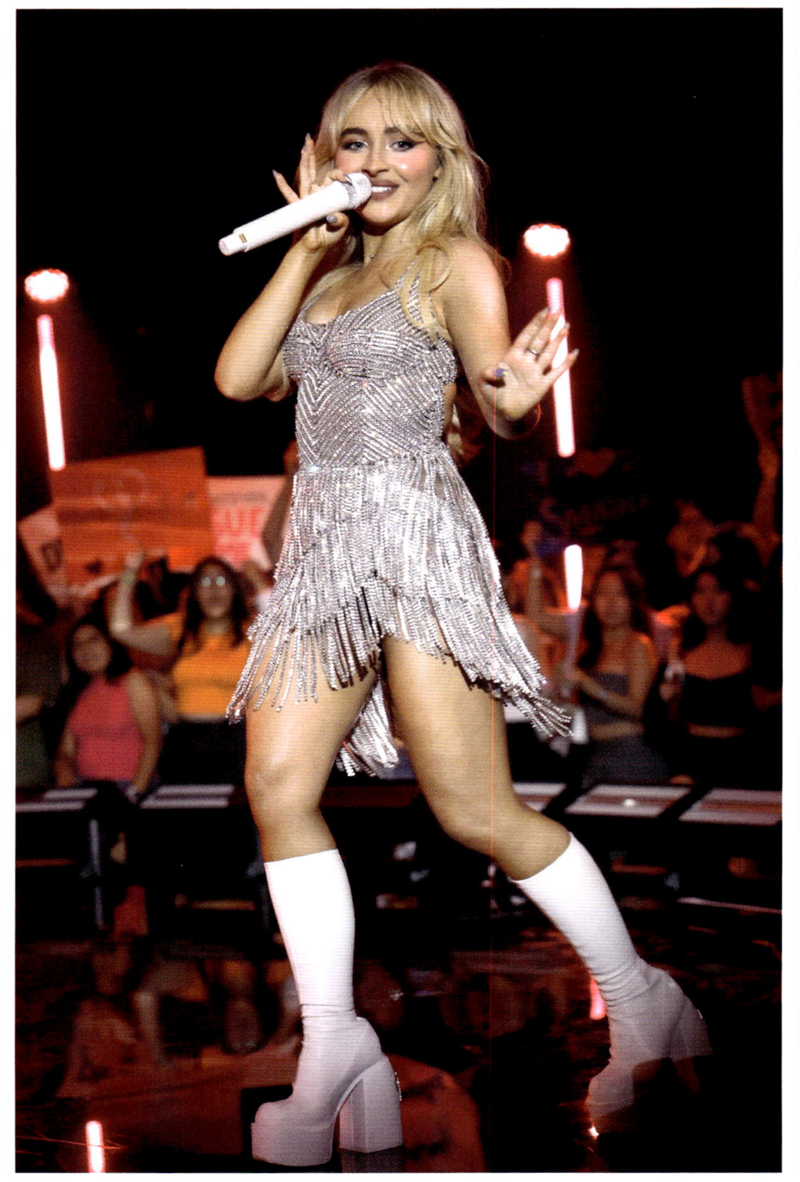

Once *emails i can't send* made it into the world, a new Sabrina – or better put, the real Sabrina – began to emerge. That transition to full-blown pop star seemed to start as she went on tour with her fifth album, but her authentic personality began to shine through even more when she released the deluxe version of *emails i can't send fwd:* in March 2023.

The updated version of the album came with the addition of four new songs, including the ethereal call-out 'opposite', the twangy guitar track 'Lonesome', and a heartbreaking acoustic love song called 'things i wish you said'. The other track, a disco dance number about the lighter-than-air feeling of finally getting closure with a toxic ex, called 'Feather', was released as a single.

She told Grammy.com that she 'wanted to make this song about all the s—ty events happening in my life, because it's so much more fun to turn it into a positive than to sit in the sadness.' The lyrics – again a mix of campy and sharp lines – tell the story of feeling lighter after dealing with an ex who sends mixed signals, asks for pics and judges you for the wine you drink; but mostly it homes in on the feeling of finally letting go and how it is not wondering where that person is every night. The song, co-written with her close friend Amy Allen and John Ryan peaked at number 21 on the Billboard Hot 100 chart and became Sabrina's first number 1 on the Pop Airplay chart. She performed the song as part of a medley at the 2023 MTV Video Music Awards pre-show. She wore a short, silver tasselled dress, and danced amid Las Vegas showgirl-style ostrich plumes, under a black-and-white retro filter, for her rendition of 'Feather', before the stage lit up in colour again for 'Nonsense'. Though it was for a smaller audience, it hinted at her VMA performance the following year, and what she'd be capable of on a larger stage.

Performing at the MTV Video Music Awards, Newark, New Jersey, September 2023

JESUS WAS A CARPENTER

She released a music video for the breezy, nonchalant song on Halloween of 2023, with a horror-film plot. In it, men catcall and follow her down the street, mansplain boxing, and one even takes a photo up her skirt, all without her consent. Each man meets an untimely, and sometimes bloody, demise. At the end of the video, Sabrina, rocking a teeny black tulle bodysuit and matching veil, dances in a cathedral in front of the pastel caskets of the deceased. Much of the video was filmed at the Annunciation of the Blessed Virgin Mary Church in Brooklyn, New York, and – after seeing the sexy visuals – the congregants there were not very pleased. It raised the same eyebrows as Madonna's 'Like A Prayer' in 1989 with its mixture of religious symbolism and provocative scenes; Sabrina wears an oversized cross in the video, much like Madonna's. However, this time around, there was more than online controversy and actual legal implications.

After the Diocese of Brooklyn condemned the video – saying that Monsignor Jamie Gigantiello, who gave it the go-ahead, didn't make a proper review of the scenes and script – Sabrina responded to the allegations. She told *Variety* that she had received permission to film, cheekily explaining: 'We got approval in advance,' adding 'and Jesus was a carpenter'. She even wore a custom 'Jesus was a Carpenter' tee during her Coachella debut.

Recording a controversial music video in a church may seem like a far cry from the Sabrina of *Singular: Act II*, who was still walking through cities in romcom-style videos, but by the time she released *emails I can't send fwd:* Sabrina was already slowly revealing – track by track, look by look and joke by joke – her true self. In fact, by that point, her signature look was nearly complete, thanks in part to the decision to snip her blonde locks into classic, and now iconic, curtain bangs. (In an interview with *Vanity Fair* she shared, 'I literally cut my bangs 'cause someone broke my heart and I was just like, "I have to do something."')

Arriving at Spotify's 2023 Best New Artist Party, West Hollywood, February 2023

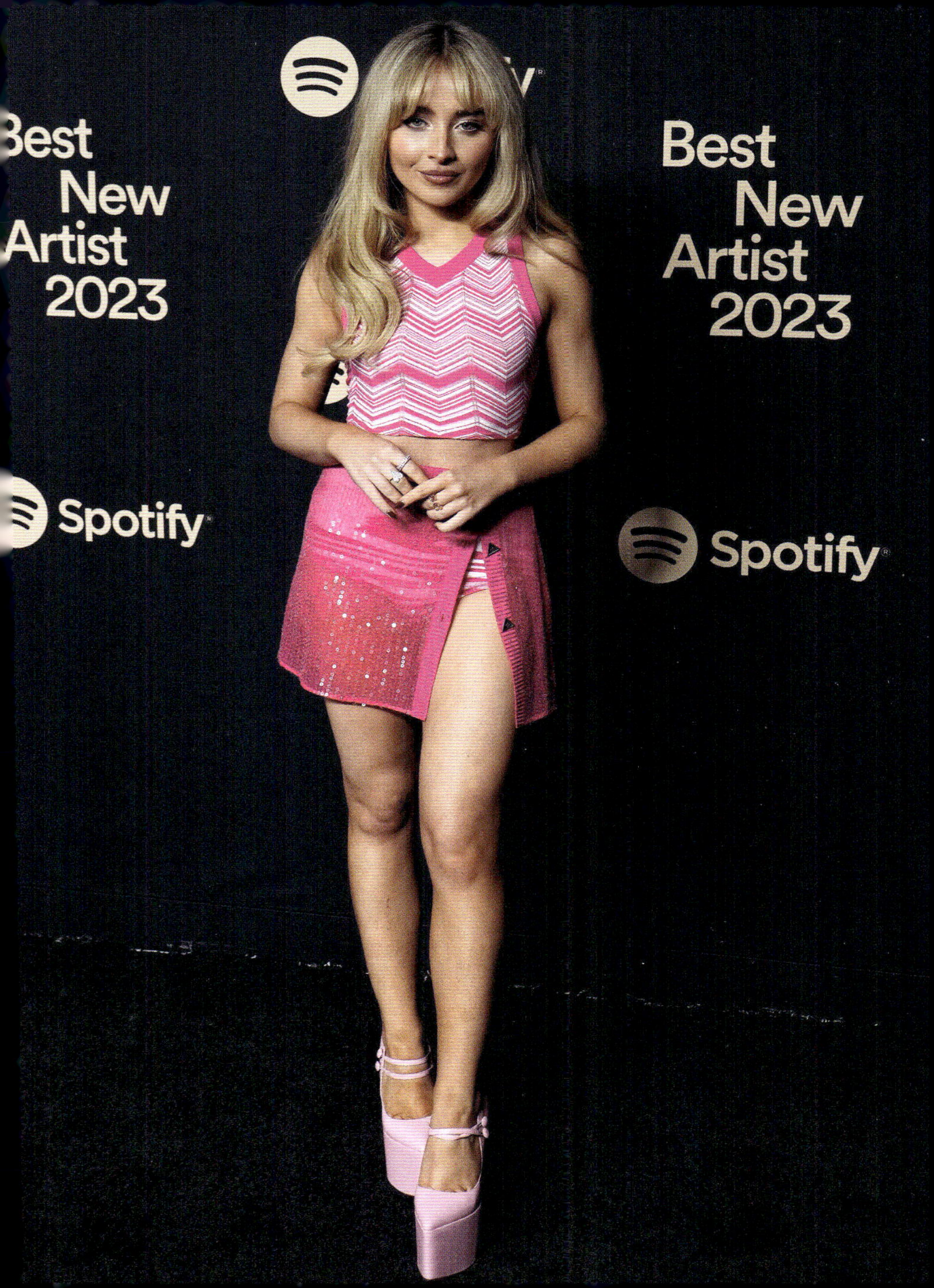

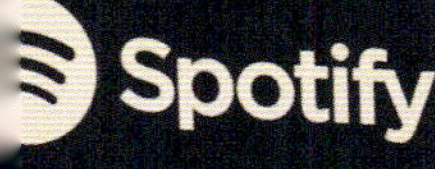
Best
New
Artist
2023
Spotify

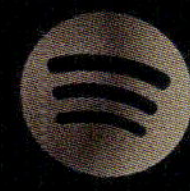

ICONIC NEW LOOK

The costumes she wore on stage changed as well, as she left behind t-shirts for more daring, glamorous, burlesque-esque fits. Her penchant for sexy silhouettes may have been there all along – see, for example, when she walked in Rihanna's Savage X Fenty show in 2021, wearing a revealing net bodysuit – and she even started to wear corsets on stage at the beginning of her *emails i can't send* tour. But as her live performances evolved, towards the end of 2023, so did her penchant for frilly lingerie and barely-there bustiers. By the time she brought her cheeky hits to New York City and Boston for iHeartRadio's Jingle Ball performances that December, her flirty corset, super short bloomers and garter belts had become canon.

Offstage, she was also morphing into a fashion icon: walking the red carpet at the Vanity Fair Oscar Party, sitting front row at multiple Paris and New York Fashion Week shows and ascending the steps of the hallowed Met Gala in May 2024.

Sabrina had explained the inner metamorphosis that was being mirrored in her look and visuals to *Vogue* in a 2022 interview, pointing to the time she spent with herself and her thoughts between *Singular: Act II* and *emails i can't send*, during the Covid lockdown.

'One thing that experience did do was that it stripped back a lot of layers of tolerating anything that's less than real,' she said. 'I didn't really have the energy to tolerate anything that was less than genuine and authentic at that time.' She'd also seen first-hand that her personality and her ability to embrace humour and sexuality led not only to a deeper connection with her fans, but to bigger success on the charts. She revealed to *Vogue* that she was thrilled when someone had listened to her fifth album and seemed to read her mind, saying 'It's almost like your music is a romantic comedy.' Her music was a match to her personality. She could finally be herself, which meant making some of her lifelong creative dreams come true.

A NONSENSE CHRISTMAS

In November 2023, she released a Christmas-themed, six-track EP called *Fruitcake*. It included a ballad called 'santa doesn't know you like i do'; 'cindy lou who', which refers to the characters in *How the Grinch Stole Christmas*; a cover of the classic song 'White Christmas' called 'white xmas'; and a song called 'buy me presents', filled with Yuletide wordplay. In 'is it new years yet?' she writes about wanting to get through the frustrations of being lonely at Christmas. The album also included the Santa-friendly version of 'Nonsense',

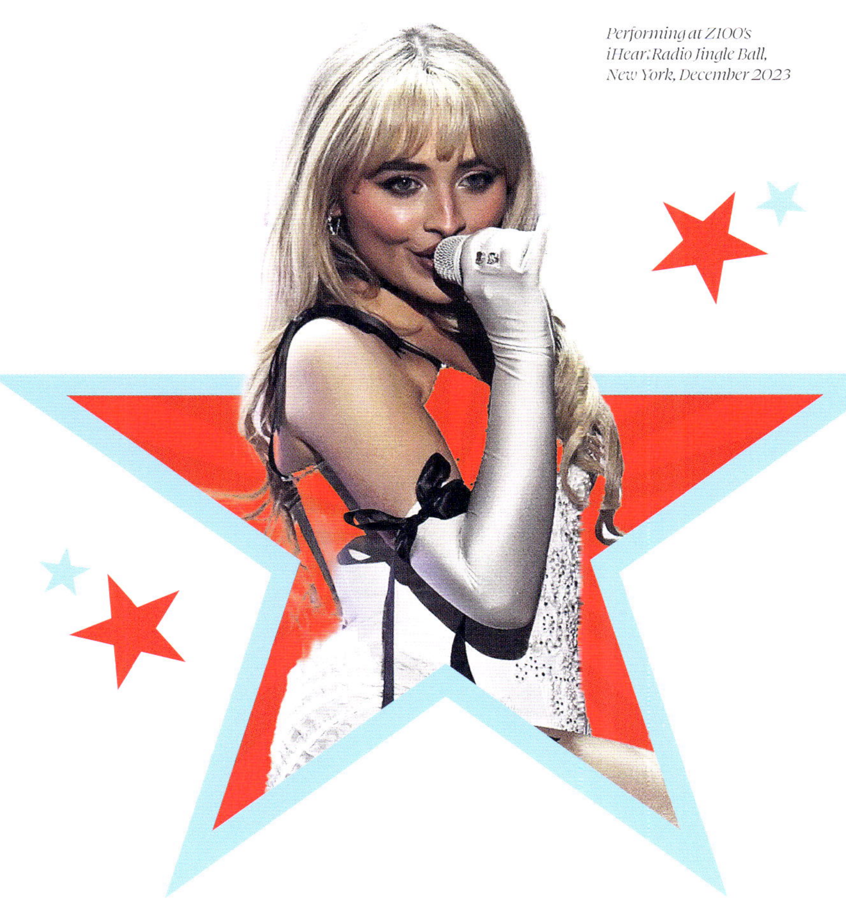

Performing at Z100's iHeartRadio Jingle Ball, New York, December 2023

called 'A Nonsense Christmas'. Critics applauded her for avoiding the trap of the typical Christmas album and instead coming up with her own, Sabrina-esque material for the season. In a *Grammys* interview, she said that the EP had been a dream of hers for a long time and that she'd originally wanted to write risqué Christmas songs because, growing up, 'Santa Baby' and 'I Saw Mommy Kissing Santa Claus' were always her favourites. She decided to do both, writing traditional songs with her own spin, sharing that on the 'very special project' there was both a lot that was new and a lot that was old.

After a banner year, Sabrina was awarded the Rising Artist Award from *Variety* in December 2023. In her speech, she looked back at how far she'd come and the mindset that had got her there. She told the audience that growing up her mum had told her she was 'the tortoise', nodding to the fable about the tortoise and the hare. 'That pissed me off a lot,' she said, adding that, throughout her life, she'd hear 'Sabrina, you're the tortoise, just chill,' and 'It's okay, you're the tortoise, just slow down.' She added that in moments of 'frustration and confusion, it can feel like a letdown, but it turns out it's actually a very good thing. And I've really loved getting to know the mindset of a slow rise.' However, after five albums, a sold-out headline tour and multiple chart-topping singles, 'slow and steady' for Sabrina Carpenter would soon be a thing of the past. And to kick off, she made a decision with big consequences – she agreed to open for one of the world's most famous pop stars, Taylor Swift.

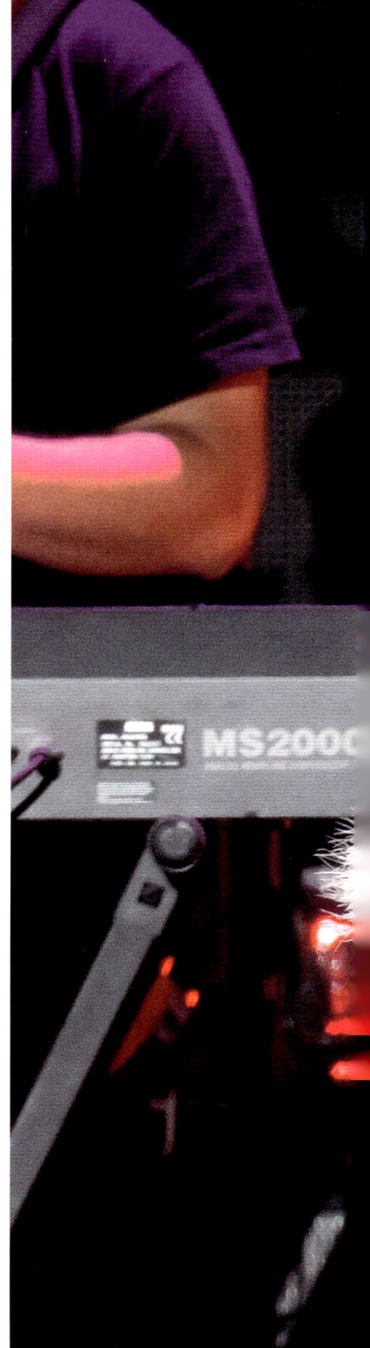

Right and overleaf: Performing at KIIS FM's iHeartRadio Jingle Ball, Inglewood, California, December 2023

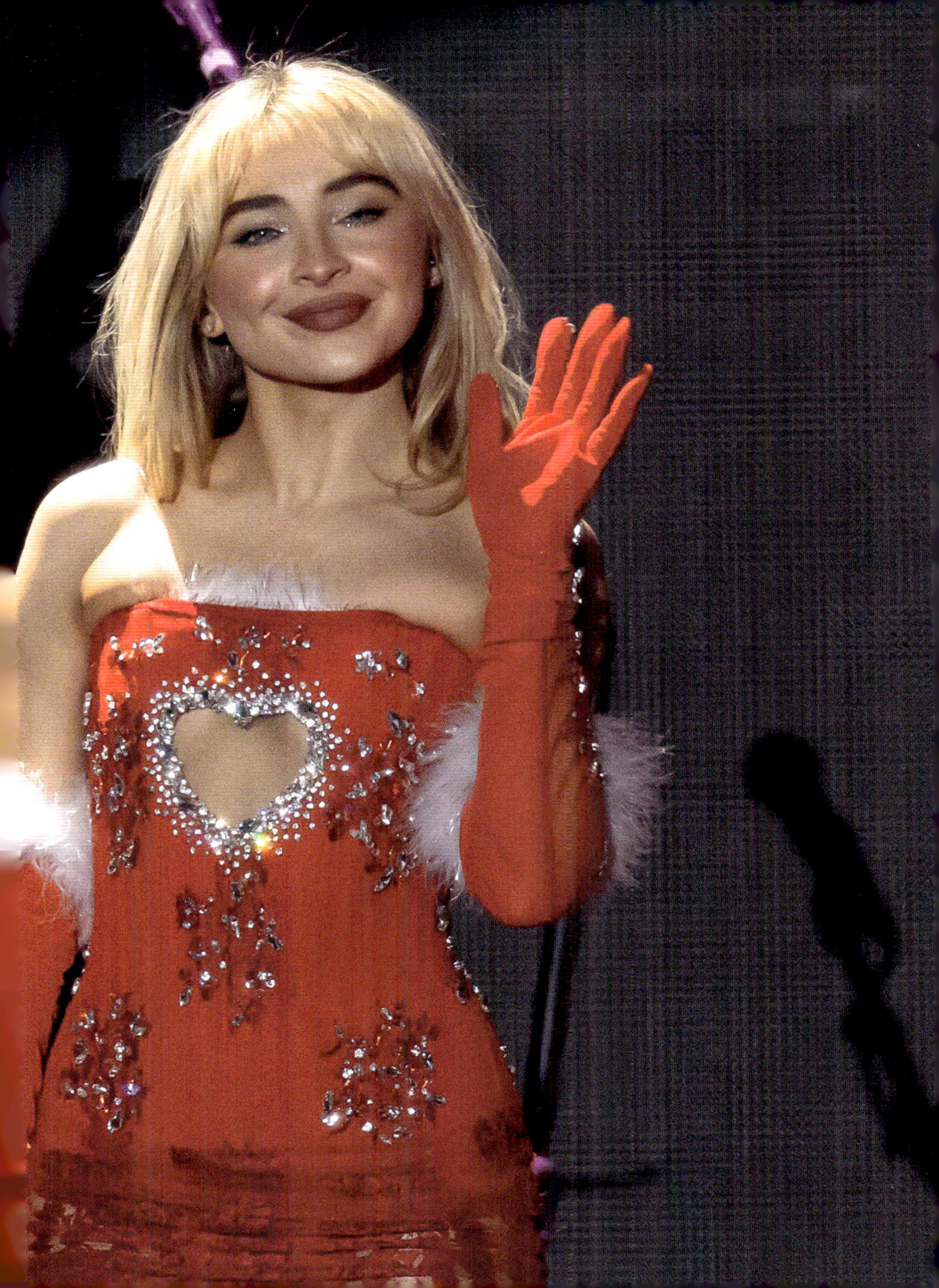

By the time she brought her ***cheeky hits*** *to New York City and Boston for iHeartRadio's Jingle Ball performances that December, her* ***flirty corset, super short bloomers*** *and* ***garter belts*** *had become canon.*

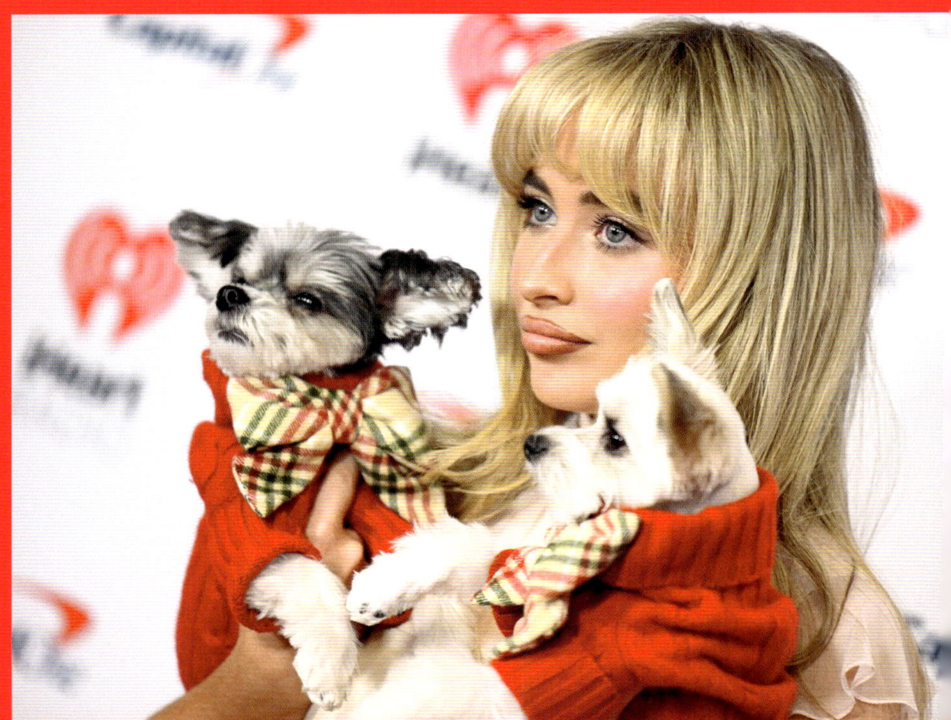

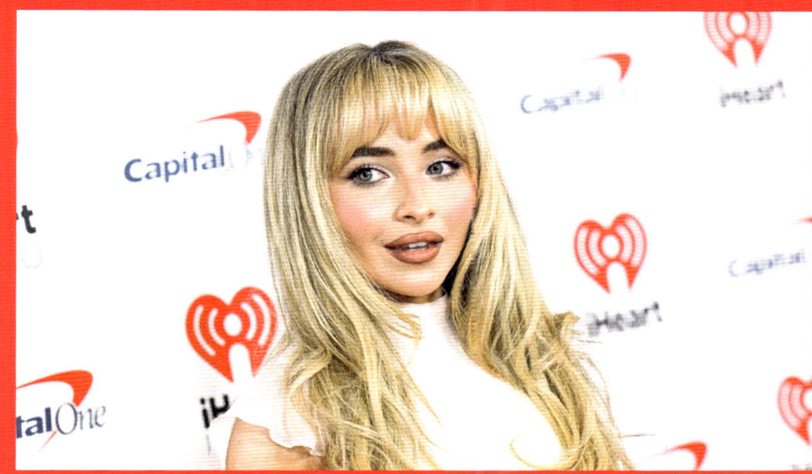

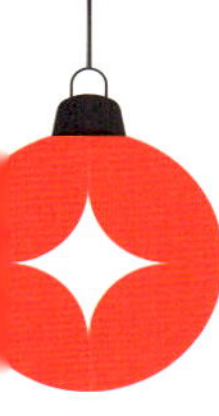

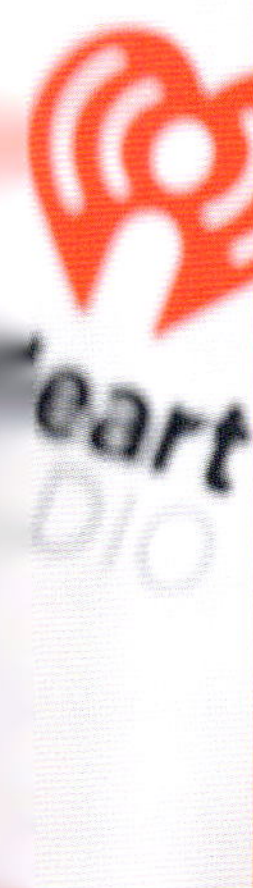

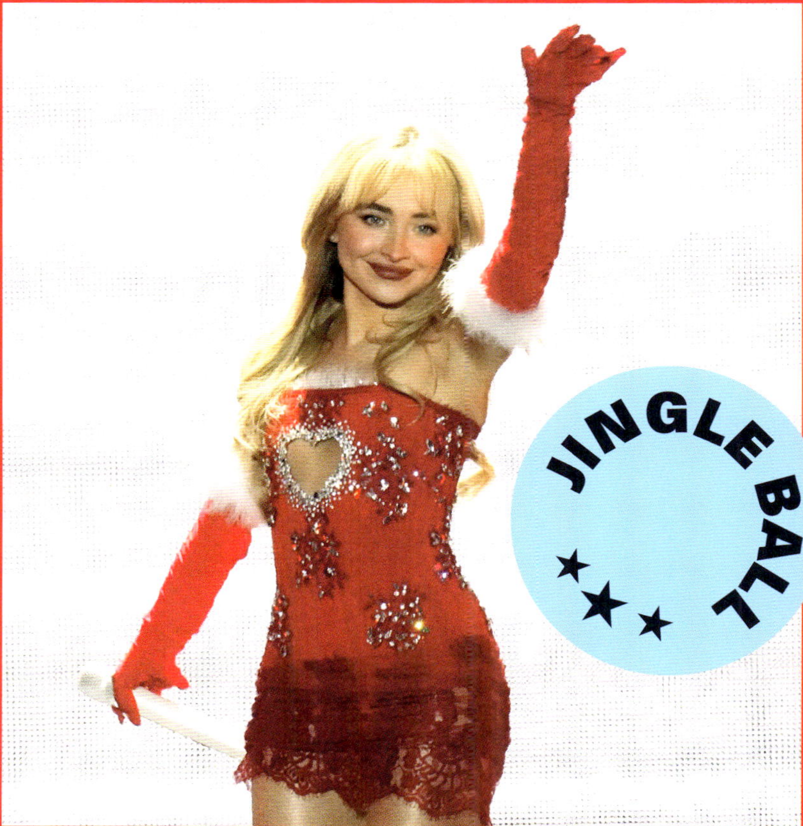

JINGLE BALL

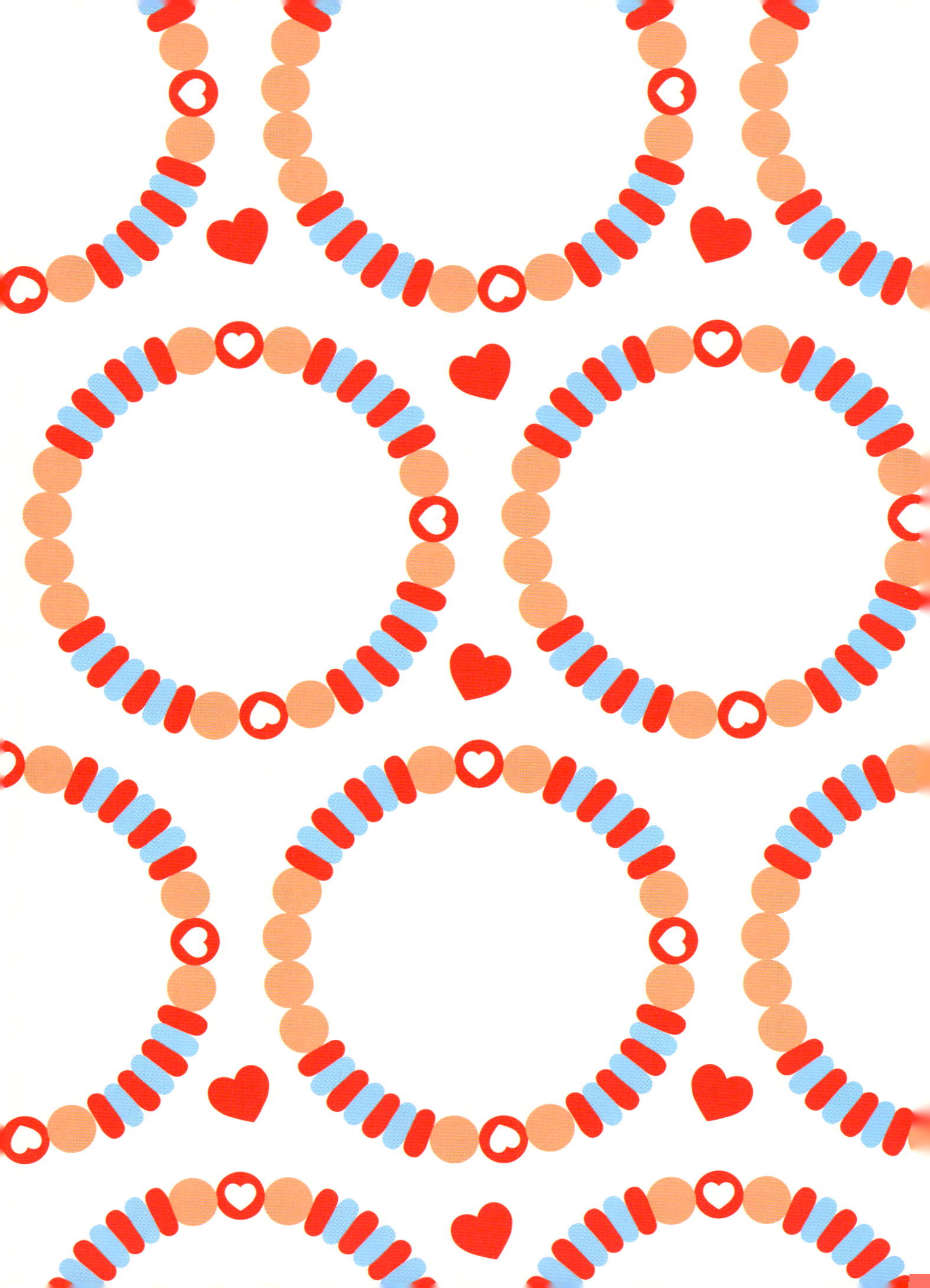

SABRINA
and
TAYLOR

Friendship through the Eras

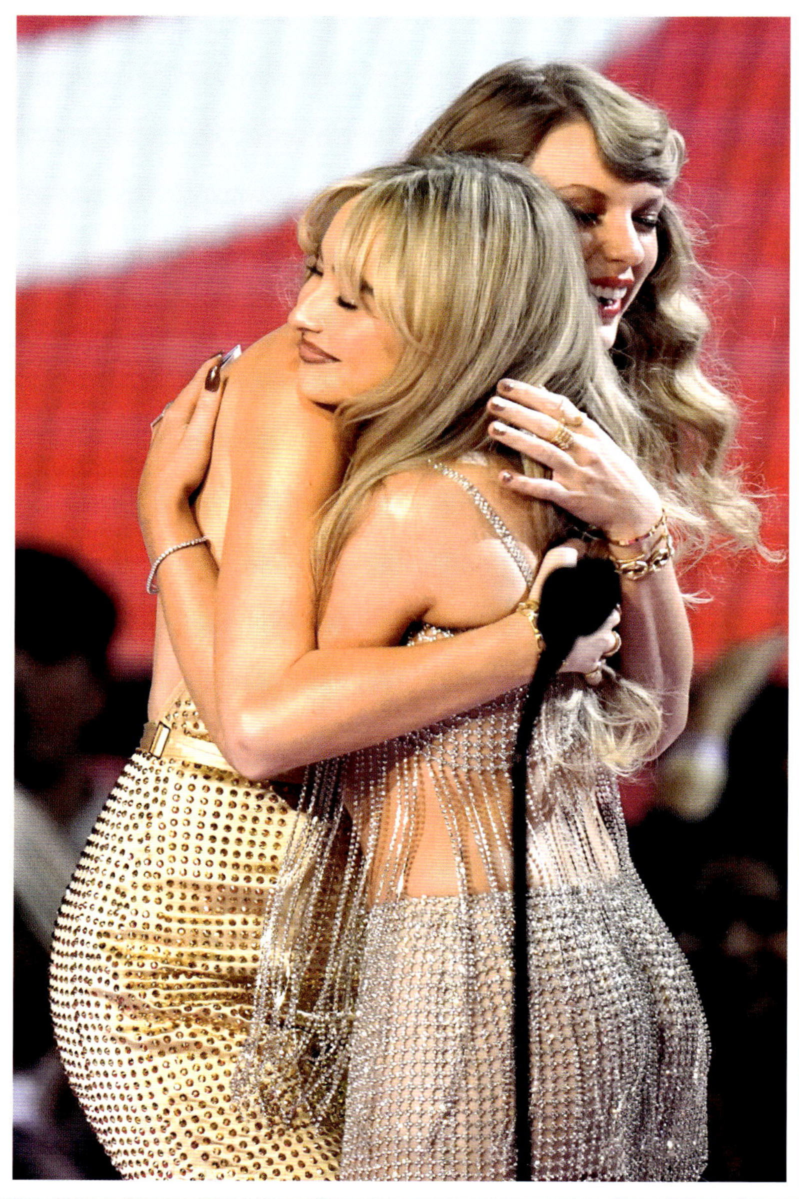

After spending a year on the road on her *emails i can't send* tour, Sabrina Carpenter got a message that would change the course of her life, career and creative trajectory forever. Her phone lit up with a text from Taylor Swift – no manager, no middleman (and, apparently, a lot of emojis) – asking her if she'd be interested in joining her behemoth, record-breaking Eras Tour.

Sabrina told Grammy.com that she threw the phone across the room (she also joked to *Who What Wear* that she wasn't going to say she peed her pants ... but that the moment really caught her off guard). She added: 'To call her a friend and be a part of something as iconic as this tour, I still can't process it.' It was a pivotal moment for Sabrina, whose admiration for Swift was based not solely on her songwriting, but also on her confidence as a businesswoman and her creativity as an artist. The tour took her to places to which she'd never travelled and placed her in front of a global audience who had never heard her songs live.

She joined Swift for 25 dates, starting in August 2023, opening for sold-out stadium shows. She played thirteen shows during the Latin America leg, six shows in Australia, and six more shows in Singapore. It was a moment 15 years in the making. 'That is one of my main inspirations ever since I was a little girl,' Sabrina said about Swift to *Billboard* before joining her on tour. 'Now, to be able to watch that show every night is going to be so special.' She also joked to Grammy.com that she almost felt bad that, as a fan, she got to see so many of Swift's shows (tickets to which were famously hard to secure), sharing that she felt lucky to have the privilege every night.

Hugging Taylor Swift at the American Music Awards, Los Angeles, November 2022

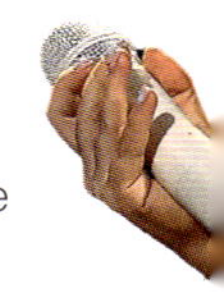

For her it was the perfect evening: performing a set she was comfortable with, having played her songs live for two years, then watching one of 'the greatest performers' she'd ever seen. She likened Swift's Eras performance to a Broadway show, calling it synchronized and yet still in the moment, referring to it as an 'art' that's 'hard to teach and hard to learn', when speaking to *Cosmopolitan*. Still, she absorbed everything she could from the star.

Her stage set-up, dreamed up over a year on her own tour, had been upgraded to fill out the larger stage. She joked that she had to bring a lot of energy to be visible, 'since I'm 5 feet tall', and had to make sure to take up space on stage. She brought special moments to the crowd as well, singing a cover of Olivia Newton-John's 'Hopelessly Devoted to You' at her first-ever show in Melbourne, Australia. She also sang a cover of Selena Quintanilla's 'Dreaming of You' on her stop in Mexico. In Argentina, she covered a track by one of her favourite acts, ABBA's 'Dancing Queen'. She also, of course, brought her 'Nonsense' outros, telling Mexico City, 'Felt so good he made me hit the top note/Eras tickets, girl you won the lotto!/Mexico, I kinda think te amo' and the Buenos Aires crowd, 'When I'm in the bedroom looking sexy/ He's having a ball, he call me "Messi"/ Argentina, will you be my bestie?'

Her glamourous garment game also got an upgrade for the bigger crowds. She worked with Ukrainian designer Frolov for some of her tour looks, including a custom-made black, short, corseted minidress with sparkling lace, white crystals and her signature heart-shaped cut-out. Her platform boots also took on their own sparkly embellishments. Frolov created a blue version of the dress with rainbow crystals, that she wore with thigh-high white socks. 'I'm in my short skirt era – no surprise to anyone,' she told *Vogue* of her look.

*'This is the **dreamiest dream** come true.'*

One of the first covers Sabrina ever did, at just nine years old – it still makes the rounds online, a black-and-white video of a small Sabrina in front of a makeshift backdrop – was of Swift's sombre song about heartbreak, 'White Horse'. Then, in 2009, Sabrina covered Swift's country-rock hit 'Picture to Burn'; it was the first song she ever uploaded to YouTube. For her tour debut with Swift in Mexico City, Sabrina opened her performance with that same video, shown up on the big screen. Next, her name, in her signature retro font, scrolled across the same video display. She spoke to *Vogue* after the set, saying it was magic, and sharing that Swift had the most welcoming fan base ever, before adding, 'I feel so lucky to be part of such an indelible tour.' The manifesting magic she'd conjured up wasn't lost on Sabrina, who in

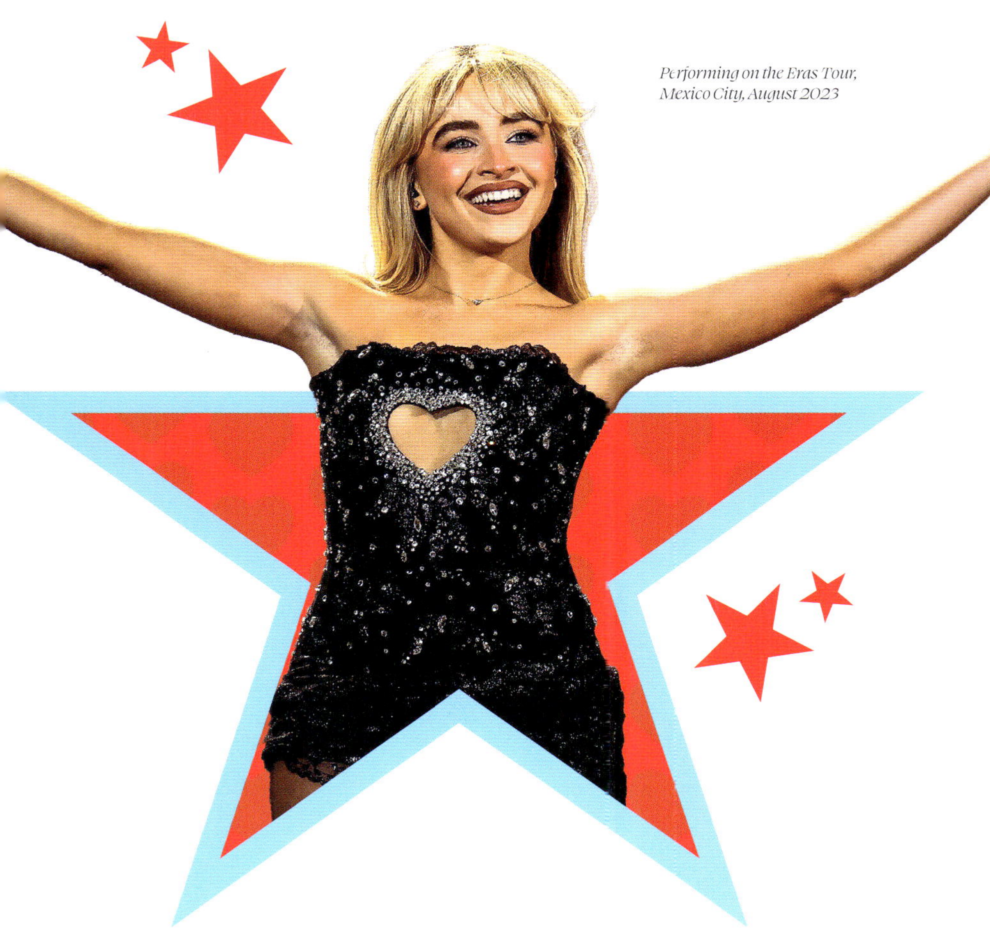

Performing on the Eras Tour, Mexico City, August 2023

2009 tweeted that she'd tried to enter a karaoke contest to win tickets to see Taylor Swift and have a chance to meet her, but was told no because she wasn't 13 years old yet. In 2010, she finally got to see Swift in concert and shared with followers that the show was amazing, adding that she couldn't wait to have a world tour someday, like hers, with sold-out shows. When Sabrina announced she'd be joining Swift's Eras Tour, she retweeted that old post, adding, 'This is the dreamiest dream come true.'

A SWIFT STAN

The fast friends first met backstage when Sabrina was 17 years old. They bonded over their love for felines (Swift had her cats with her; Sabrina has two white British Shorthairs). Sabrina has also said that her friendship with Swift felt like the relationship she has with her older sisters, a familial bond. Even then, Sabrina was a true Swifty. When Taylor sent her a ring and scarf as part of her *Red (Taylor's Version)* release, Sabrina shared a photo of the gift and of herself crying to 'Nothing New (Taylor's Version)' on her Instagram stories, with the caption 'thanks blondie' and 'being 22 is hitting very differently now', a nod to Taylor's track '22'.

In 2022, Sabrina was spotted with Swift at a VMA's afterparty, and told *GQ* plainly, 'I love Taylor Swift.' Shortly after, the pair were seen shoulder to shoulder as they attended the American Music Awards. Their friendship seemed to tighten as they took photos at a 2023 Grammys afterparty, and that May, Sabrina attended Taylor Swift's Eras Tour stop in their shared birthplace of Pennsylvania. Then, in June, buzz around their friendship hit a peak when Swift shared the announcement that 'angel princess' Sabrina Carpenter would be joining her on tour. Off the road, they continued to hang out, posing together at the 2023 VMAs and going together to a Kansas City Chiefs game to support Swift's beau, Travis Kelce. Sabrina later joked that after one vodka cranberry she wasn't thinking about football. For fans, seeing two of

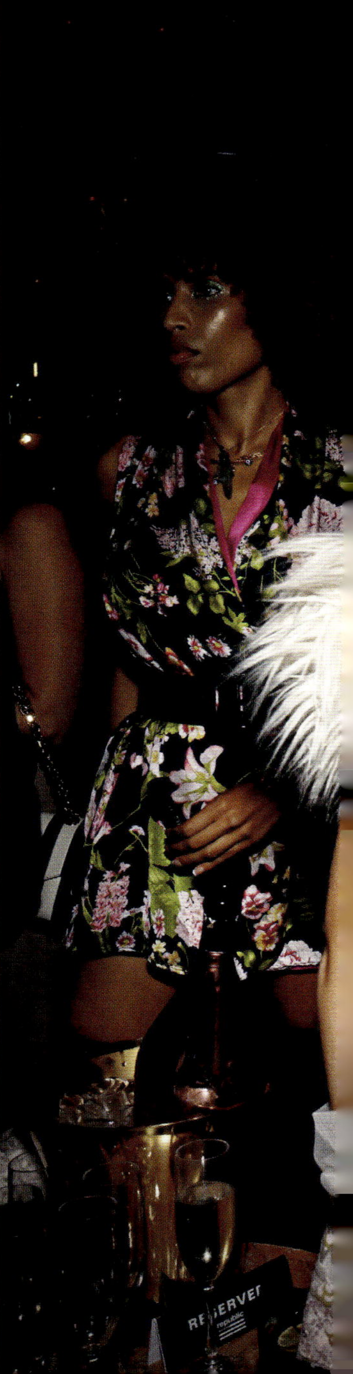

With Taylor Swift (centre) and Rosé (right) at the 2022 Republic Records VMA afterparty, New York, August 2022

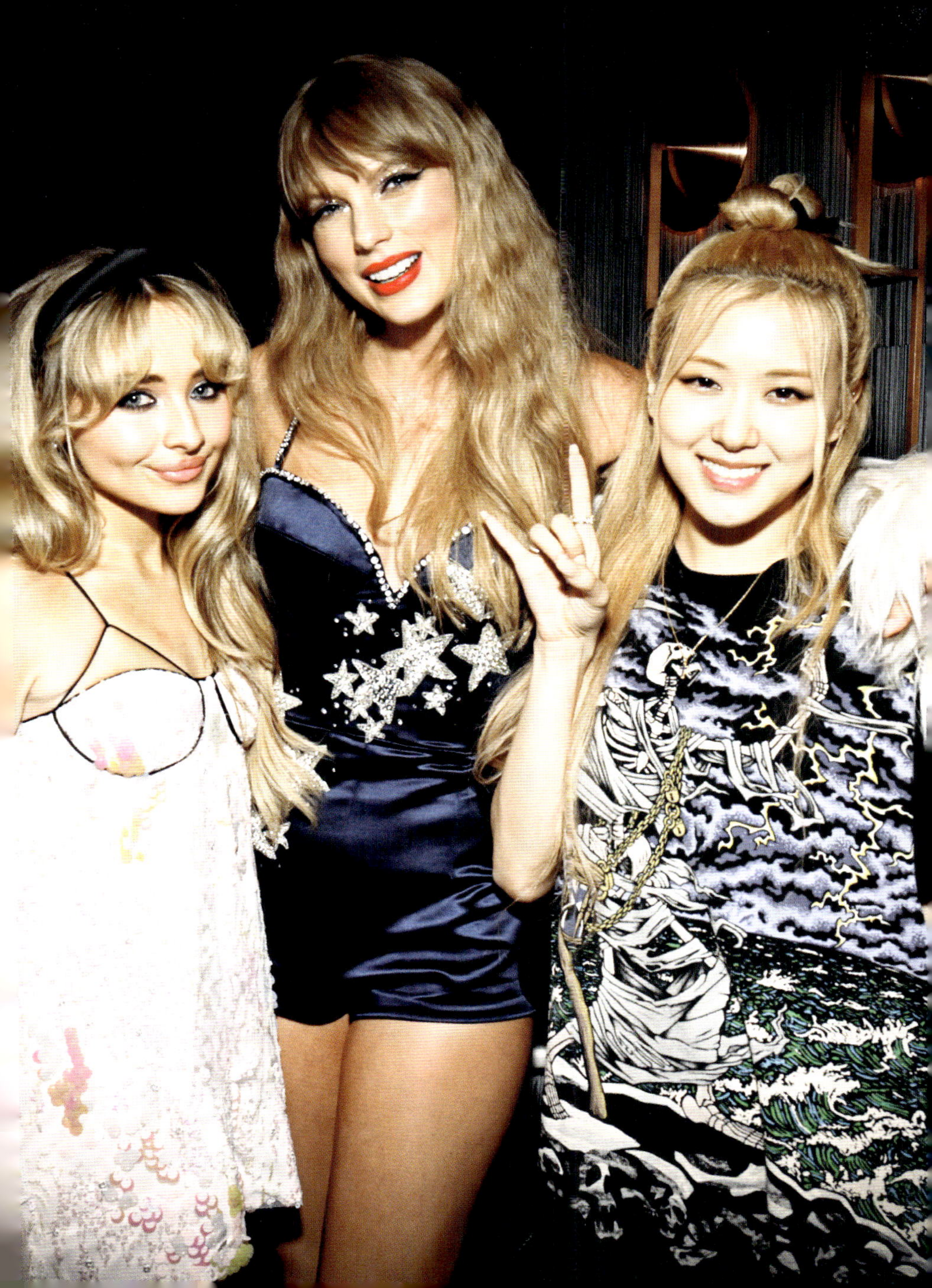

their favourite pop stars bond was exciting. For Taylor and Sabrina, it was a combination of mentorship and friendship that allowed them to share experiences and have conversations about a reality of fame and music-making few others could relate to.

In 2023, Sabrina told *Rolling Stone* that being around Swift was a masterclass, adding 'she's very good with words', before sharing that she had plans to watch her and study. That October, Sabrina released her first Swift cover in nearly a decade for Spotify singles: a stripped-back rendition of her synth track 'I Knew You Were Trouble'. Swift reacted to the cover via her Instagram stories: 'Well she nailed it.'

> ***'Love you*** *so so dearly* ***Taylor.*** *Always have* ***always will.'***

Their close bond continued to grow, with Sabrina spotted at Swift's intimate birthday party celebration in December, and joining Swift for dinner in Sydney, as well as hanging out with Swift and Kelce on a trip to the Sydney Zoo during their Eras Tour stop. Sabrina's sister Cayla also took part in the outing, as they fed kangaroos and snapped selfies in front of koalas. One of the sweetest full-circle moments, however, was a duet of 'White Horse' and 'Coney Island' on 23 February 2024. After the songs, Swift wrapped her arms around Sabrina in a sisterly embrace. In an Instagram post immortalizing the otherworldly moment, with photos of them hugging each other behind a piano, Sabrina joked her nine-year-old self would never have seen this coming. She added, 'love you so so dearly Taylor. Always have always will.' Later, she told the *Today* show in Sydney that 'White Horse' was the first song she ever learned on guitar. She added that her mum called her the next day saying 'I don't know how you just didn't start sobbing.'

In March 2024, Sabrina officially wrapped her run of shows opening for Swift. She wrote a heartfelt note about the 'taybrina era' on an Instagram post, calling the tour a 'whirlwind' and saying thank you, to fans for giving her some of the most impressive friendship bracelets she'd ever seen and, of course, to Taylor.

In April, Swift, Kelce, Sabrina and Barry Keoghan were seen dancing at Coachella during rapper Ice Spice's set, the same weekend of Carpenter's debut at the festival. However, that same month, there were internet whispers that attempted to pull the two apart. Sabrina featured in Kim Kardashian's SKIMS Stretch Lace and Fits Everybody styles campaign, rocking a '90s bombshell look with her signature big blonde locks, and wearing both delicate lace lingerie and a comfy two-piece set.

Kardashian called her 'the pop star of the next generation'. In a statement from the brand, Sabrina said she loved the creative and femininity behind the looks and the campaign, adding that she had always been a fan of the brand.

Fans were wary of Sabrina's connection to Kardashian, as Swift and the shapewear mogul had famously feuded in 2016. But Sabrina was clear when speaking to *Rolling Stone* that she'd spoken to her close friend and was very communicative about the situation, and loved her and supported her 'til the end. In short, there was no 'weirdness'; rather, Sabrina felt that people say things because 'that's all they have time to do.' It confirmed what Sabrina had said all along, that Swift knew her well outside of just their music, and that their connection couldn't easily be tarnished. 'To work with someone [who] cares about you as a person as well as an artist ... that's been the biggest gift for sure,' she told *Who What Wear* of their friendship.

By July the rumours had died out, with Sabrina telling *Variety* that her and Swift were the type of best friends that grab dinner and text, and catch up. She also shared that they always play each other their music, and get advice from each other, because 'you can't just ask the internet.'

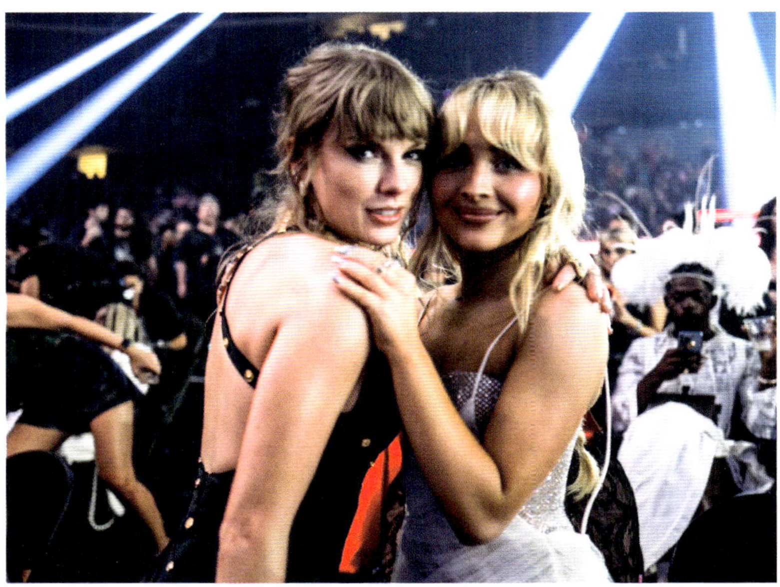

With Taylor Swift at the MTV Video Music Awards, Newark, New Jersey, September 2023

HOW TO BE A STAR

When asked on *CBS Mornings* if Swift had given her advice about handling fame, Sabrina said that most of what she learned from the megastar was through her example – the way that she's composed, graceful and gracious when she walks into a room. She also told *Billboard* that she'd grown up taking advice from Swift's songs, calling them a 'how-to book on how to survive as a young woman'. When, that same month, Sabrina had her first number 1 hit and an entire sold-out tour at the same time, Swift couldn't be happier, commenting on the post: 'Summer of Sabrina may it continue forever' in all caps.

That October, fans got another chance to see 'taybrina' take the stage. During her Eras Tour New Orleans stop, Swift took a moment to ask a fan in the crowd if she could borrow their phone to make a phone call. She then asked everyone to be quiet, because she was going to put it on speakerphone. That's when Sabrina answered, her voice filling up the stadium. Taylor joked that she was somewhere really loud, and asked Sabrina, 'What are you doing, why aren't you here with us?' Sabrina quipped back, 'I'm somewhere everyone is screaming so loud too.' Taylor then asked Sabrina how long it would take her to get there. The crowd erupted as Sabrina responded, 'Probably like five seconds.' The duo played a medley of songs, including Sabrina's 'Espresso' and 'Please Please Please' and Taylor's 'Is It Over Now?' Later, Swift reflected on Sabrina joining her at the show in an Instagram post, writing 'She's as real as they come, and I'm thankful she did that for us.'

In February 2025, when Sabrina picked up her Grammy for Best Pop Vocal Album, Swift was in the audience. The moment that she heard Sabrina's name, she burst from her seat and started hopping up and down. She also couldn't stay seated during Sabrina's performance, beaming up at her while dancing to 'Espresso'.

But playing on such a big stage, supporting one of the world's biggest artists, didn't come without its fair share of nerves. Sabrina told *Who What Wear* that the experience was vastly different to playing with an audience that's there for you, knows your songs and came to see you. Still, she leaned into the pressure, learning how to work the larger-than-life room. 'I go into it with a little bit more excitement, being playful and just really singing and interacting with the crowd as much as I possibly can,' she said. 'There's so many of them – I can't see them all.'

Performing on the Eras Tour, Singapore, March 2024

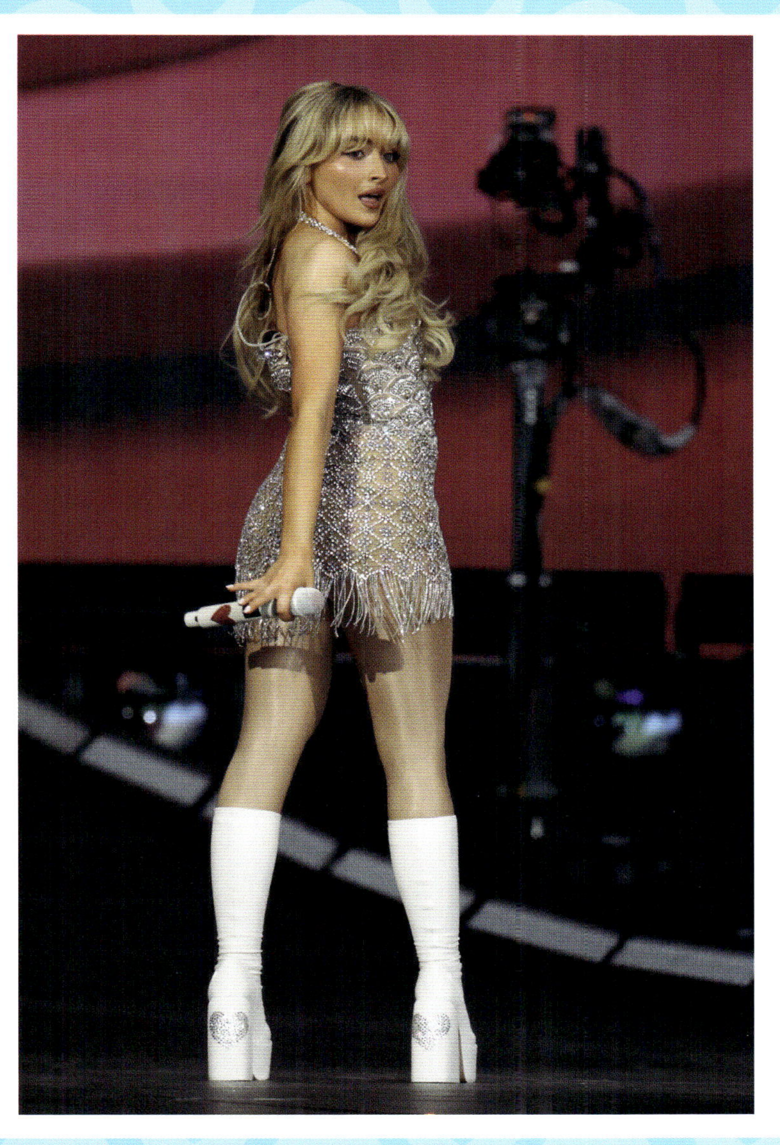

Going on the road with Swift was a study in what it takes to be a world-class pop star, and Sabrina was ready to pass the test as she got closer to her own headline tour. She told *Cosmopolitan* that the Eras run made her want to tour the world again. Though many fans have dubbed her a 'Taydaughter' because of her songwriting and stage presence, clearly influenced by Swift (she told *Rolling Stone* that she sees Swift in 'such a different echelon' and 'could never compare my life, my career, my trajectory to anything close to what she's done'). Sabrina, at that point, was ready to create a world all her own.

She told *Vogue*, 'Her stadiums make my shows look like clubs. Watching her keep their attention as if she's playing in their living room ... I told her this, "Your tour enabled me to do mine".' And Sabrina brought what she learned on tour with Swift to her own meteoric next chapter, with even bigger songs and even bigger crowds, and her first-ever number 1 Billboard hits.

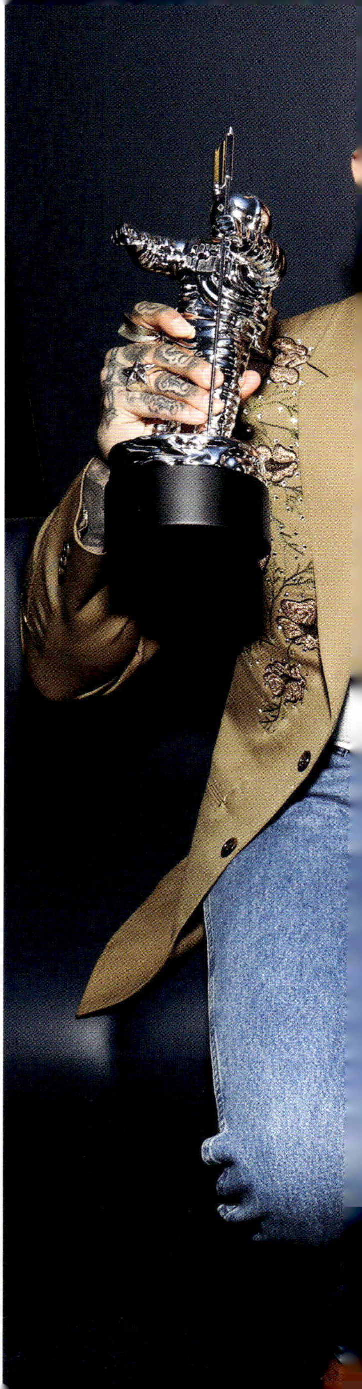

With Post Malone (left) and Taylor Swift (centre) at the MTV Video Music Awards, New York, September 2024; overleaf: Performing on the Eras Tour in New Orleans (left and below right) and Sydney (top right) in 2024

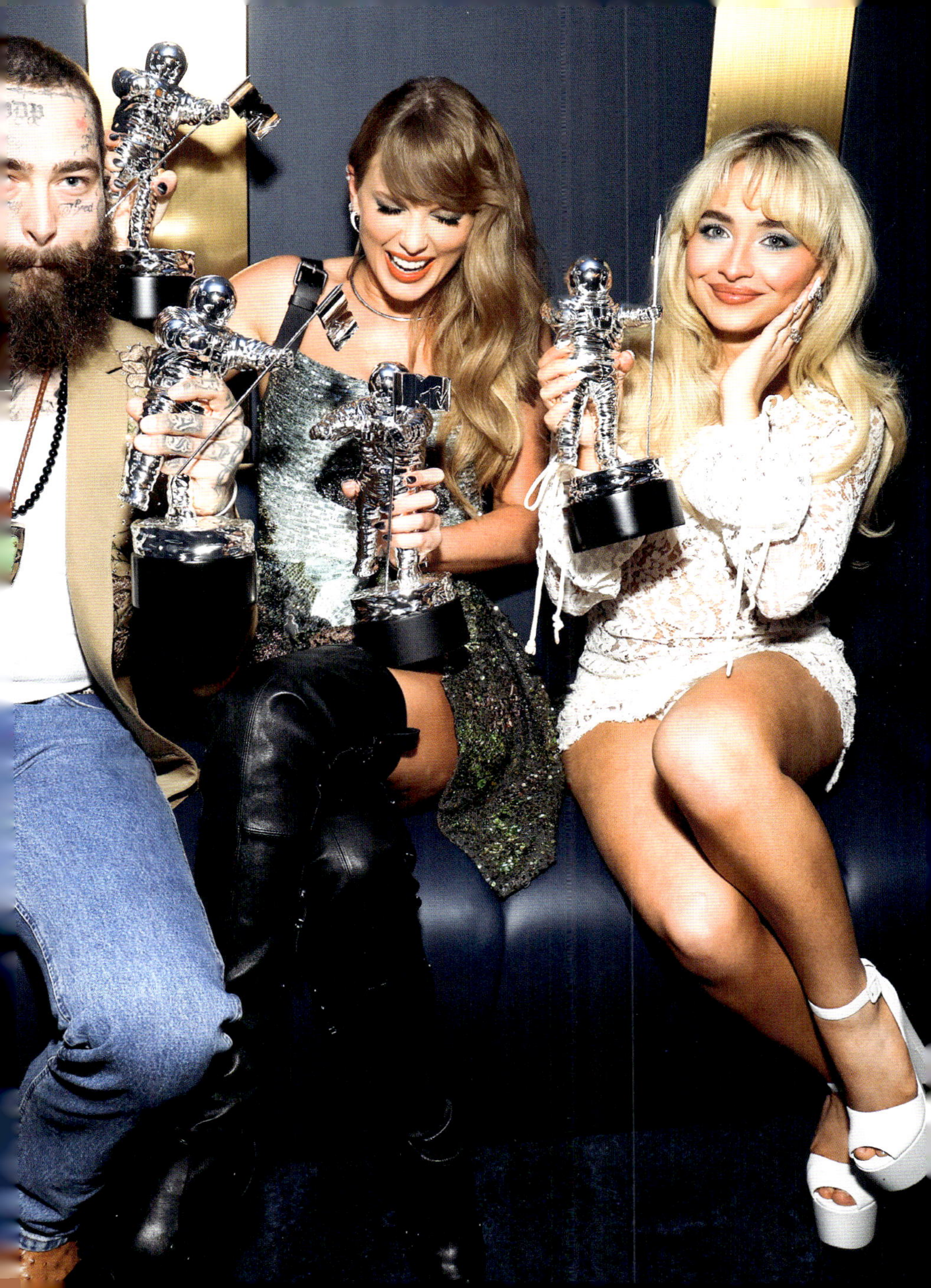

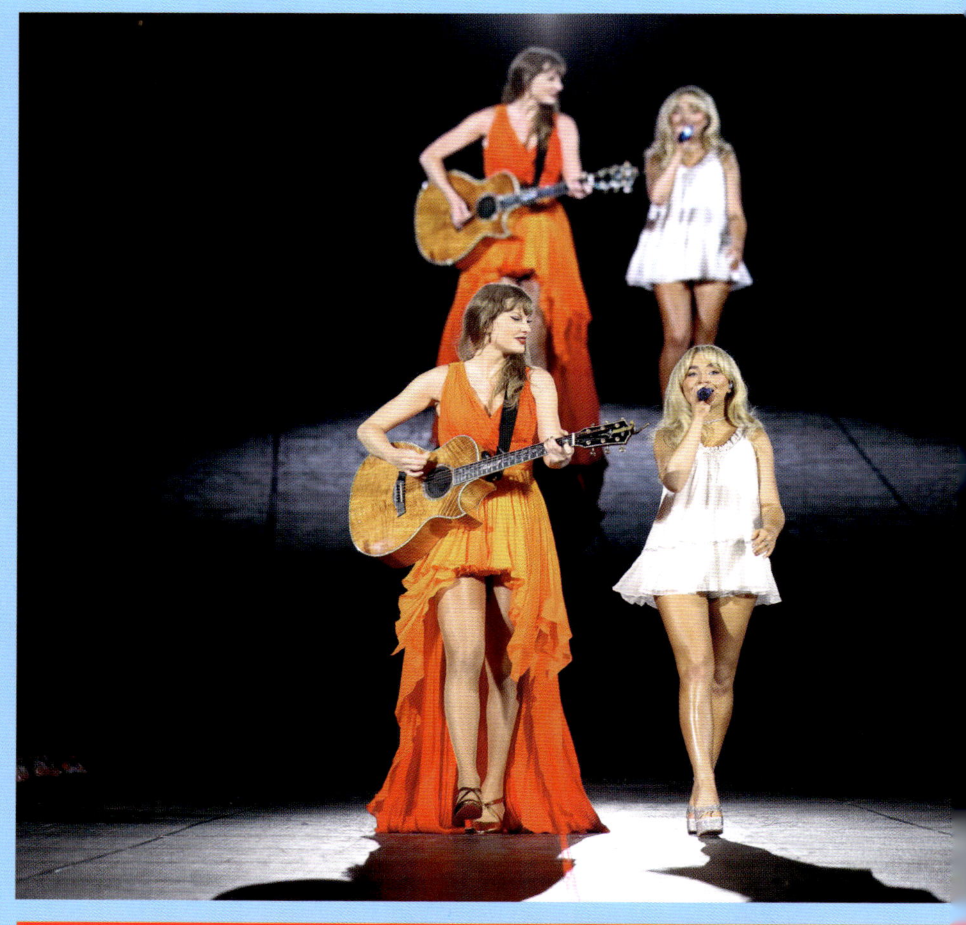

'I feel so ***lucky*** *to be* ***part of*** *such an* ***indelible tour.'***

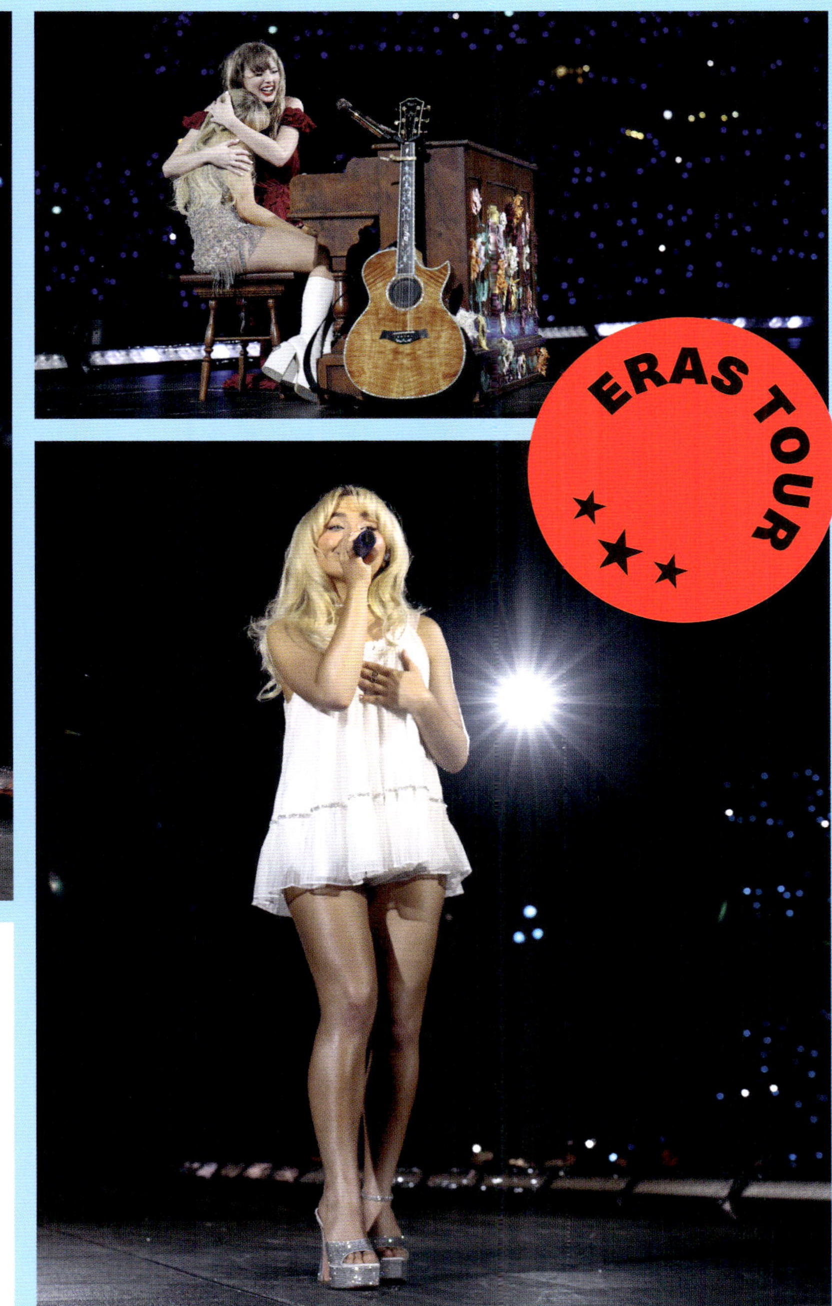
ERAS TOUR

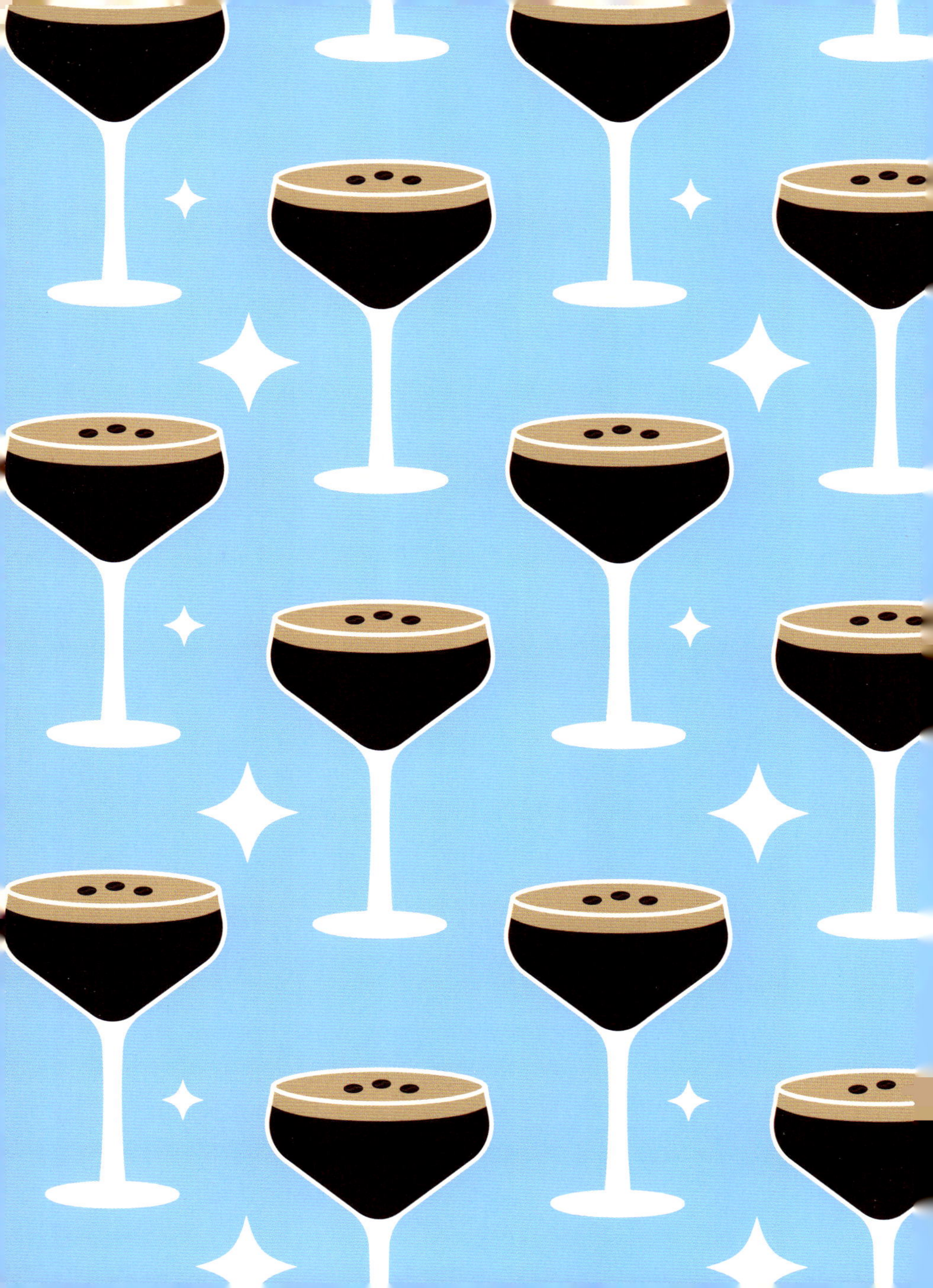

A *Caffeine* HIT

Surging to the Top

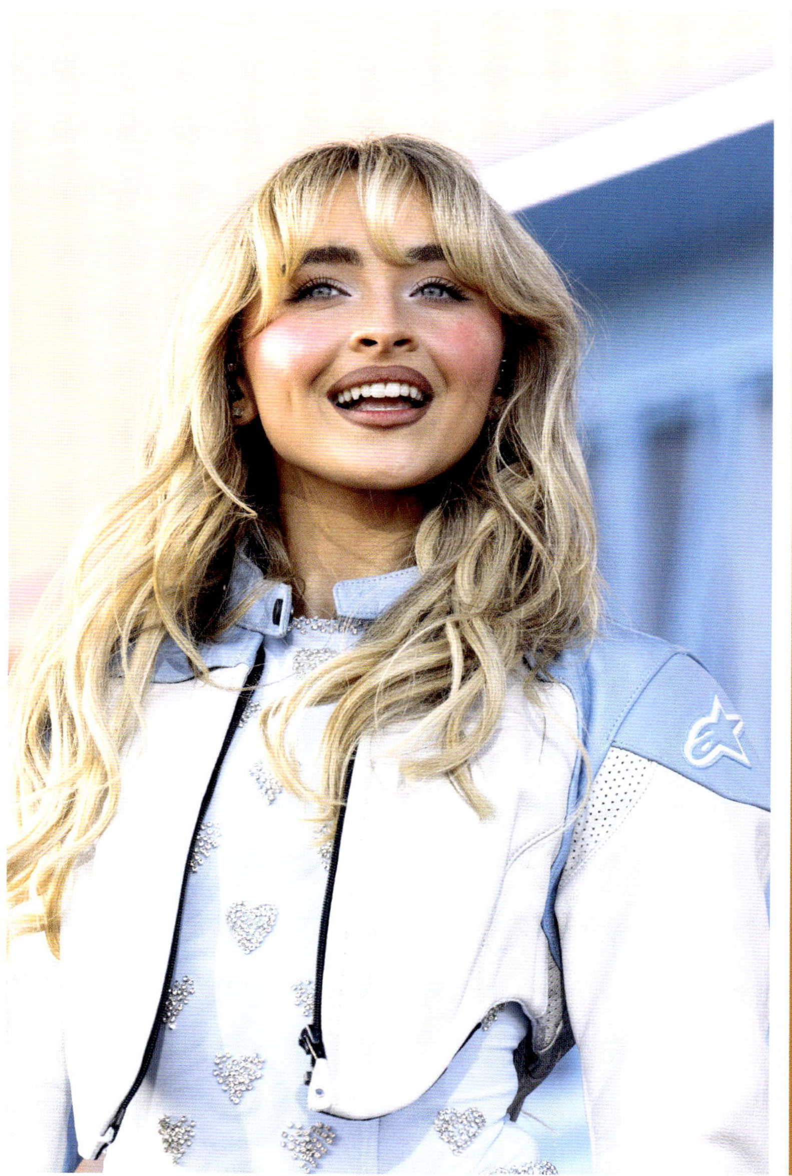

On 11 April 2024, Sabrina Carpenter released 'Espresso', the lead single from her sixth studio album. Written with her friends and co-writers Amy Allen and Steph Jones, and Julian Bunetta, who had previously worked with her on 'Nonsense', the track took inspiration from the highly caffeinated beverage, taking self-assured, seductive lyricism and pouring it over a bouncy, Italo disco melody.

A few days before she dropped the stimulating single, she teased the album art on her Instagram: a photo of herself in glam curls wearing a vintage denim Chanel dress with white trim, against a white background, with the word 'espresso' in brown, spiralling letters across the top-left corner. 'Just wanted to put out a little song before Coachella,' she wrote in the caption, adding a brown heart.

Just one day after the 'Espresso' release, she gave the addictive, nu-disco pop track its live debut on Coachella's main stage. It was a pivotal moment for Carpenter, as she presented the world with a new level of stage design, fashion and performance; back-up dancers and charming choreography played out in front of a two-storey, light-blue desert hotel set, with kitsch signage – a heart with her name written across it on a ribbon – and a convertible 'crashed' into the side of the makeshift building.

The old-Hollywood aesthetic she'd been teasing on tour with Taylor Swift, and her fresh sound and flirty delivery were on full display – there was no turning back. That day marked a new era for Sabrina officially dubbing her the next pop It girl. In a post she put up on Instagram following the performance, she thanked her family, friends and crew for a special night she'd always remember, adding 'just a blue hotel and a dream'.

At Coachella Valley Music and Arts Festival, Indio, California, April 2024

CAFFEINE ADDICTION

'Espresso' became Sabrina's biggest hit to date, peaking at number 3 on the Billboard Hot 100 and becoming her first top-five hit single on the chart. It also became Spotify's most streamed song of 2024, with 1.6 billion listens, making it one of the fastest songs to hit that many streams in the platform's history. Gone were the days of critics predicting Sabrina as the 'next big thing': she had officially arrived.

'Espresso' was written in Chailland, a small village in France, while Sabrina was enjoying time off between dates on the Eras Tour (she posted a series of photos from the town, while she was writing at Flow Studios, on her Instagram, with the caption 'dtf (down town france)'). Sabrina told Zane Lowe on Apple Music 1 that writing in France had been something she'd wanted to do her whole career, noting that she felt it would be 'creatively inspiring'. But when she finally had around 11 days to make that dream come true, she felt like she was going crazy. Eventually, she sank back into writing and began to create songs she described as 'so honest, so emotional, and so important to me'. One of those songs was, of course, 'Espresso'.

Sabrina says that during her time in Chailland there was only one restaurant in town, a crêperie. 'I had my shot of espresso, and then I might have had some champagne, and before I knew it, the song was written,' she told *W Magazine* of visiting the local spot. The song was written in just 30 minutes, as the team played around with ridiculous lyricism, throwing in a mention of switching it up like 'Nintendo', and adding 'I know I Mountain Dew it for ya'; there's even a nod to Sabrina's 'twisted humour'. There were also the much-talked-about lines 'That's that me espresso' and 'I'm working late 'cause I'm a singer'. Sabrina recalled that the speed with which she wrote the song, plus the excitement she felt from travelling around the world; both impacted the song's overall energy. 'For me, there was something really exciting about the fact that there was so much personality throughout the entire song,' she told Lowe. 'Those are the ones that are really fun to sing live with a crowd. Those are the ones that people, when they don't know my music or who I am, they can just tune in to a single song and leave with a better idea of my sense of humour.' Plus, as someone with a love for coffee, equating espresso to infatuation just made sense for her. 'I definitely have a caffeine addiction as it is, so it ends up being a full circle for me,' she told Lowe, noting that the song had been stuck in her head from the moment she wrote it. 'I decided to put that burden on other people,' she joked.

Performing at BBC Radio 1's Big Weekend, Luton, May 2024

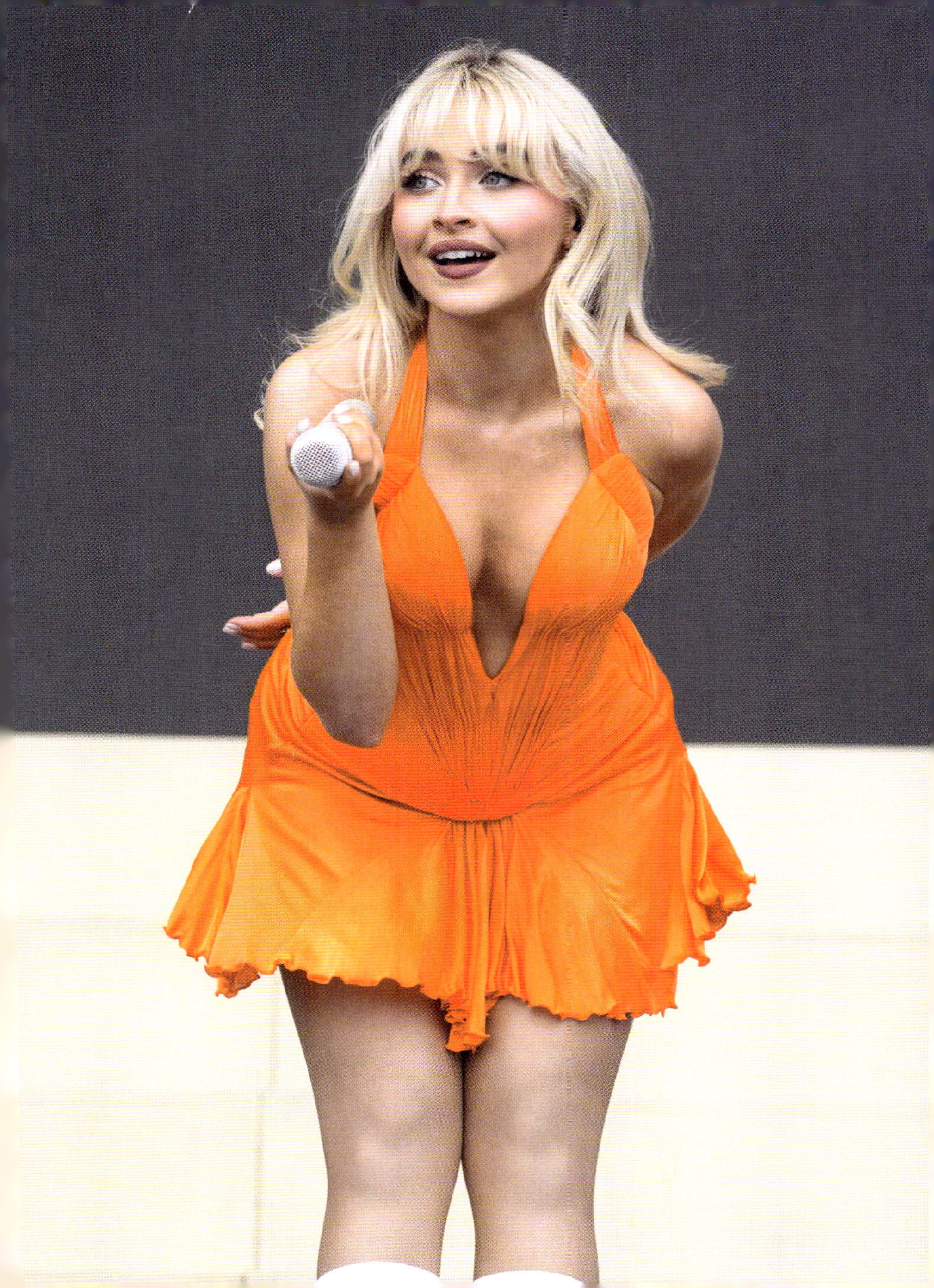

Carpenter also defended the silly syntax of the song during an interview on *Hot Ones*, telling host Sean Evans, 'I've heard a lot of people that were like, "She should've said, *That's that blonde espresso*, duh." And I'm like, "Well, yes. That is another song as well that deserves its spot in the world, but … "me espresso" just felt like the right thing to say, and it rhymes with the line before it.' It was another example of what fans found magnetic: her ability to stand out in her writing, be outlandish in her lyricism and, of course, confidently back her work.

Finding a groove with collaborators who understood her personality and musical goals was also at the heart of 'Espresso''s genesis. She told *Rolling Stone* that working with Allen, Jones and Bunetta – writers and a producer she felt comfortable and loved 'making music with' – made it possible to confidently share some of the most 'idiotic-slash-funniest' lyrics she'd ever written – mixing nonsensical wordplay with affirmations about how irresistible, hypnotizing and inescapable she is. Though some of the lyrics can be heard as absurd, Sabrina told *Vogue* that the deeper meaning of the track was about 'seeing femininity as your superpower'. And although there's clearly an obsessed lover at the centre of the song's story, she told the *Guardian* that it was written not from reality but as a manifestation tactic because no one liked her romantically at that point; she said she's 'always been a bit delusional, in that sense'.

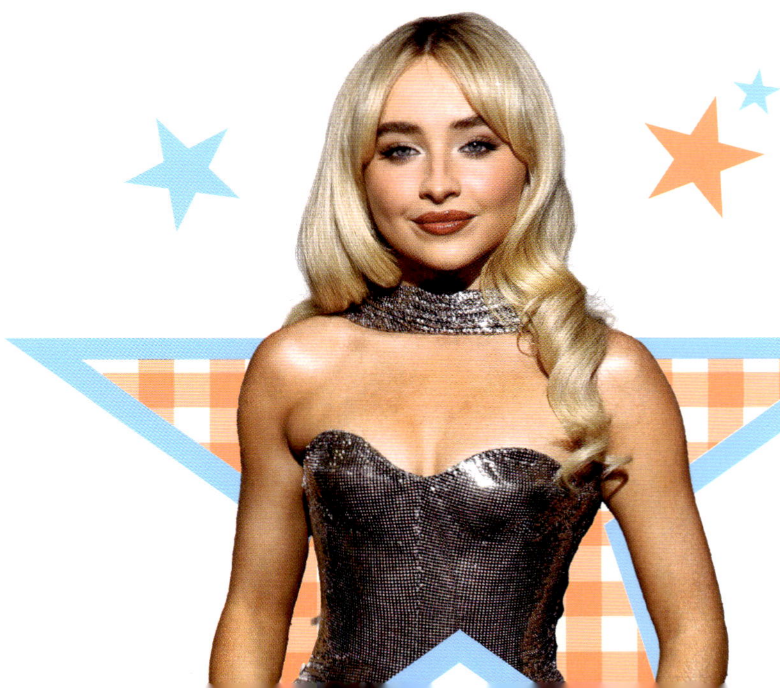

Despite putting all of her creative and manifesting energy into the track, Sabrina was a little apprehensive about whether or not 'Espresso' would actually resonate with fans. She told *The Hollywood Reporter*, 'I really didn't know if it would connect, but the sentiment and the sound of the song and the confidence that it carries along with it was something I really believed in.'

The timing of the release also gave her pause, since she felt like a song about a hot beverage may make more sense in the autumn as opposed to the summer. Still, she decided to trust her instincts. But even after she convinced herself, she still had to convince her label. 'I was completely alone in wanting to release "Espresso". Not so much from my immediate team. But when it came to "the powers above",' she told *Variety*. 'There was a lot of questioning behind whether it made sense. But they trusted me in the end, and I was happy that I believed in myself at that moment.' She went with her gut, and once again, she was right.

On 12 April, Sabrina released the official music video for 'Espresso', directed by Dave Meyers and filmed in Castaic Lake, California, with visuals as playful and cheeky as the song itself. 'Since the day I heard the song, I saw a beach atmosphere,' she told *Vogue*. In the short film, Sabrina drives a speedboat with a romantic interest before lifting his wallet and credit card and driving recklessly so that he falls into the water. She takes a lifesaver to the shore, where she goes off to enjoy her day: reading, getting a pedicure, riding in a vintage convertible-turned-pool, and sunbathing with a group of girls who are also wearing pin-up-style swimsuits, matching her Brigitte Bardot-esque aesthetic. In true Sabrina fashion, the video ends with her being apprehended for her crime, waving as she's cheerfully hauled off in a cop car. 'I did want to make it a little bit ridiculous,' she said of the video, 'because that's up my alley.' The video, then, was a perfect encapsulation of the song's sound and energy.

Never one to rest on her laurels, she released multiple shots of the hit in May with an *Espresso* EP, containing the original track as well as five other versions: 'Espresso – Double Shot Version' (sped-up version), 'Espresso – On Vacation Version' (an instrumental), 'Espresso – Decaf Version' (slowed down), 'Espresso – Mochapella Version' (an a cappella spin on the hit) and the 'Espresso – Espressooooo Version'. On 31 May, Mark Ronson and FNX released a 'Working Late Remix'. The duo won the Grammy for Best Remixed Recording for their take on the buzzy track. It gave fans a chance to play with the song, adding versions to their playlists that best suited the moment: a serving of the 'Mochapella Version' while laying on the beach, or perhaps a dose of the 'Double Shot' while getting in a hot girl workout.

Opposite: Arriving at TIME 100 Next, New York, October 2024

HOT SHOT SUMMER

As the summer of 2024 rolled in, it was impossible to escape 'Espresso', whether it was on the radio, TV, streaming sites or, especially, while scrolling social media. Lyrics and photos from the track and video took over X, Instagram and TikTok, one of which – a screenshot of shelves at the grocery store with the words 'Excuse me, where is the me espresso?' written over it in bold letters – Sabrina even shared herself on Instagram, while announcing that the song was number 1 globally on both UK and US charts.

Her then partner, Barry Keoghan, even got in on the fun, posting a photo on his Instagram stories of a small cup of espresso, with a blonde queen emoji floating in the middle of it. Fans started using the lyrics in their internet vernacular, posting things like 'don't talk to me until I've had my me espresso', with one user posting a photo of a crime scene with a joke about a chain restaurant, writing 'do NOT drink that me espresso from chili's'. Sabrina shared a few of the most viral 'Espresso' tweets and memes to her Instagram story, including one that said 'when we exchange our vows and that me espresso becomes that us espresso'. She also reposted a tweet she'd written in 2016 but forgotten about, and that fans had found after the success of the track. It read 'ppl r always scared to give me caffeine !!!? I don't know whyyyyy those little espresso things taste cute and I likemmmm.' After her interview on Amelia Dimoldenberg's *Chicken Shop Date*, the song inspired another trending sound, after a clip of Dimoldenberg standing up with a microphone, miming Sabrina's Coachella intro for 'Espresso' while the pop star sits behind her looking a bit embarrassed, was posted on TikTok. Fans made their own viral versions, with captions like 'my married friends watching me go on another first date' and 'me posting like an influencer when I'm on vacation'.

In October of 2024, iconic US comedy revue *Saturday Night Live* used the hit song in a sketch where bridesmaids – including Ariana Grande, purposely singing off-key – did a rendition of 'Espresso', changing the lyrics to focus on a wild bachelorette trip. The hilarious song and clip went viral, amassing tens of millions of views on YouTube alone and soundtracking millions of clips on TikTok. In February 2025, Sabrina joined the *SNL* cast for their 50th Anniversary Special, performing an updated version of the skit, where she sang her own flat version of the track. When asked about the viral nature of 'Espresso', she told *Rolling Stone* that the memes were her favourite 'niche part of the internet', adding 'love that for me.'

Arriving at SNL 50 - The Anniversary Special, *New York, February 2025*

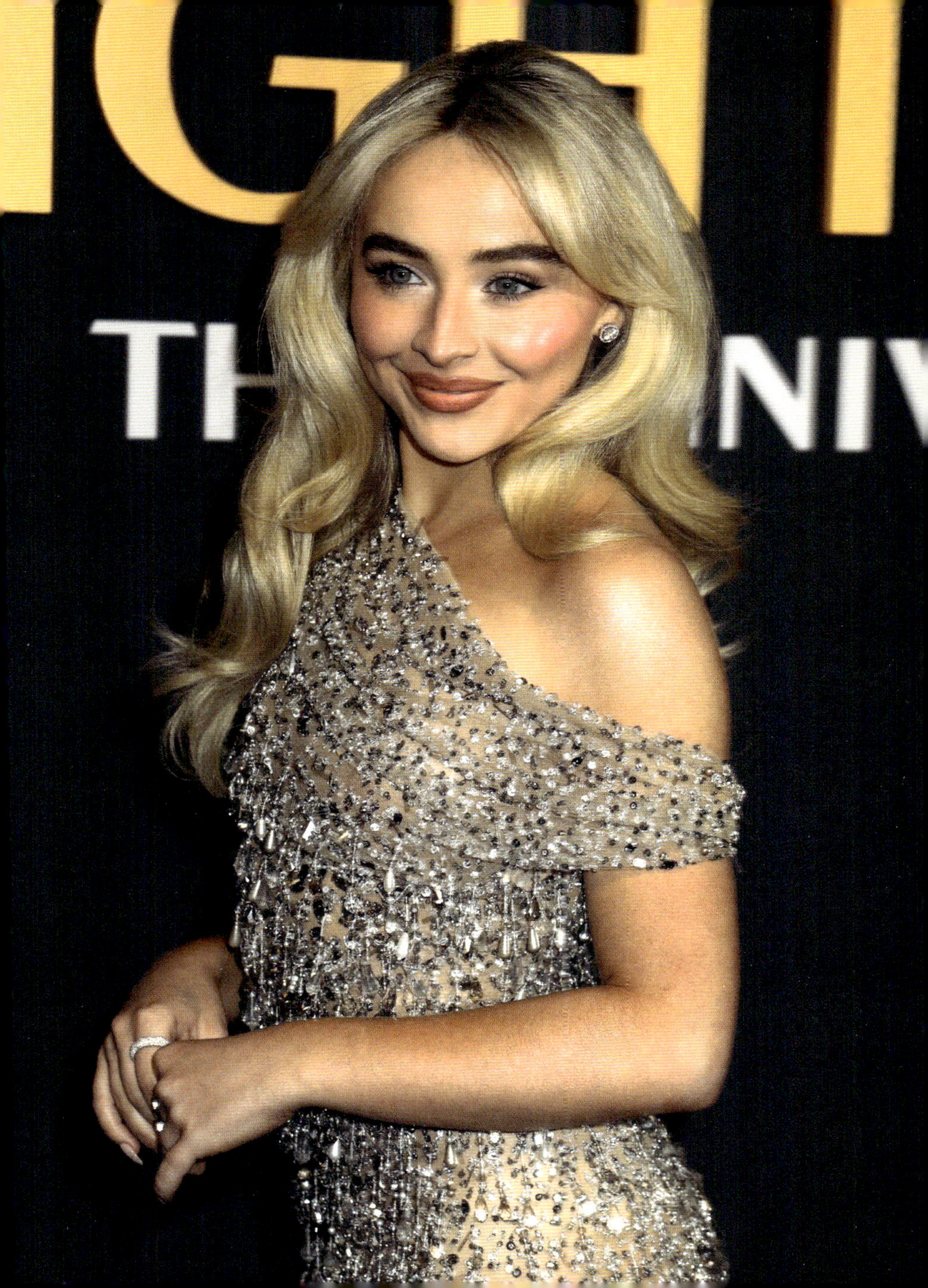

STARRY SHOUT-OUTS

She also performed 'Espresso' on the season finale of *Saturday Night Live* on 18 May 2024. She opened the performance holding a newspaper with the headline 'Sabrina Loves To Be On Top', while sitting in a chair on a bar-themed set. She wore a red minidress, dancing with men in black suits. She also sang 'Feather' and 'Nonsense' during her *SNL* debut. Sabrina showed off her comedic acting chops in the episode, playing the character Daphne in a Scooby-Doo-themed horror sketch with actor and host Jake Gyllenhaal. Later that month, she performed the track at BBC Radio 1's Big Weekend Festival. Coldplay closed out that night of the festival, and brought Sabrina back on stage to perform their hit song 'Magic' with them, with Chris Martin saying, 'What we'd like to do, to say thank you to you for being so wonderful for the whole three days, is bring on a singer who's much younger, more beautiful, more successful, better in every way, and sing a song of ours that is okay but make it really good.' Martin paid homage to Sabrina a second time during the set as well, slipping lyrics of 'Espresso' into the band's hit song 'Fix You'.

Coldplay weren't the only artists singing Sabrina's praises. On one night of her Las Vegas residency, Adele told her audience that as she was falling to sleep at night, she found herself singing 'I'm working late, 'cause I'm a singer. That Sabrina Carpenter song, that song is my jam!' Trent Reznor of Nine Inch Nails also gave the singer a shout-out, sharing that 'Espresso' was his song of 2024 during a red-carpet interview at the Golden Globes.

Sabrina, of course, made the rounds on the late-night circuit, performing the hit on *The Tonight Show Starring Jimmy Fallon* and famously climbing on the host's desk. During her visit to *The Late Show with Stephen Colbert*, she was offered an espresso martini to celebrate her Grammy nomination, and she challenged the host to a chugging contest; as he tried to continue the conversation around her noms, she responded, 'I'm very drunk now'.

But 'Espresso''s cultural reign didn't just come in the form of live interviews and performances. Carpenter had multiple brand deals thanks to the Java-inspired tune. In June 2024, she announced a collab with ice-cream company Van Leeuwen for a limited-edition 'Espresso' ice cream with chewy brownies, chocolate chips and swirls of fudge, with packaging emblazoned with the single's artwork. That same month, she did a shift at Blank Street Coffee in London, surprising fans by giving them free espresso drinks that had her signature red-kiss graphic on the cups. In November she worked with Absolut Vodka and Kahlúa to release the 'Short n' Sweet Espresso Martini Kit', which came with a DIY espresso martini-making set.

Performing at the MTV Video Music Awards, New York, September 2024

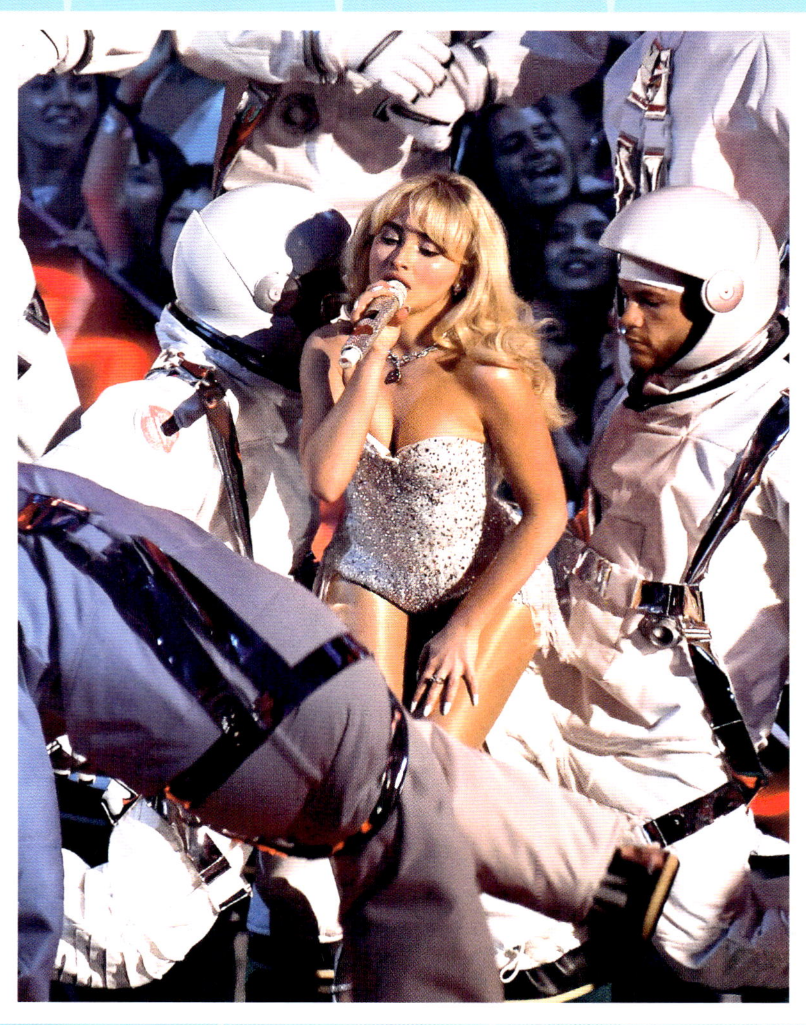

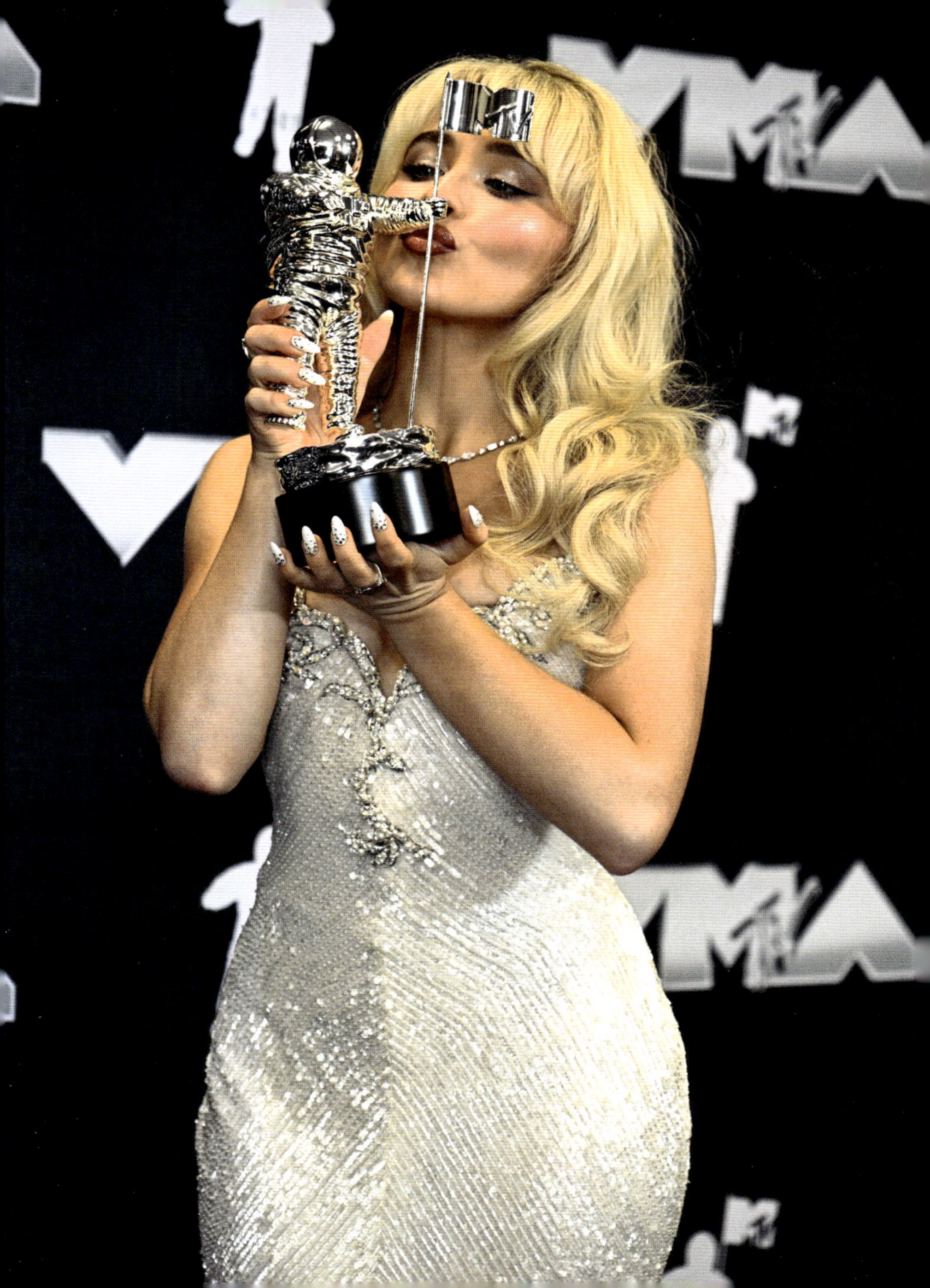

The following December, she collaborated with Dunkin' Donuts, releasing an iced beverage called 'Sabrina's Brown Sugar Shakin' Espresso'. The release came complete with a viral commercial, in which she holds a coffee shaker while saying 'I love shaking that Ess', as people around her also share in her love for shaking that 'Ess'. At the end of the commercial, she laughs cheekily, saying 'Oh, shaking that Ess sounds a lot like...', as the clip cuts off. That December, she shared a fragrance tied to the song, called 'Me Espresso'. In a post, she used the song's lyrics as a caption, writing 'soft skin and i perfumed it for ya', with photos of the scent, which comes in packaging made to look like a chocolate bar and smells like espresso bean infused with cocoa powder, buttery biscotti, caramel and sugared amber. Despite leaning into the song's global admiration as part of her music marketing, Sabrina joked with Zane Lowe that she's now hesitant to order espresso, knowing that every barista is just waiting with bated breath for her to say the magic word. It was a global phenomenon.

'I ***definitely*** *hear it now in* ***every car*** *I get into.'*

'Espresso' was and still is one of the biggest hits the world has ever seen, and for Sabrina, timing had, once again, been everything. It had taken her five albums, global tours, vulnerability in songwriting and finding a creative team that trusted her instinct; 'Espresso' was evidence that slow and steady really does win the race.

'I definitely hear it now in every car I get into,' she told *W Magazine*. 'Being on the radio, to me, is still – it's like fate. You have to be at the right place at the right time.'

In September of 2024, Sabrina Carpenter picked up her very first MTV Video Music Award for 'Espresso'. She thanked her fans. 'You guys are the reason that I get to do what I love, but also the reason that we get to have so much fun and share music with each other. I just feel so grateful to have the best, truly the best, fans in the world. I know it sounds cheesy, but I love you.' As part of a three-song medley, she gave a space-themed performance of the song, singing 'Espresso' as she was surrounded by a dozen men in spacesuits.

At the MTV Video Music Awards, New York, September 2024

BEST POP PERFORMANCE

The following February, 'Espresso' nabbed Sabrina a nomination for Best Pop Solo Performance at the 67th Grammy Awards. She performed a medley of the track along with her hit 'Please Please Please' at the show, opening with a glamorous, jazz version of the song and a comedic intro that saw her wearing a retro sparkling black suit, pretending to accidentally drop a baton after twirling it, and making fun of her short stature by disappearing behind stairs as she walked down one too many steps. At one point, she tap-danced to the track with multiple dancers, before hiding behind a green hedge to do a cheeky outfit change. The vaudeville-inspired performance showed off Sabrina's stage prowess and comedic timing, a perfect display of her personality. 'Espresso' went up against some of the biggest pop stars and songs of the year for Best Pop Performance that night: Chappell Roan's 'Good Luck, Babe!', Billie Eilish's 'Birds of a Feather' and Beyoncé's 'Bodyguard'. 'Espresso' won.

The song continued its pop culture reign well into the following year, and by its one-year anniversary 'Espresso' was still on the menu, having spent 52 weeks straight on the Billboard 100. By following her inspiration, her taste and her wit, Sabrina got us hooked on 'Espresso'.

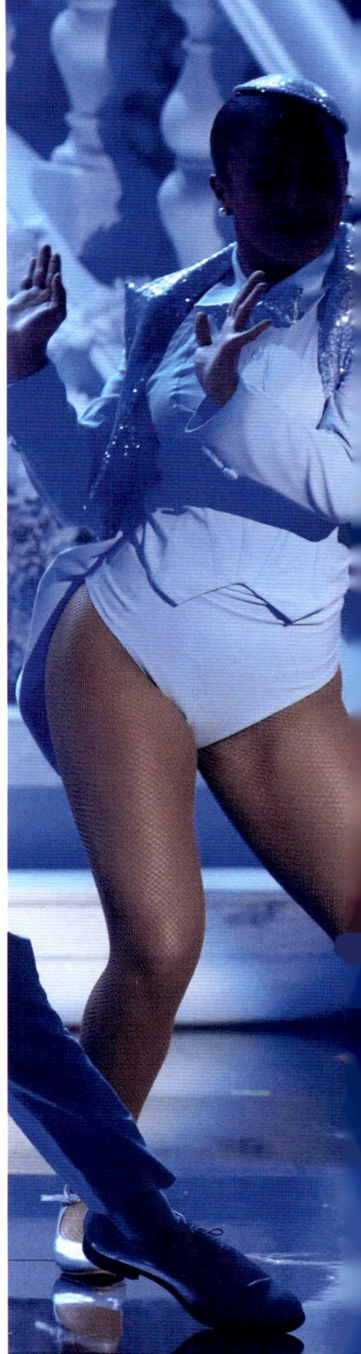

Performing at the 67th Annual Grammy Awards, Los Angeles, February 2025

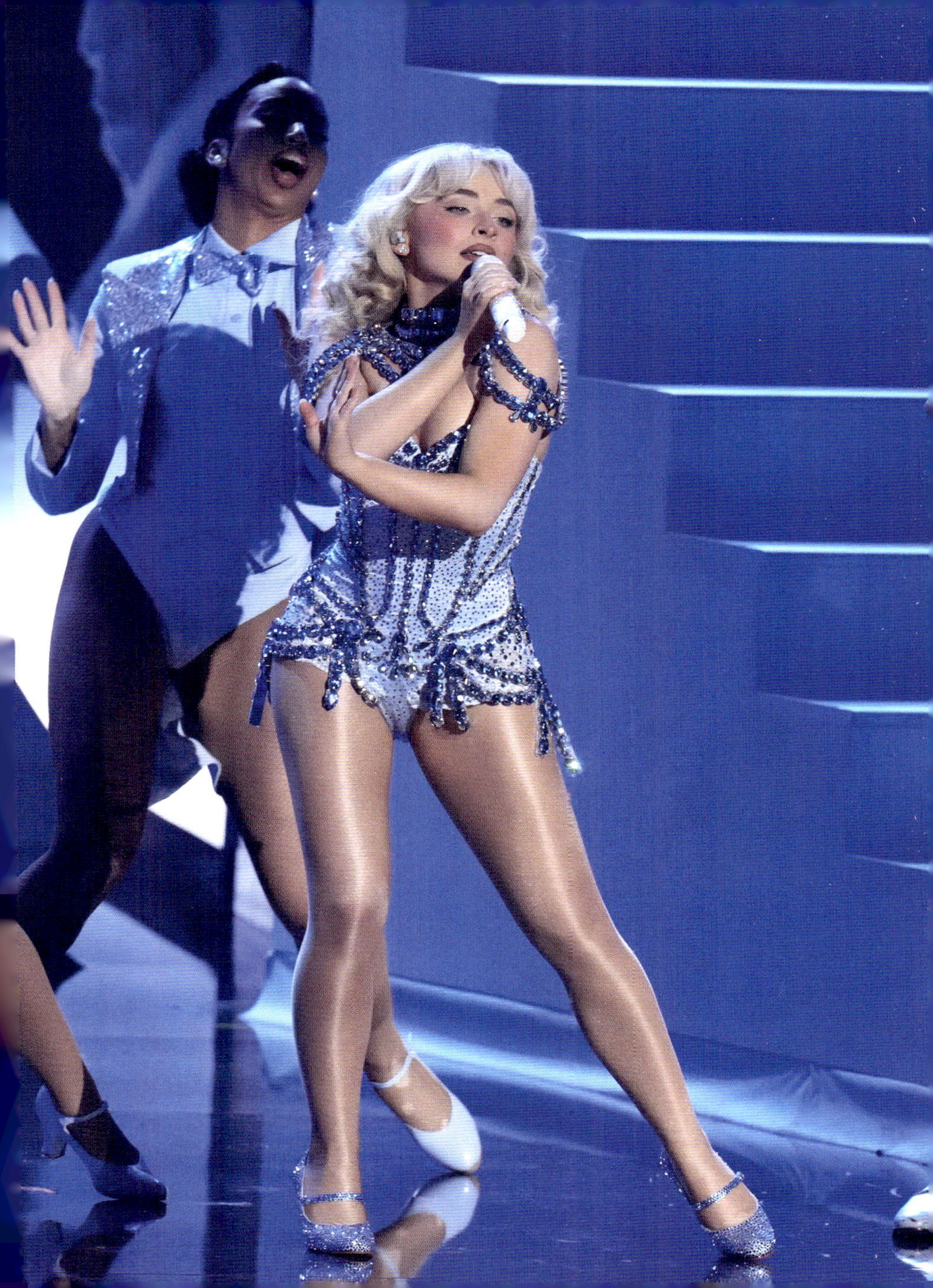

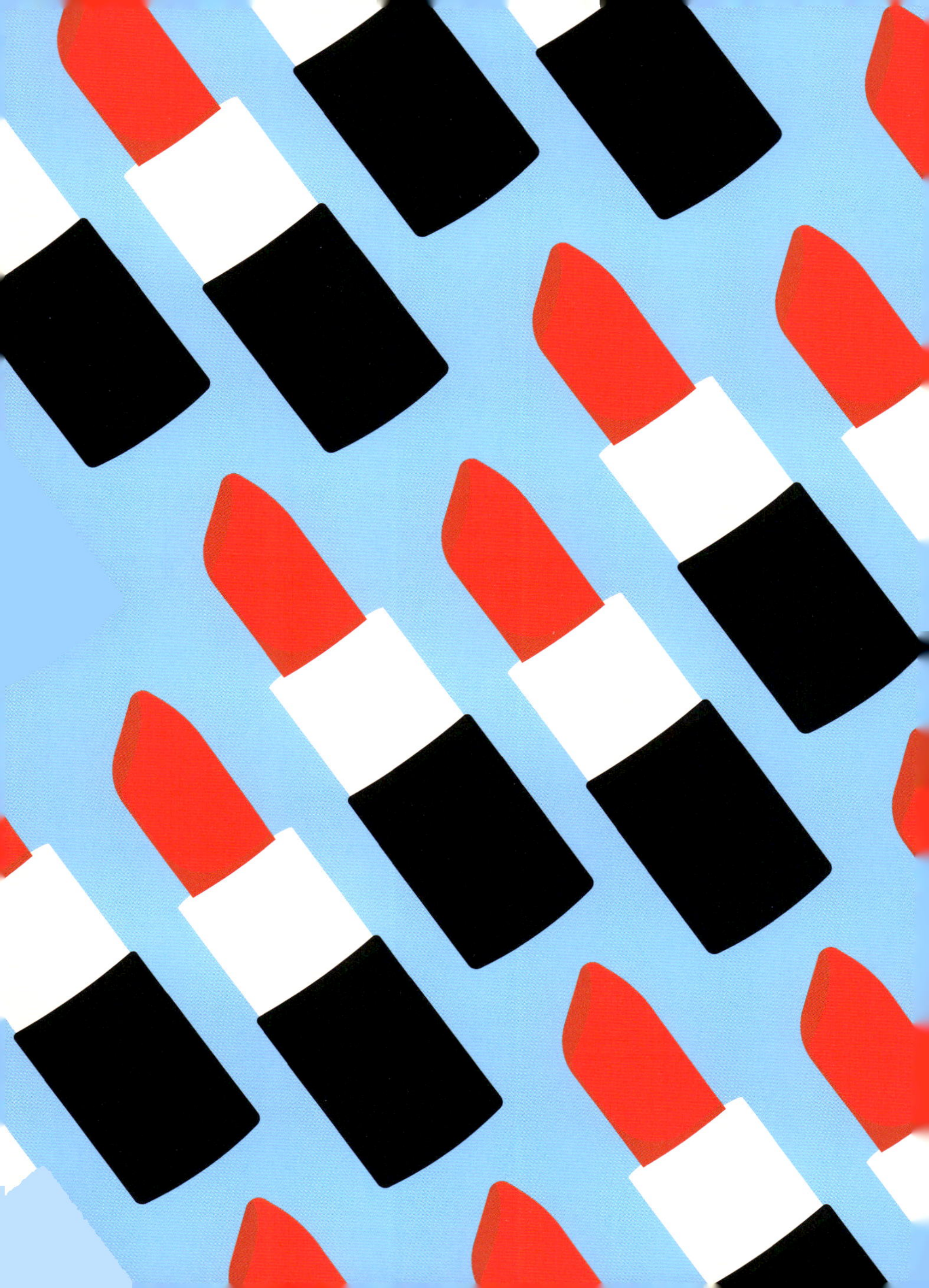

BUILDING

★ A ★

BOMB-SHELL

Creating an Iconic Look

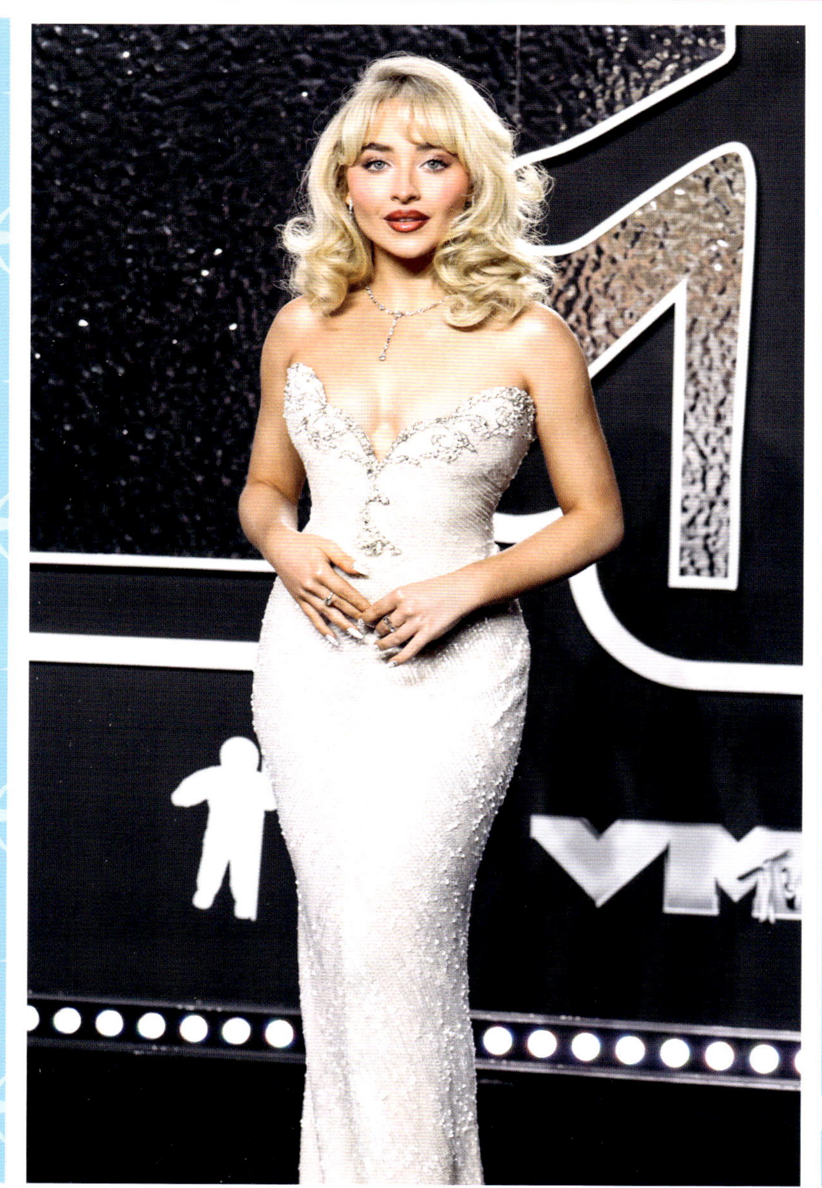

Polly Pocket. Bratz Doll. Vintage pin-up in platinum curls. Pop princess and purveyor of coquette-core. As Sabrina Carpenter's fame continued to rise, so did the number of terms fans used to describe her petite, retro, doll-like aesthetic.

As a Disney teen, Sabrina stuck to the typical, layered bright colours and bold patterns the channel and its up-and-coming stars were known for. But, towards the end of her *Singular: Act II* album cycle, her colour palette began to shift towards pastels, her skirts got shorter. Her hair? Blonder. And her platform boots got even higher. By the time she took to the stage to promote *emails i can't send*, fans were catching on, taking part in her new era of style by creating their own wardrobes of heart cut-outs, blush-pink crop tops, sequins, minidresses and corsets. While her style signature has changed over time, it's important to note that, deep down, Sabrina was always walking in this direction. She told *W Magazine* in 2024 that the first time she wore high heels was when she was just six or seven years old, playing dress-up in her mum's closet. 'My mom was a dancer,' she shared. 'So costumes were very much everywhere in my household.' When she was 14 she would go to set every day in 'chunky big heels'. She said she was comfortable walking in them because she could see people eye to eye. 'Ever since then I've been a big heel lover,' she added.

By 2023, Sabrina's sphere of influence had grown to colossal dimensions, and the fashion world took notice. Her Instagram following clocked in at 40 million engaged followers, and fans across the internet were desperate to mimic the pop star's style, making videos on 'How to Style Your Curtain Bangs Like Sabrina' and posts on 'What to Wear to Sabrina Carpenter Concerts'. The chokehold she had on Gen Z was undeniable. And though brands had taken notice early on – she was asked to walk in Rihanna's Savage X Fenty Vol. 3 fashion show in 2021 – as her cultural impact increased, so did the frequency of her collaborations with luxury fashion houses.

Arriving at the MTV Video Music Awards, New York, September 2024

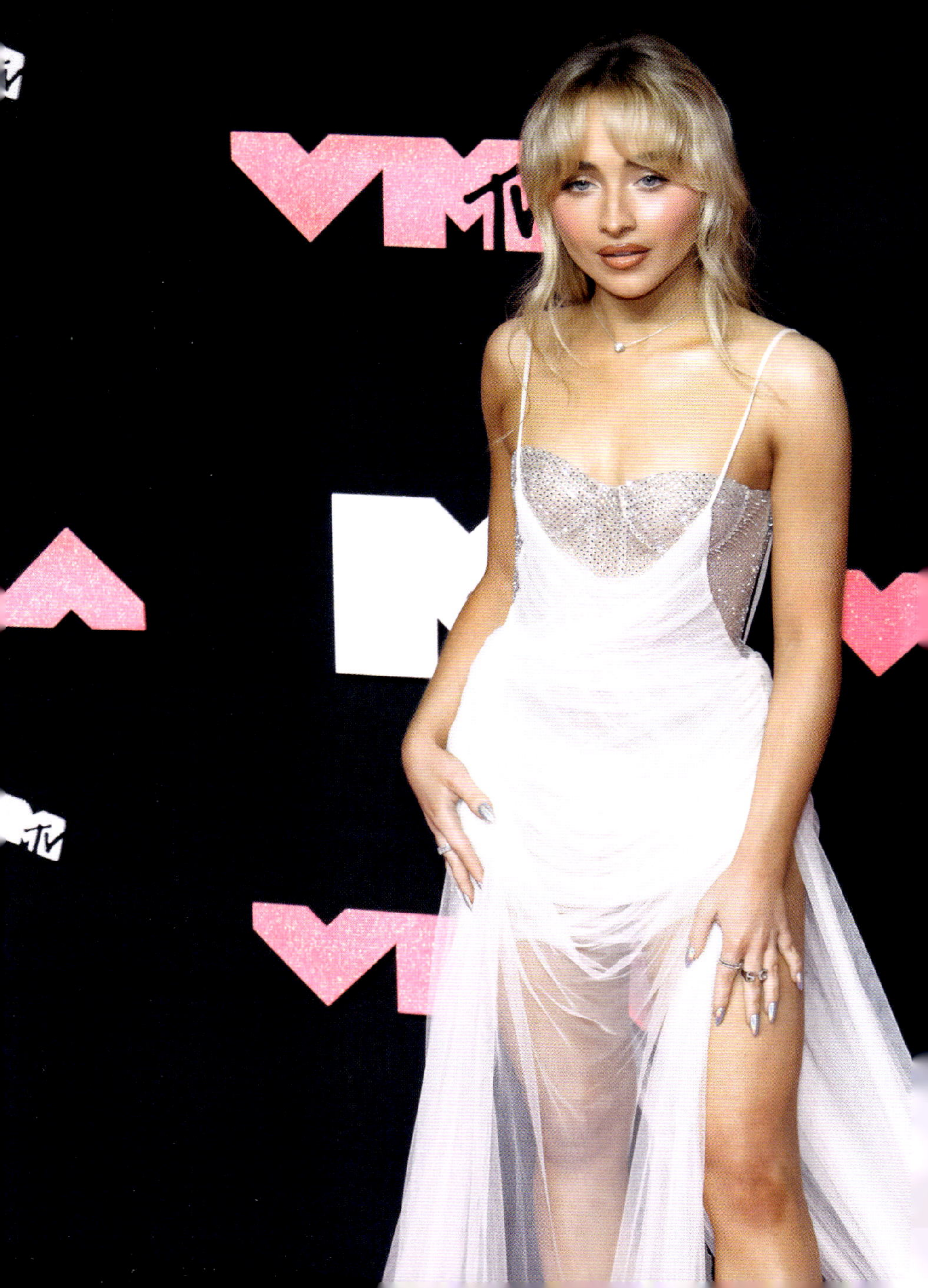

In June 2023, while playing in London during her *emails i can't send* tour, she gave a hint at silhouettes to come, showing that she knew how to build a risqué but sophisticated, one-of-a-kind wardrobe. She told *Who What Wear* how the outfit came together, sharing that she'd mixed pieces like a crystal bedazzled top with heart cut-out over subtle heart bra, pairing it with 'a little skirt that's too short for me'. 'There's a part of me right now that's like, "I'm going to wear short skirts for as long as I can",' she added. She tied the look together with chunky, '60s-style go-go boots.

In September 2023, she wore custom Vera Wang on the MTV Video Music Awards red carpet. She told *Who What Wear* during their 'Truth, Wear or Dare' series that she'd directly worked with the designers, who made a Swarovski-crystal corset for the star, draping it with sheer white fabric to give it the outline of a fuller dress. 'I felt a bit like a fairy,' she said. The love for flirty high heels and feminine fashion ideals was Sabrina at her core. As she prepared to share her sixth studio album, *Short n' Sweet*, with the world in 2024, her signature, iconic look was complete, as was her transformation from style novice to fashion icon. From her hair to her rosy cheeks and even her on-stage costumes, Sabrina didn't just create a signature style. She gave fans and onlookers a step-by-step guide as to what it takes to build a bombshell.

Arriving at the MTV Video Music Awards, Newark, New Jersey, September 2023

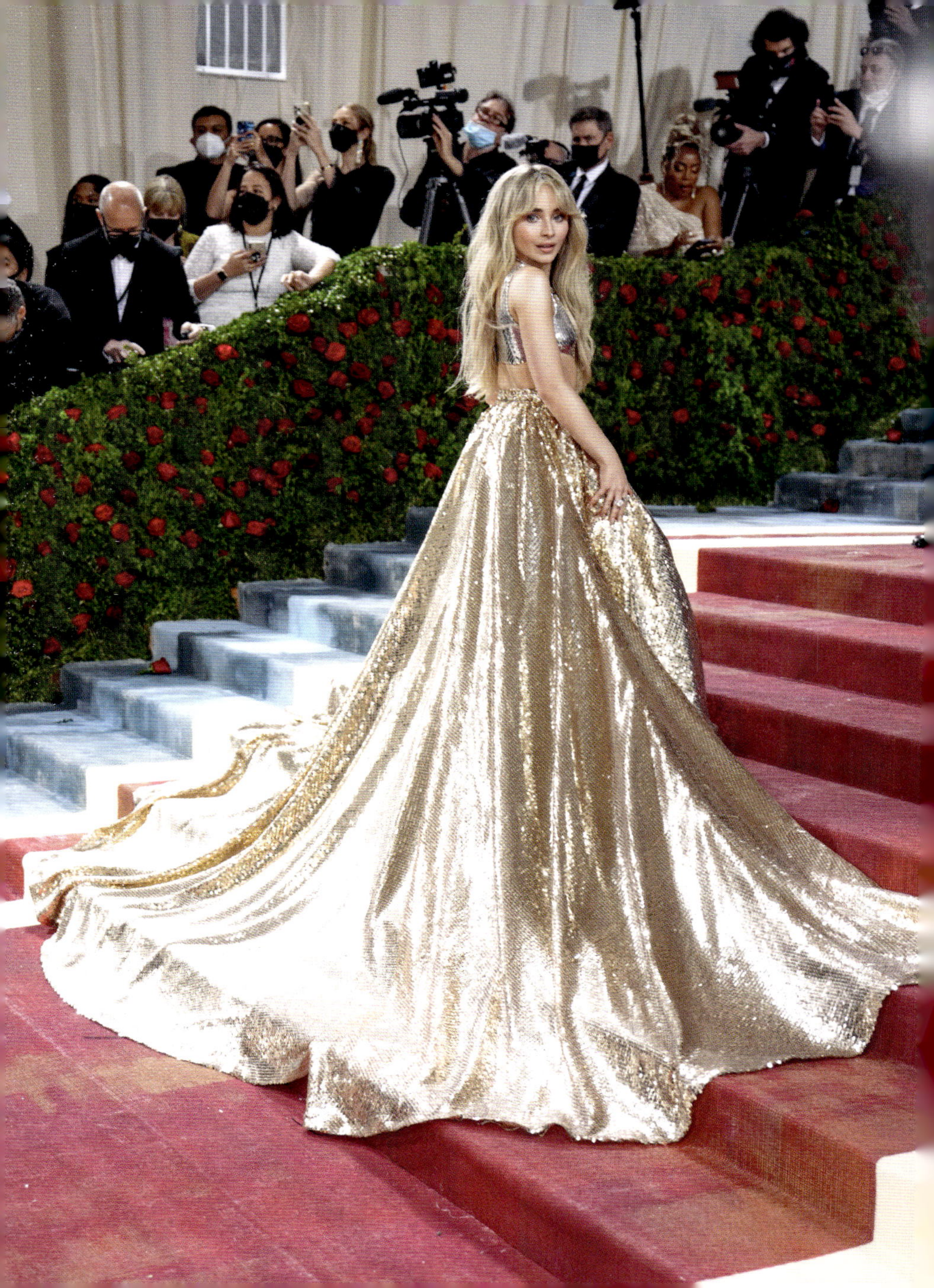

RED CARPET GLAMOUR

One of the strongest indicators of Sabrina's status in the hierarchy of fashion and culture are the highly coveted invites she's received from former *Vogue* Editor-in-Chief Anna Wintour for the annual Met Gala. Getting your name on the guest list for the exclusive event, held at New York City's Metropolitan Museum of Art, is quite the feat. In 2022, she made her first appearance at the gala. The theme was 'In America: An Anthology of Fashion', and she wore a glistening two-piece gown designed by Julien Dossena for Paco Rabanne. She was thrilled to be attending, telling *Vogue* that the night was like her Super Bowl, since she was able to spend time with so many incredible people coming together for art and fashion. Sabrina worked closely with Dossena on the gold voluminous skirt that spread behind her on the carpet and a fitted silver brassière embroidered with crystals from Maison Lesage. She said that the look was surprisingly comfortable, yet timeless and boundary-pushing – 'the epitome of glamour'.

In 2024, to meet the gala's 'Sleeping Beauties: Reawakening Fashion' theme, Sabrina wore a black and sky-blue strapless dress by Oscar de la Renta, with a fitted velvet bodice and a billowing azure satin skirt. *Harper's Bazaar* referred to the look, with its ombre blue, orchid flower inspiration, as the 'perfect match for pop royalty', calling Sabrina, who took notes from Aurora in Disney's *Sleeping Beauty*, a 'real-life pop princess'. Sabrina's stylist, Jason Bolden, called the look a combination of 'romance and edge', what he referred to as 'quintessential Sabrina'. It stood in contrast to her previous Met Gala look; it was more mature, more (dare we say it) *fashion*. It was the type of dress that demanded confidence, and walking the carpet that night, she exuded it. Bolden noted the look was inspired by one of Carpenter's favourite icons, Brigitte Bardot, and her hair stylist Scott King told *Vogue* about his treatment for her hair, making the hue whiter and icier to contrast the Met's crimson-red carpet, and teasing it to embody 'romantic, fluffy, '60s vibes'.

Sabrina first began working with Ukrainian label Frolov in 2023, creating custom stage costumes for her *emails i can't send* tour – costumes that would come to be identified with the pop star's performance persona. She first debuted a look by Frolov at her sold-out show at the Greek Theatre in Los Angeles, in a strong indication of her future fashion It girl trajectory. Sabrina and designer Ivan Frolov, along with Bolden, worked together closely on the look, creating a mini version of a blush corset dress from Frolov's fall collection that, as Sabrina told *Who What Wear*, he 'graciously allowed me to shorten and bedazzle'. The number featured a shimmering bodice with a heart-shaped cut-out that revealed her underboob, and a short, draped, lace skirt. The pink version was only the first iteration Sabrina would wear.

Opposite: At the Met Gala ('In America: An Anthology of Fashion'), New York, May 2022
Overleaf: Arriving at the Met Gala (Sleeping Beauties: Reawakening Fashion), New York, May 2024

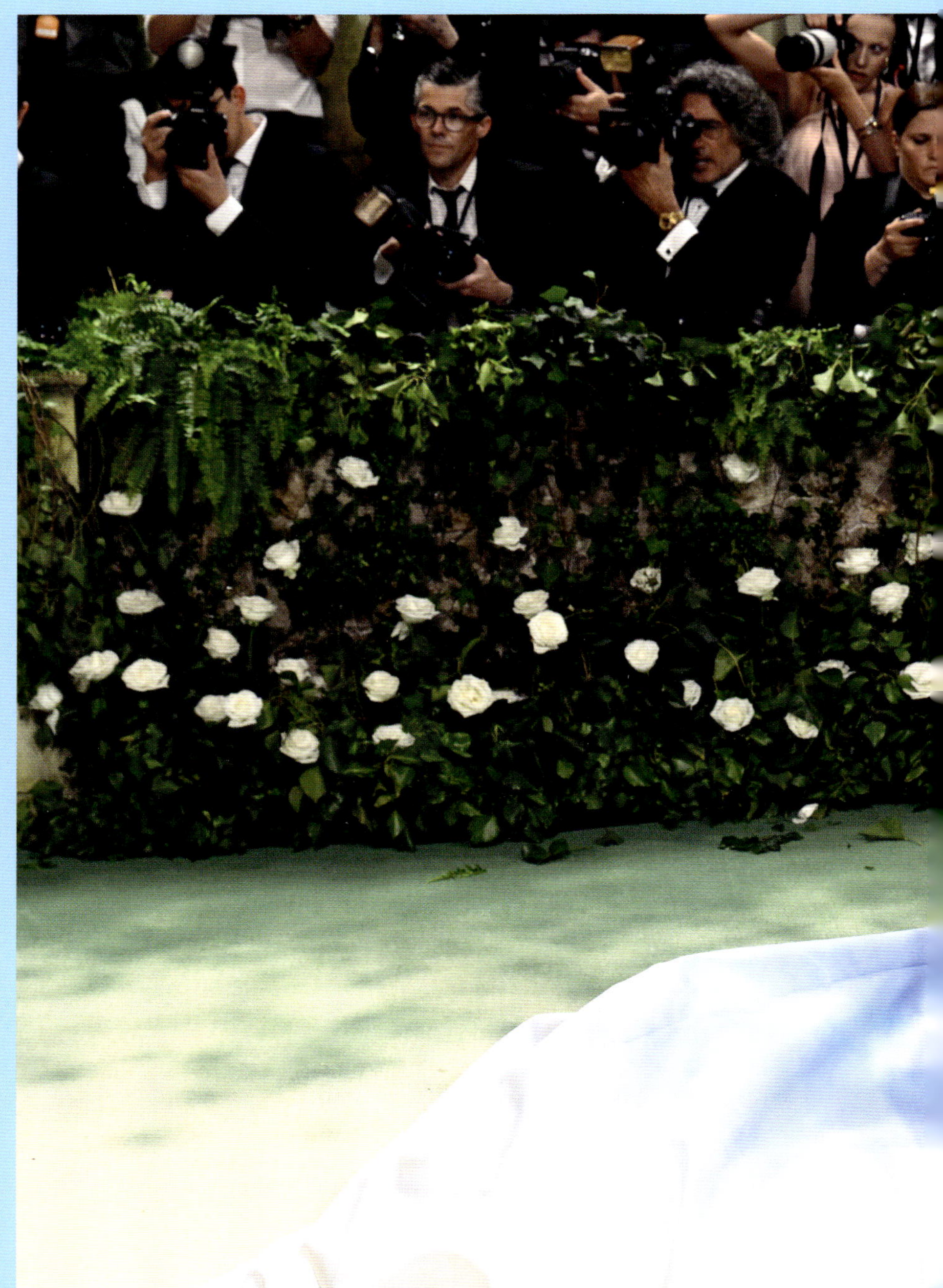

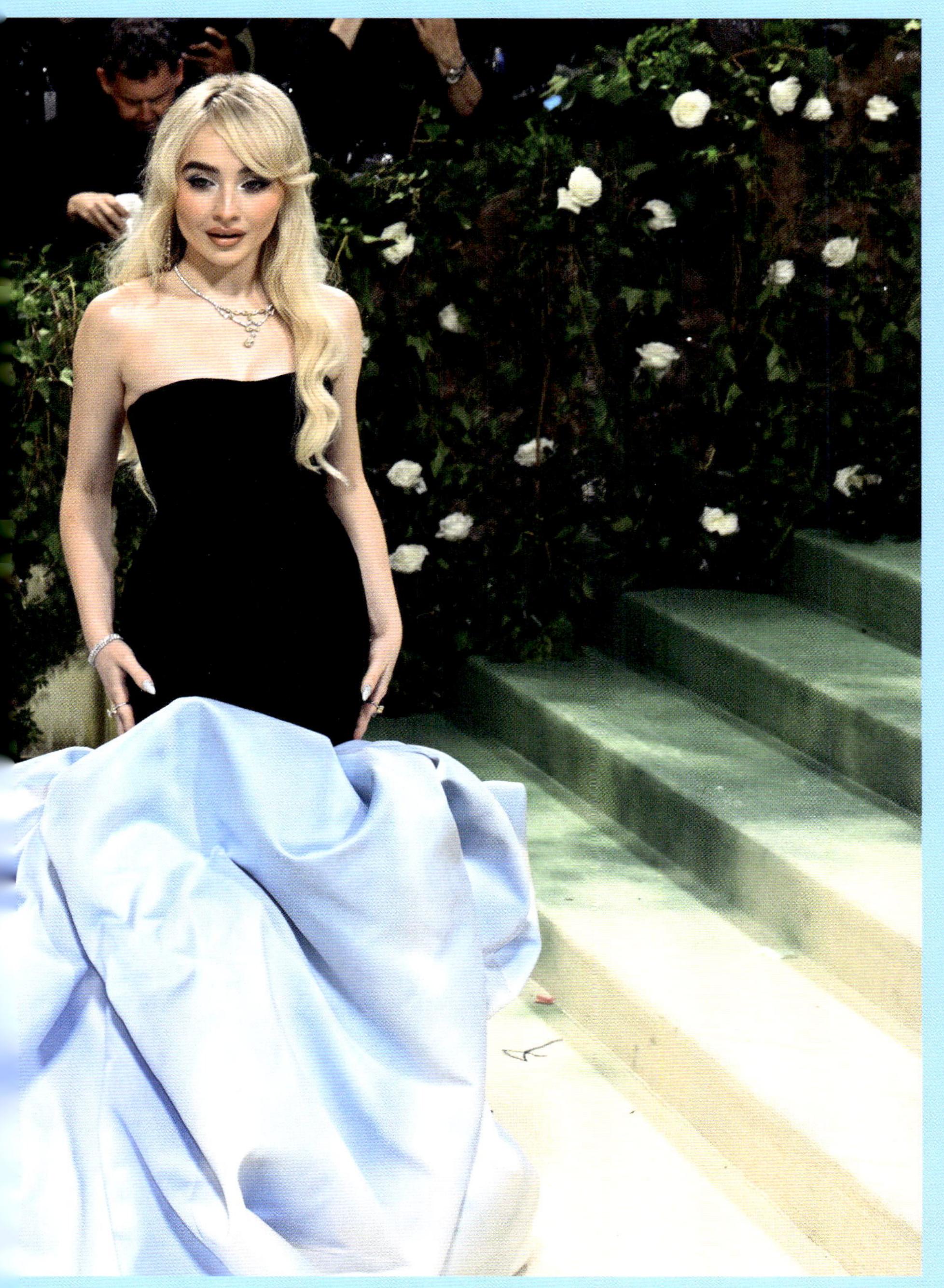

Speaking to *Fashionista*, Frolov talked about the powerful connection between him, Sabrina, her team and his brand. He went on to say that they shared 'the same vibe, the same ideas and built a very warm relationship during the creation of all the looks'. He also went into their process, explaining that the looks would begin with a short conversation about what Sabrina wanted the garment to look like, and adding that much of their collaboration is organic: 'I just do what I feel and Sabrina likes it ... it's magic to tell the truth.' Though he rarely meets with his clients face to face, he personally delivered her Greek Theatre dress to Sabrina in Los Angeles. 'When we met, I was so happy and inspired by her personality and her talent,' he said.

Sabrina loved that first design so much that she asked for the mini moment in multiple colours, wearing versions of Frolov's custom designs – including a baby-blue and black version of the Swarovski-crystal dress – during her Eras Tour performances, and a holiday-red version of the signature look for her 2023 Jingle Ball show.

Frolov's designs became the uniform for big moments in Sabrina's on-stage career. For her Coachella debut, she wore two of his designs. One was a light-blue dress with a lace skirt and silver hearts on the bodice. The other was a blush dress, worn while giving audiences their first listen of 'Espresso' – a deep V-cut dress, with crystal heart and crystal rose details, draped sparkling detail across the bodice, and a pleated super-short miniskirt with a crystal belt. During her June 2024 Governors Ball performance, she wore a canary yellow version of the dress as she performed her second single from *Short n' Sweet*, 'Please Please Please', live for the first time. Frolov credits his relationship with Sabrina and her insatiable young audience for making his brand famous in the United States.

VINTAGE BEACH BABE

Off stage, Carpenter was still making fashion waves. In June 2024, she made a surprise appearance at Vogue World 2024, walking the runway in a custom look by Jacquemus that in some ways seemed inspired by the retro swimwear she'd donned for her 'Espresso' video. The red-striped headscarf, swimsuit-like bodysuit and matching skirt were also said to be inspired by Brigitte Bardot's classic style. Sabrina's desire to embody the French actress's *je ne sais quoi* has been well documented. She has recreated multiple iconic looks worn by the starlet, including photos captured of Brigitte smoking a cigarette while playing cards, and wearing pigtails with red ribbons on set while filming the 1965 film *Viva Maria*. Sabrina's hair stylist, Scott King, has shared photos of Sabrina in this mode on Instagram, with the caption 'Brigitte is always the inspo.'

King, an enthusiast for vintage hair styling, gave *The Quality Edit* a behind-the-scenes look at how he styled Sabrina's hair for her *Short n' Sweet* tour – making it as bouncy as possible, and her curls as voluminous as could be, 'almost like an amped-up version of her signature blowout but with more of a '60s "doll" aesthetic'. He also discussed just how long it takes for her hair to be stage-ready, sharing that, after an hour to an hour and a half of blow-drying, curling and setting Sabrina's hair, he lets it sit for three hours, then brushes everything out, sprays it, and does final touches that take around 20 minutes.

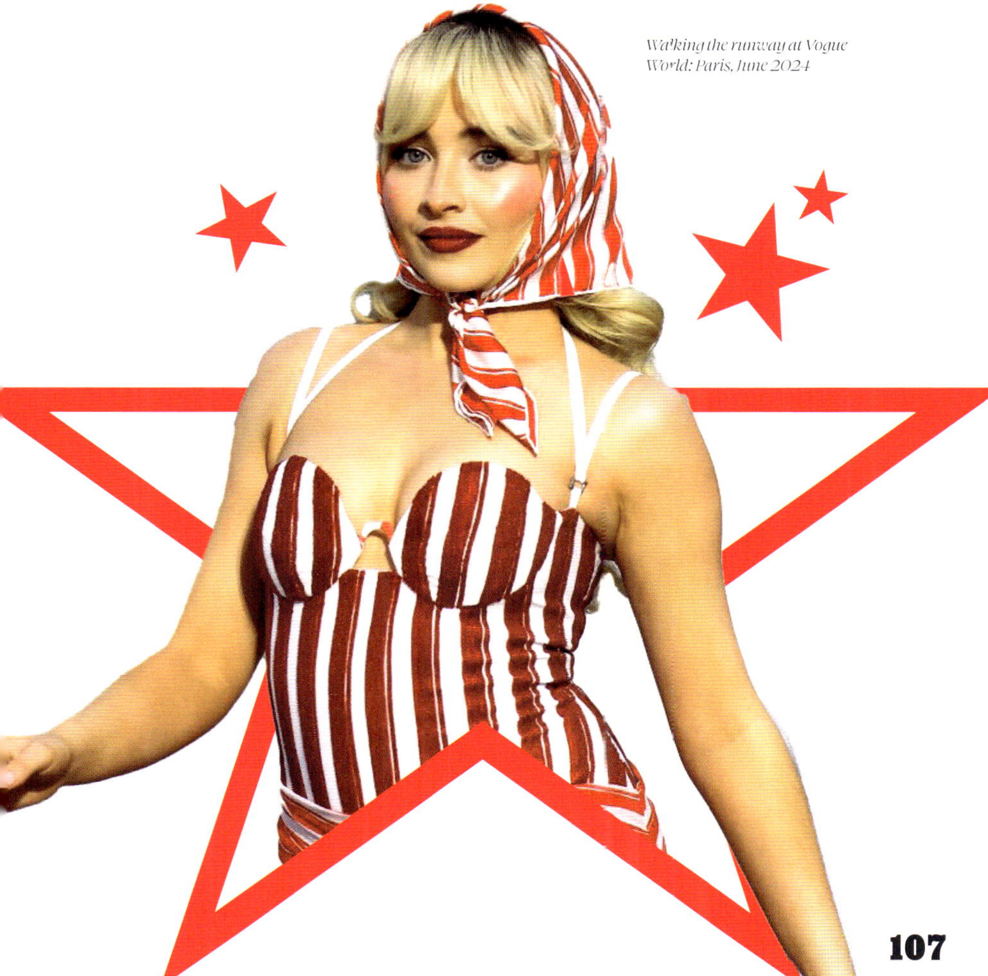

Walking the runway at Vogue World: Paris, June 2024

SABRINA AFTER DARK

The *Short n' Sweet* tour ushered in a new era of stage design and costume for Sabrina. She worked closely with her stylist, Jared Ellner, from the time she got off stage at Coachella until the tour kicked off in September 2024 to come up with each outfit. In a backstage video with *Vogue*, she shared that Jared takes the ideas she has in her head and knows how to elevate them 'times a thousand'. They decided on different looks for each act that they would change by colour for different shows. It was the first time that Sabrina had implemented multiple wardrobe changes during each show, and they leaned into film and classic iconography to find inspiration. She wore babydoll dresses, inspired (again) by Bardot and the sleepover scene from *Grease*. She also donned a black custom catsuit by Patou – made of lace and embellished with crystals and a small bow – as inspired by Audrey Hepburn in *Funny Face* (1957) and Marilyn Monroe in *There's No Business Like Show Business* (1954). The show opens with Sabrina in a tight glittery corset, which she reveals by opening a towel after a sketch in which the audience interrupts her while she's in the middle of bathing. She wears a vintage-style babydoll dress in acts where she's getting ready for a party. 'It's inspired by *Playboy After Dark*,' Sabrina told *Vogue* while explaining the vibe of her late-night scenes. 'But, it's *Sabrina After Dark*.' She dons fur boas and a heavy, glistening fabric inspired by ABBA's *Voyage* show, where the singers, played by holograms, wear sparkling, iridescent looks. She brought her iconic red-lip kiss stamp to the looks, decorating her tights, corsets and accessories with the smooch. She worked with Victoria's Secret, Patou and Ludovic de Saint Sernin to curate each act of the show.

Sabrina continues to stun on the carpet by keeping a tight, creative relationship with her favourite designers, like Roberto Cavalli, whose orange V-neck minidress she wore while performing at BBC Radio 1's Big Weekend in London. She also wore Cavalli as one of two outfits for Coachella. She later shared, in a recap post of the performance, 'it was an honor to wear 2 custom @roberto_cavalli looks on this day in his memory ... rest in peace'; this was a special thank you to the designer, who died the month of the performance. One of the looks was an embellished sleeveless top with a raw hem, matched with an army-green pleated skirt, with panther-head emblems ornamenting the waistband. The other was a minidress with a heart-shaped bodice and feather skirt. Cavalli's designs made an appearance during Sabrina's Outside Lands Festival performance in San Francisco. She stepped in last minute as a headliner at the show, replacing Tyler, The Creator, and the Cavalli black corset with a tinsel-decorated hemline was a perfect fit, as she showed the audience just how much she deserved to be at the top of the bill.

Performing on the Short n' Sweet *tour, Barclays Center, New York, September 2024*

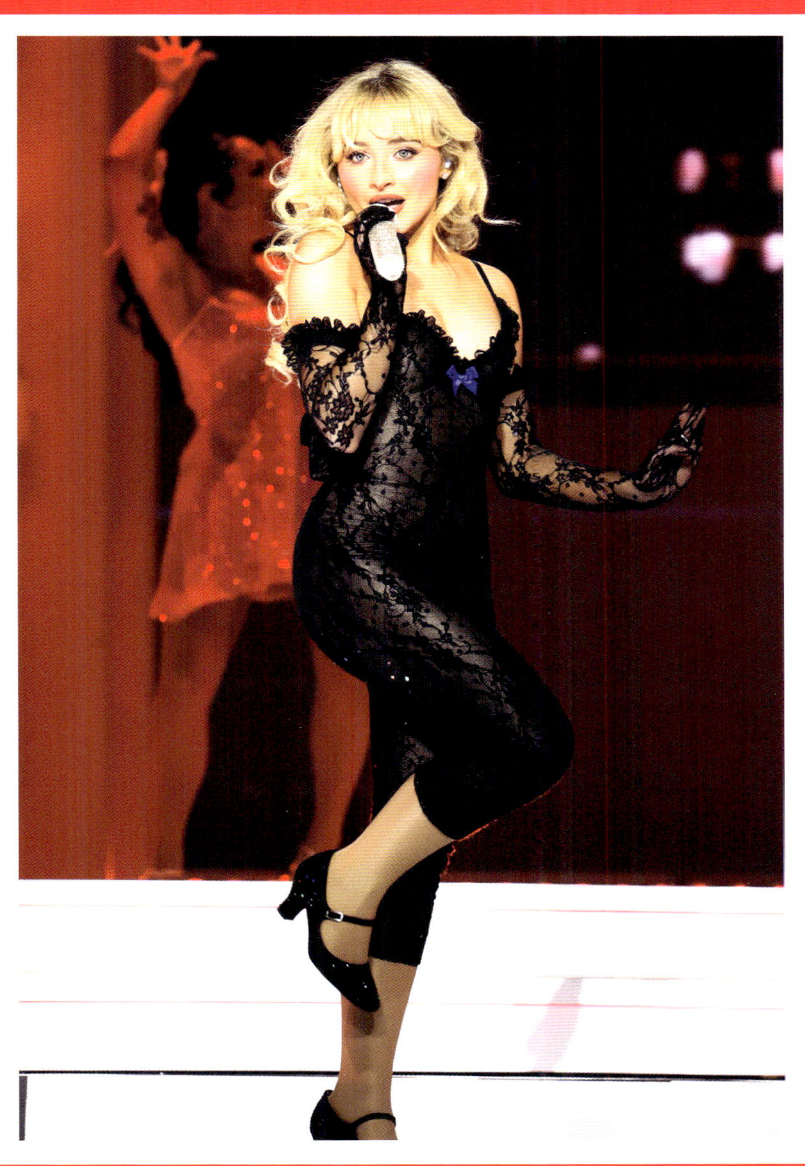

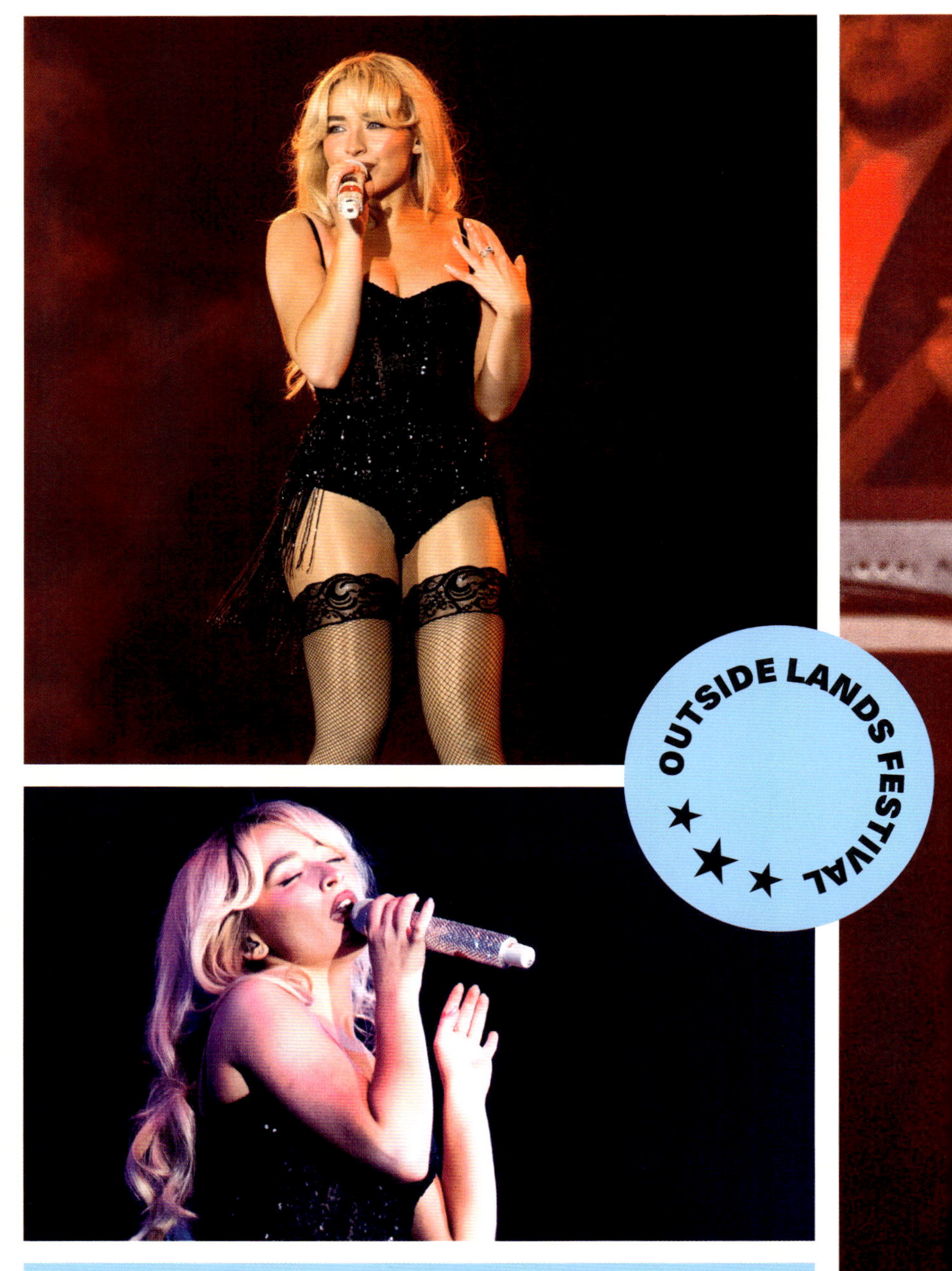

Performing at the Outside Lands Music and Arts Festival, San Francisco, August 2024

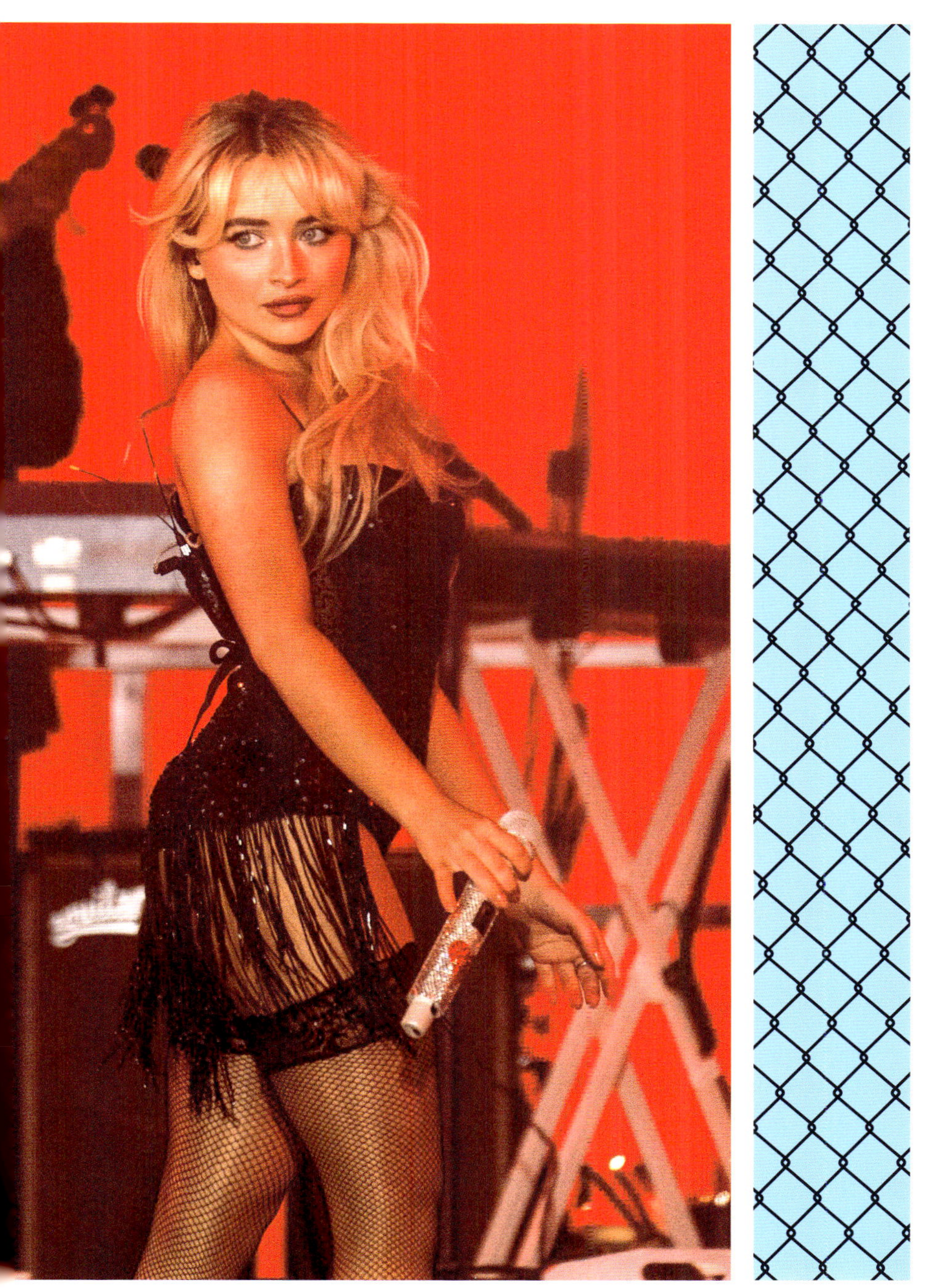

BLONDE AMBITION

Looking to the past has always been at the centre of Sabrina's mood board. At the 2024 MTV VMAs, she paid homage to pop icon Madonna by wearing the same custom silver strapless sequin gown the megastar wore to the Oscars in 1991. The original Bob Mackie dress, with its sweetheart neckline, was inspired by Marilyn Monroe in *Gentlemen Prefer Blondes* (1953), giving Carpenter's donning of the dress multiple layers of Blonde-spiration. She styled it in a similar way to Madonna, rocking the same crimson red lip and blonde, tight curls. That same evening, after the awards show, Sabrina was seen leaving an Electric Lady Studios afterparty wearing a 1996 Gucci dress by Tom Ford with similar material and shaping to Britney Spears's iconic blue lace minidress, which she wore to the 2001 VMAs. The dress, which has '70s-style bell-shaped sleeves, was originally worn on the runway by Kate Moss.

Even on her birthday, the pint-sized pop star couldn't help but play homage to fashion. In May 2024, as she celebrated turning 25, she put her own spin on the yellow dress Kate Hudson's character Andie Anderson wears in *How to Lose a Guy in 10 Days* (2003). Sabrina's stylist, Jared Ellner, confirmed that he sourced a mini (and bedazzled, of course) version of the sunny-hued dress on peer-to-peer reseller platform Depop. The original, featuring an open back and deep V neckline, was designed by Carolina Herrera and costume designer Karen Patch, and worn during the climax of the hit movie. Hudson, for her part, praised the nod, commenting on Sabrina's Instagram post, 'that's that Andie Anderson Espresso'.

In September 2024, Sabrina's blonde ambition paid off when she was announced as Redken's first-ever global brand ambassador. In a video series for *Vanity Fair*, as she painted her self portrait, talking about how her dark eyebrows and curtain fringe have become part of her trademark, she discussed cutting her hair into this specific style after a break-up, sharing that she's not usually the type of person who makes 'rash decisions' when her feelings are hurt but that she wanted to do something. 'But I never wanted to dye my hair,' she explained. ''Cause I always felt comfortable blonde, the way I was born.' In the interview, she also showed the flipside of the confident Sabrina we've seen on stage, discussing the dichotomy between feeling confident in her skin, and also how hearing one thing could make her feel like 'the ugliest person to ever exist'. Despite being under the magnifying glass of the industry at all times, she added, 'I just think I have better things to worry about than the way that I look.'

Arriving at the MTV Video Music Awards, Elmont, New York, September 2024

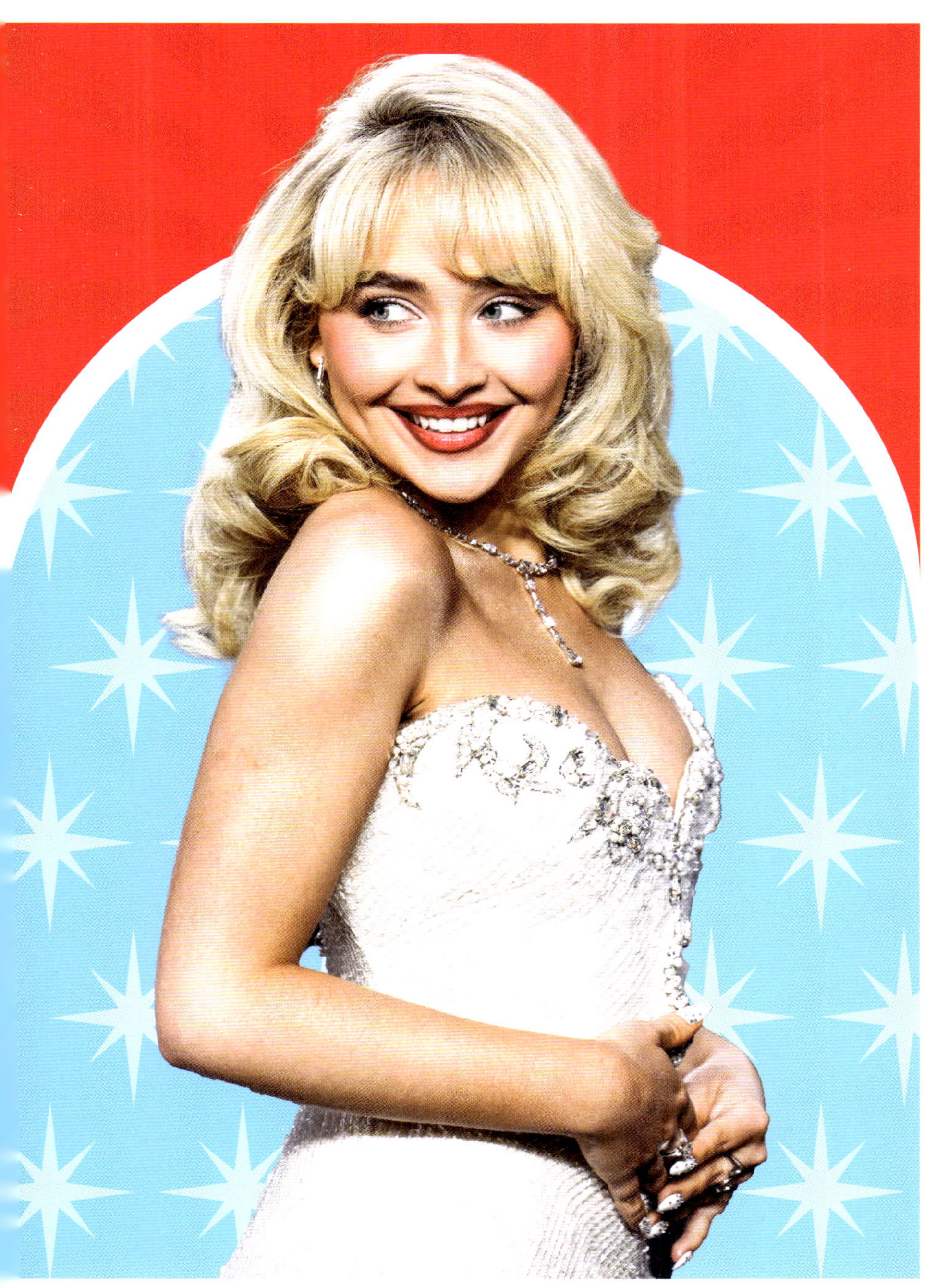

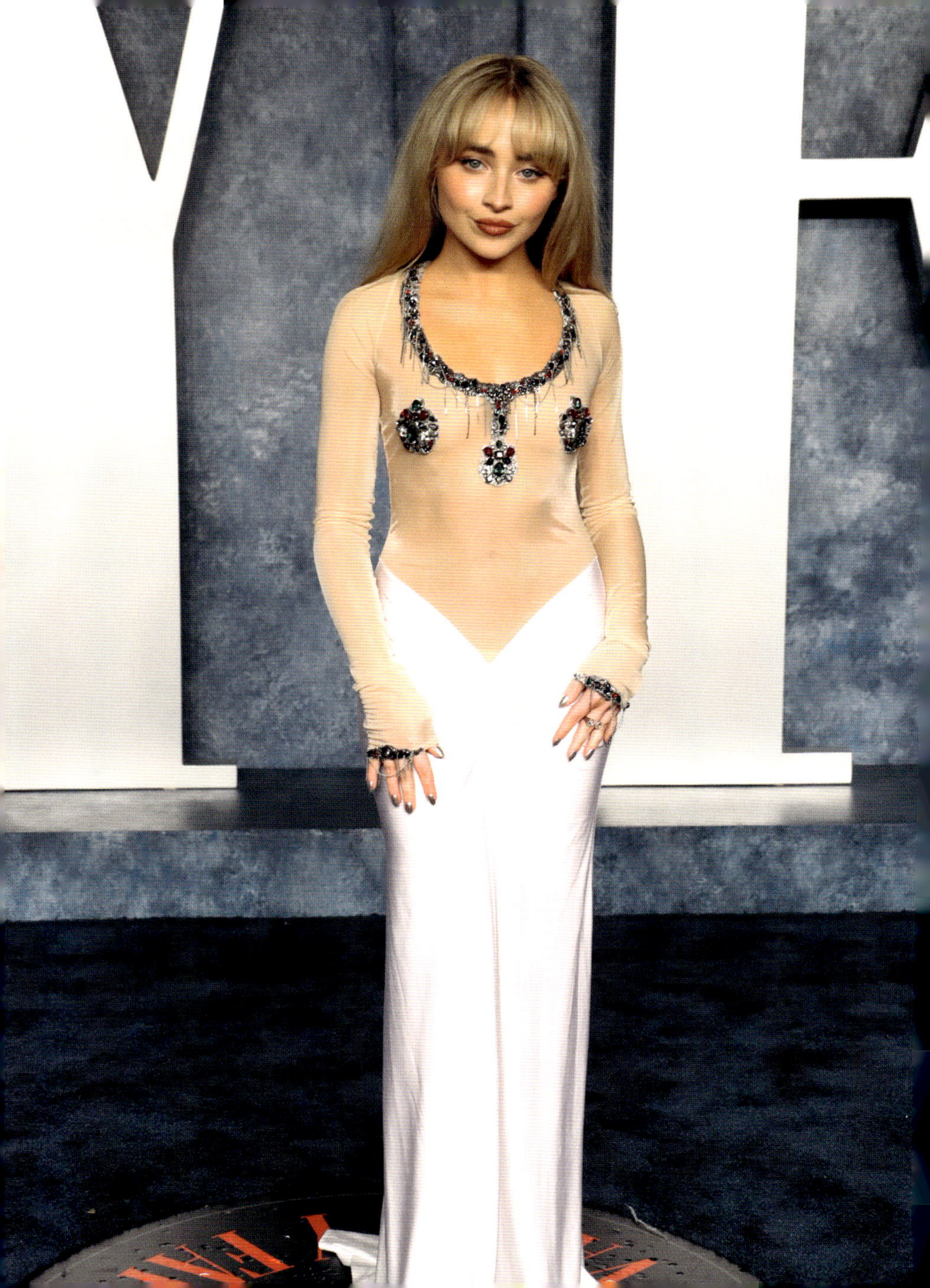

Still, fans have been eager to match her energy by matching her beauty routine – specifically her go-to make-up look, characterized by flushed cheeks, flirty lashes and rosy lips. Her make-up artist, Carolina Gonzales, told *People* some of Sabrina's style secrets, saying that for a red carpet, Sabrina's glam must withstand 'all the elements', since the lighting of the carpet doesn't lie: 'what you see is what you get.' She feels the same way about performances, but takes extra care when it comes to lip colour, because it needs to 'withstand the microphone'. Since so much of Sabrina's Hollywood aesthetic has to stay on during long work days and dance numbers, Gonzales sticks to make-up that's 'buildable, plus setting spray and setting powder' to keep the star looking flawless. Layering is also key to achieving Sabrina's highly coveted blushing look. 'The secret to that rosy glow is a cream-based blush, the layering of the blush, and the mixture of the combo,' Gonzales said. The make-up artist had shared previously that she uses two different Armani Beauty liquid blushes and plenty of highlighter to create the singer's timeless glow.

*'The secret to that **rosy glow** is a cream-based blush, the layering of the blush, and the mixture of the combo.'*

In March 2025, Sabrina made it to the cover of *Vogue*. Hands in her platinum, pinned hair, with lined lips and thick, brown brows, people immediately thought the mag had time-travelled and placed Madonna on the cover, or at least Madonna as inspired by Marilyn Monroe. However, it was Sabrina, sat pin-up style, wearing a custom baby-blue corset by Dolce & Gabbana. Gonzales gave readers a deep dive on what was used to create Sabrina's iconic cover-girl look. She told *Vogue* that she took inspiration from Alberto Vargas's pin-up paintings, wanting to replicate a look that was 'watercolored, sensual, feminine and universally flattering'. She described how she starts by prepping Sabrina's skin, before moving on to blush, lipstick and, finally, eyes, because working on her cheeks and lips inspires the make-up look she chooses for her eyes. 'I like to see what she looks like before she's full-on glammed and go from there to ensure everything is cohesive,' Gonzales said, adding that no matter the occasion, Carpenter's go-to look is 'a vixen eye with a fluffy lash, angelic cheek, and pouty lips'.

It's hard to capture all of Sabrina's red carpet, and even candid fashion moments, but some of the standouts – where she leaned into the classics

Arriving at the Vanity Fair Oscar Party, Los Angeles, March 2023

while pushing the style envelope – are easy to spot. At the 2025 Grammys, in honour of her six nominations, Sabrina walked the carpet in an icy-blue satin dress by JW Anderson, with a halter neckline, backless silhouette and feather accents on the hem as well as at the drop waist. When it was time to pick up her award for Best Pop Vocal Album, she was in a golden sparkling, strapless Versace gown that matched her Grammy gramophone. She'd worn a similar Versace silhouette, on that occasion in silver, at the Time 100 Next gala in 2024. The form-fitting gown came with a matching scarf, giving it peak Hollywood drama and glamour. She also wore a mini (of course) version of one of the designer's 2024 pieces – a chequered yellow-and-silver dress, first worn on the runway by fellow iconic blonde Claudia Schiffer – during her first performance at London's Wembley Stadium as part of Capital FM's Summertime Ball in June 2024. Her love affair with Versace didn't stop there, as she wore a bejewelled sheer gown by the designer while walking the carpet for the 50th Anniversary Special of *Saturday Night Live* in February 2025.

Paco Rabanne has also had lots of love from Sabrina. After wearing the designer to her first Met Gala, she also rocked Rabanne at her first *Vanity Fair* Oscars afterparty, in 2023. The dress came with a sheer top decorated with red, blue and silver crystals. Sabrina told *Who What Wear* that they'd sent her a black and white version of the revealing dress, but the white just felt 'special', and that it stood out as different from her typical fashion choices. She wore a short, gold, tasselled, strapless dress by Paco Rabanne for his show in Paris back in 2022, sharing in a post, 'it's so romantic in @pacorabanne'.

PIN-UP PERFECTION

Not only has Sabrina's style story hinged on relationships with brands and her own, singular look, she's also embraced fashion that has shown off her personality (i.e., her twisted humour). She embodied '90s comedian Fran Drescher of *The Nanny*, wearing a vintage Lillie Rubin leopard-fur-lined number with matching beret, for her appearance on *The Late Show with Stephen Colbert*. There was also the furry minidress from Karl Lagerfeld's 1990s Chanel runway she wore while running around New York City in December 2024. Poised, in a flurry of black and white fake fur, she prompted many on the web to call this her revenge dress, since she wore it not long after her split from beau Barry Keoghan was confirmed. Originally worn by Naomi Campbell on the runway, the monochrome dress stopped traffic.

Sabrina's fashion sense has undeniably shaped her pop star persona, but her music – particularly her sixth album, *Short n' Sweet* – has kept her permanently in the spotlight.

Arriving at The Late Show with Stephen Colbert, *New York, December 2024*

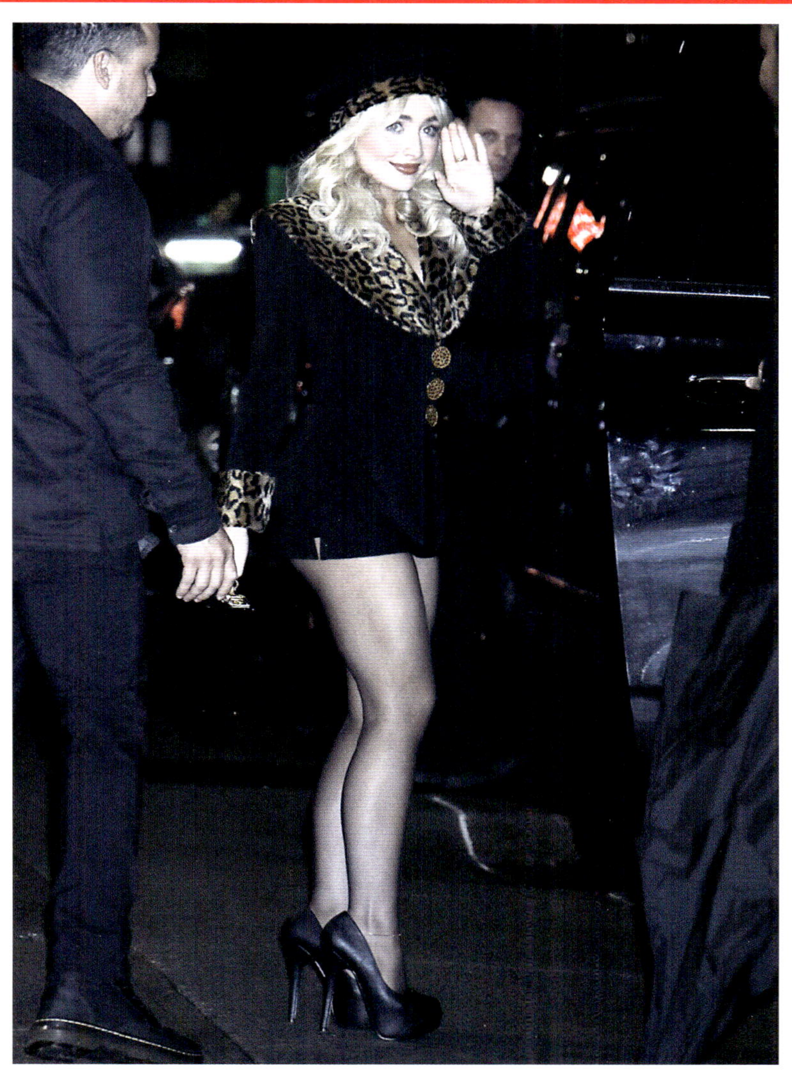

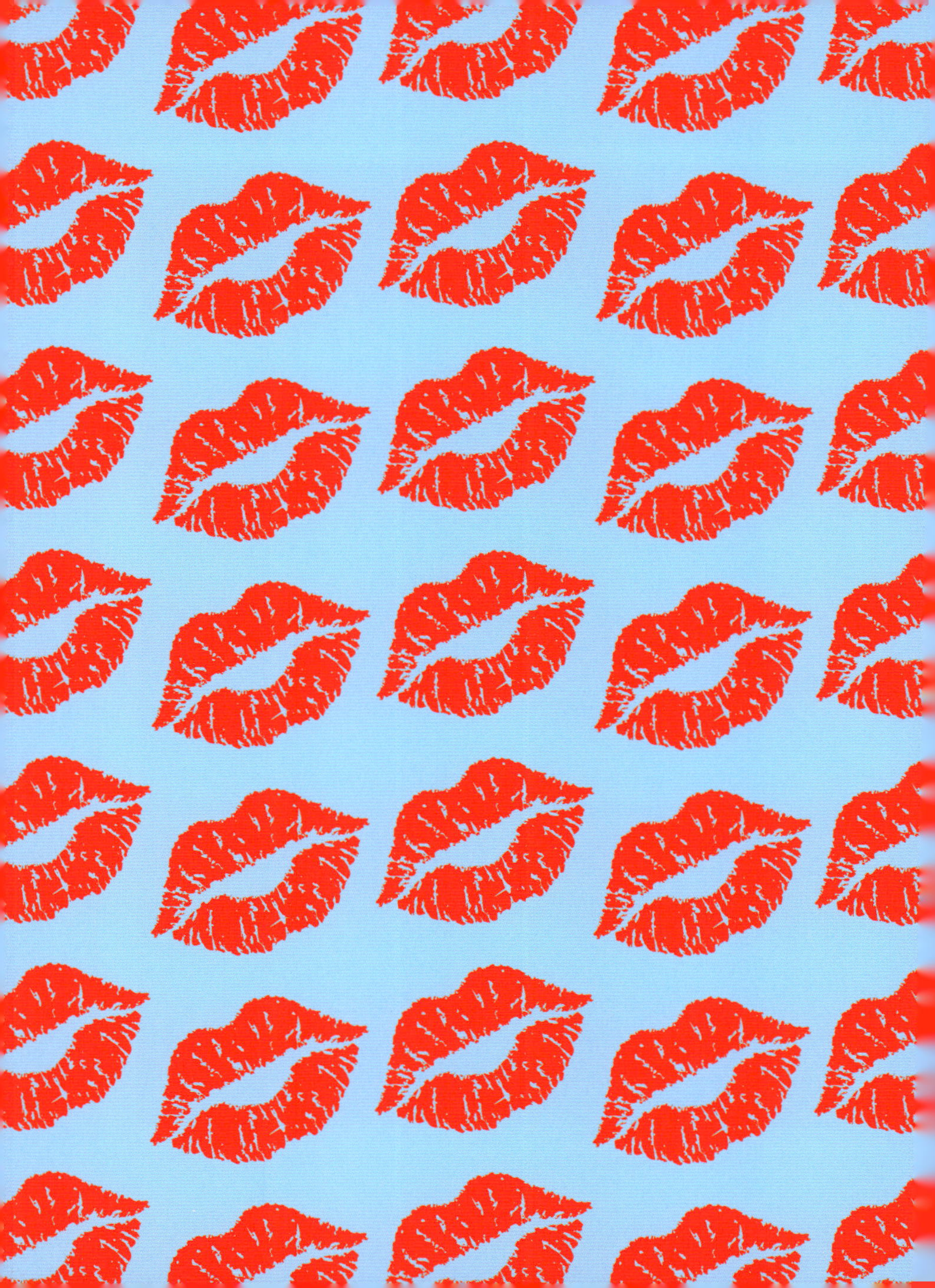

SHORT, *Sweet* AND SITTING AT THE TOP

The Phenomenal Sixth Album

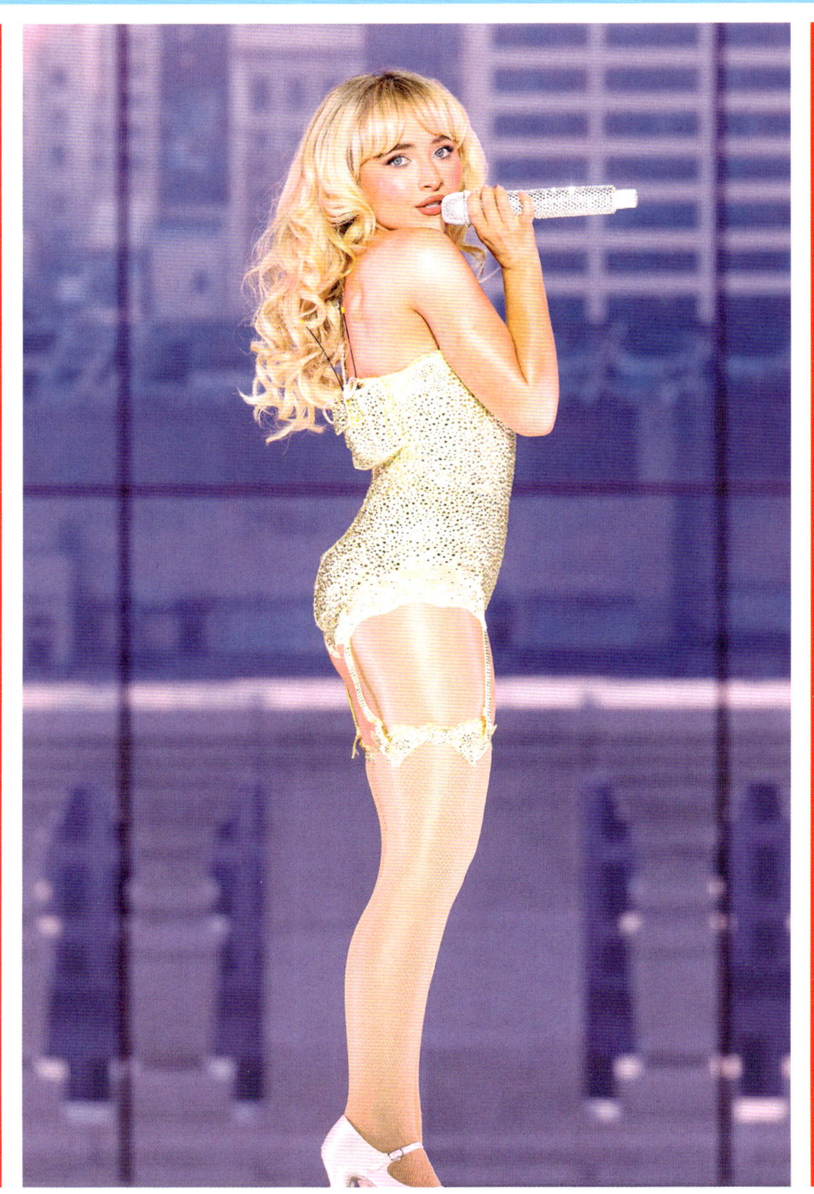

In May 2024, billboards in New York City and Los Angeles began to tease an announcement of sorts from Sabrina. In true Carpenter fashion, fan responses were all quips about her height, with one saying 'sabrina carpenter has charmed me. I don't know anything about her but i think waking up every day and being 4'11 is an act of bravery.' Another read 'when i say i hate short people, sabrina carpenter is NEVER included.'

On 2 June, Sabrina shared a cryptic video on Instagram; it showed her walking up to the camera in a light-blue bodysuit, kissing it and leaving her red lipstick mark before flipping her hair. She confirmed the release officially on 3 June, via Instagram, letting fans know it would be out on 23 August: 'this project is quite special to me and i hope it'll be something special to you too.' The album cover art shows Sabrina against a deep blue backdrop, her back towards the camera, her blonde hair bright and cascading past a denim halter top, and a bright red kiss mark on her shoulder. Like many of Sabrina's previous visuals that nodded back to a particular model or star, the artwork seemed to pay homage to a similar snap of French model Tiffany Collier, taken for *Cosmopolitan France* in 2018. Both have the same hue as the backdrop, with the blonde model also sporting a kiss on her shoulder.

Summertime steamroller 'Espresso' was now followed by 'Please Please Please', dropped on 6 June and, it turned out, another historic notch on Sabrina's sonic belt.

Performing on the Short n' Sweet *tour, Madison Square Garden, New York, September 2024*

Produced by Jack Antonoff, who also co-wrote the song with Sabrina and frequent collaborator Amy Allen, and recorded at New York City's Electric Lady Studios, the song leans into pop, country and disco. The singer weaves a tale of fear, anxiety and yearning in a new romantic relationship, as she begs her partner to disprove her assumptions and show her he's able to be faithful, the whole thing sung with a Southern lilt and teardrop in the throat. Antonoff told *Variety* that they wanted to make sure that Carpenter's voice floated above the music – that her story was the main focus, on top of the lush strings and layered orchestration beneath it. He also shared that the song was made after they talked about referencing ABBA and Dolly Parton, and wanting to create a song that can go from 'roller skating with a disco ball overhead then five seconds later you're weeping in bed'.

Like its predecessor, the song came with its fair share of meme-able lines, particularly the moment when Sabrina sweetly delivers 'Heartbreak is one thing, my ego's another/I beg you, don't embarrass me, motherfucker', before going back to the earnest plea of the chorus. During a surprise appearance on singing coach Eric Vetro's 'BBC Maestro' course, Sabrina said that 'Please Please Please', both sonically and lyrically, felt like a 'fraction' of herself that she'd been wanting to share her whole career, noting that it was aligned with the music she grew up listening to, while also being very much of herself. She shared the song was 'based on real-life events'.

A STAND-UP GUY

Speaking of real life, Sabrina sourced her actual romantic partner for the music video: Irish actor Barry Keoghan. The pair are thought to have met at Givenchy's spring/summer 2024 show in Paris, in September 2023, a rumour that Sabrina seems to confirm in her song 'Bed Chem' (more on that later). They made their first official public appearance as a couple at the *W* Grammys afterparty in February 2024, cutely covering their faces while having a photo taken together for the mag. The next month, he was spotted at the Eras Tour as Sabrina opened for Taylor Swift in Singapore, and was also photographed wearing a friendship bracelet that read 'sabrina'. That same month, the singer told *Cosmopolitan* that any relationship she would actually want to put energy into had to be 'so interesting and invigorating', and that it's 'fun and messy' and she was 'really enjoying the newness of all of it'. By April, the couple seemed to be comfortable in the public eye, as Keoghan was seen holding up his phone recording Sabrina's Coachella set, where she made a reference to his film *Saltburn* in her 'Nonsense' outro that day. Later, Barry and Sabrina were seen hanging out with Swift and Travis Kelce at a festival afterparty. That May, the couple walked the carpet of the Met Gala together, with Barry accenting Sabrina's Oscar de la Renta gown with a Victorian-style brown velvet Burberry suit. He was also behind her surprise birthday party that month, according to *People*.

Then, in June, Barry and Sabrina played a modern-day Bonnie and Clyde for the 'Please Please Please' video, directed by Bardia Zeinali. The casting makes perfect sense, seeing as even the lyrics ('I heard that you're an actor, so act like a standup guy') seem to reference Keoghan. The video picks up where 'Espresso' left off, as Sabrina gets out of jail, fixing her lipstick before making eyes with Barry as he gets thrown in the cooler. Filmed in Staten Island, with much of the footage shot at Arthur Kill Correctional Facility, the video captures a well-dressed Sabrina (think: mini mob wife but in bright colours and coquettish looks) in multiple scenarios where Barry's character commits crimes as she begs him not to. It ends with her taking the law into her own hands, handcuffing Barry, taping his mouth shut and leaving her iconic kiss mark on the tape before walking away.

The next month, she told *Variety* that Barry loved the song and gave him kudos for being one of the best actors of his generation. But by August, the pair's public appearances began to dwindle and online speculation that they'd called it quits started to increase. By the end of the year, Barry had deactivated his Instagram, citing online harassment and asking people to be respectful; with that, much of the Barry and Sabrina lore died out. However, 'Please Please Please', the song to which the relationship will forever be tied, made a permanent mark. It debuted at number 2, before peaking at number 1 on the Billboard charts, making it her first hit to do so. Sabrina also made history for being the first solo act to have two simultaneous top-three hits. The only other time that had happened in the chart's 66-year history was when the Beatles did the same in 1964 with 'I Want To Hold Your Hand', and 'She Loves You'. 'Please Please Please' took the number 1 spot on Spotify's charts, dethroning 'Espresso'. Sabrina cheekily joked about the news, retweeting it with the words: 'this bitch'.

Overleaf: Vanity Fair Oscar Party, Beverly Hills, March 2024

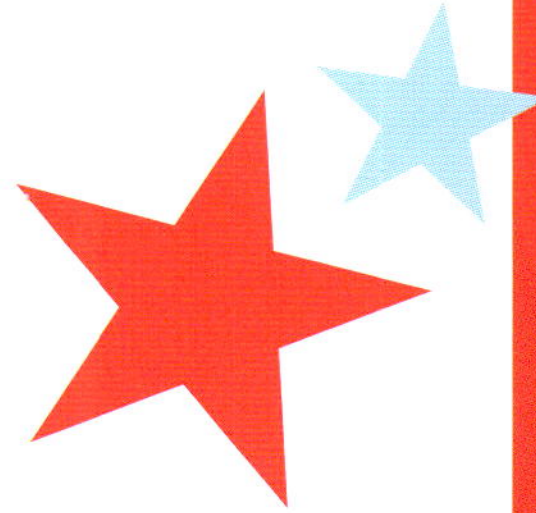

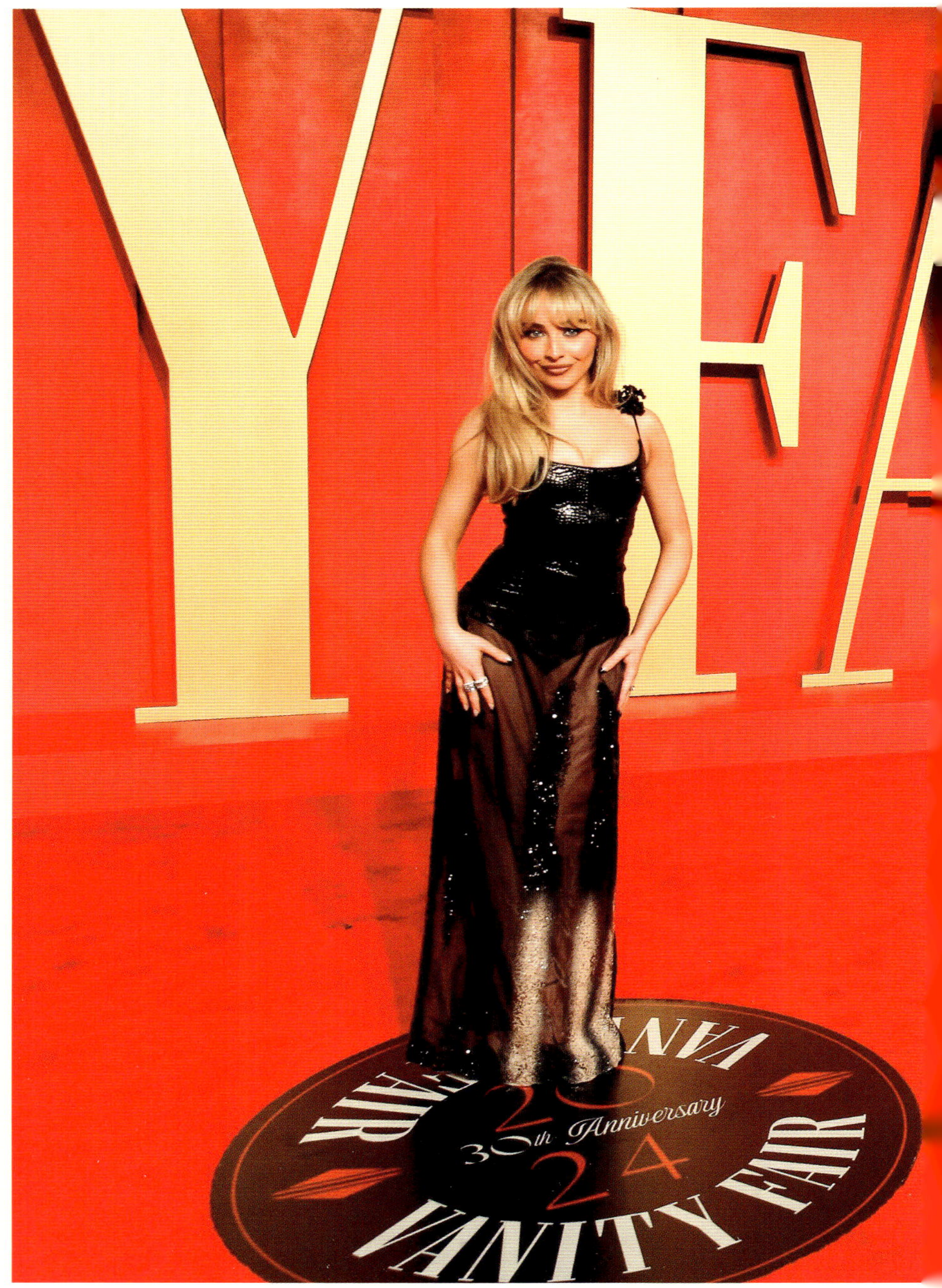
30th Anniversary
VANITY FAIR

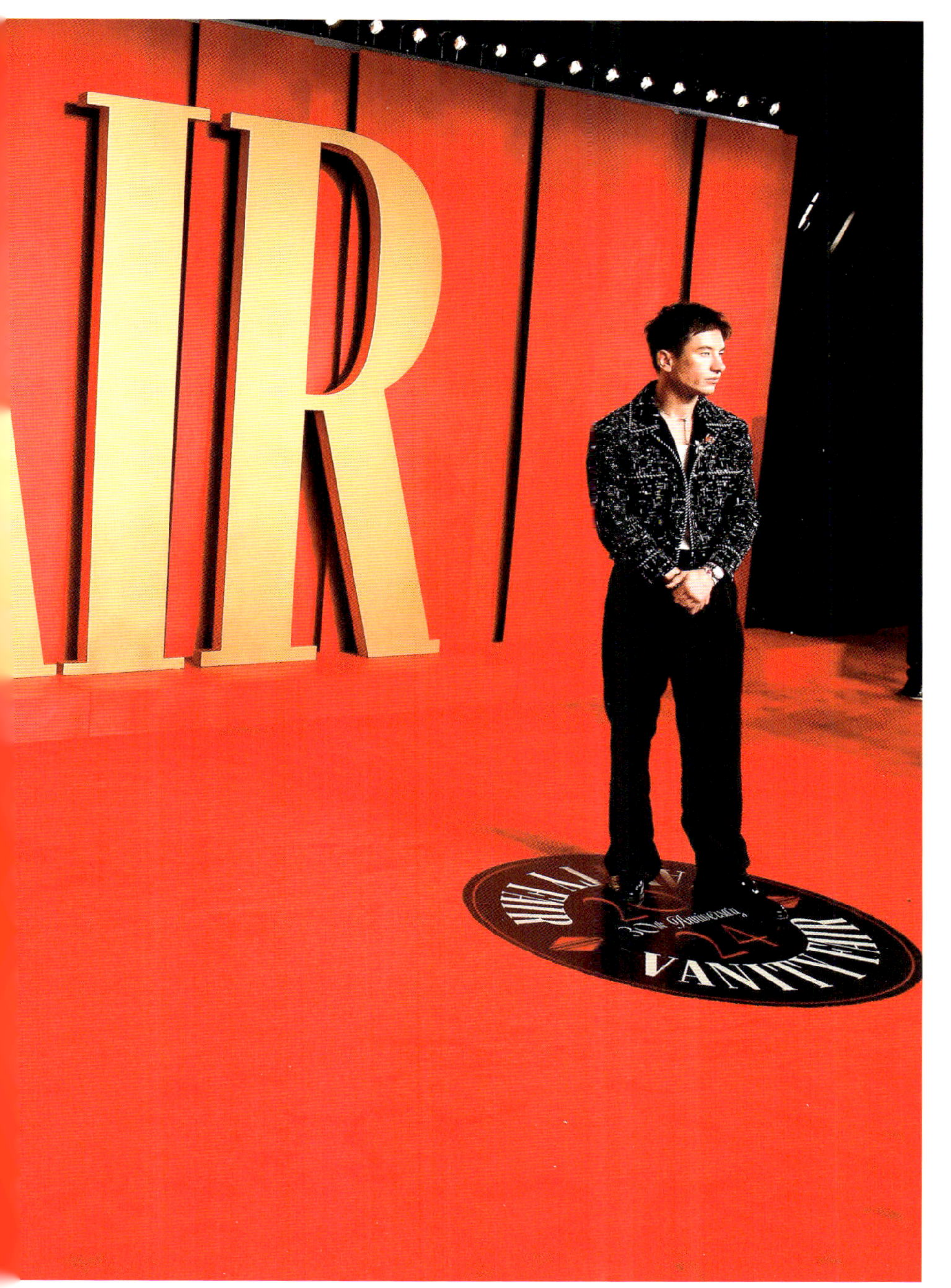
IR
VANITY FAIR
30th Anniversary

SHORT AND SWEET

On 10 June, not long after dropping 'Please Please Please', Sabrina announced her *Short n' Sweet* tour. She shared a photo of the tour dates as well as a Polaroid of herself holding a newspaper, the 'Carpenter Times', with the headline 'SHE'S GETTING AROUND!' She initially announced US dates, before promoting the European leg of the tour in July.

In July 2024, Sabrina dropped an '80s-style infomercial on her Instagram account, dancing in a blue bodysuit and black tights (the same fit she was wearing in the teaser she shared on 2 June) and dancing while each album track scrolled up across the screen.

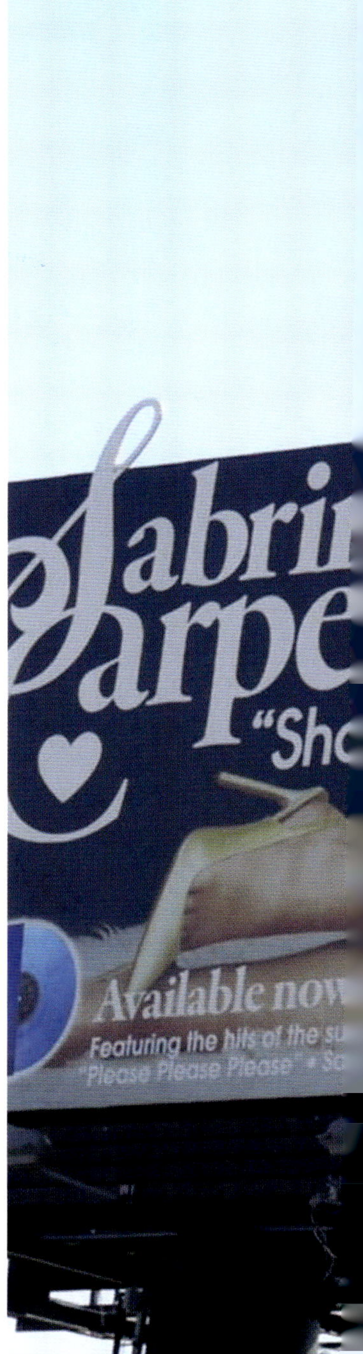

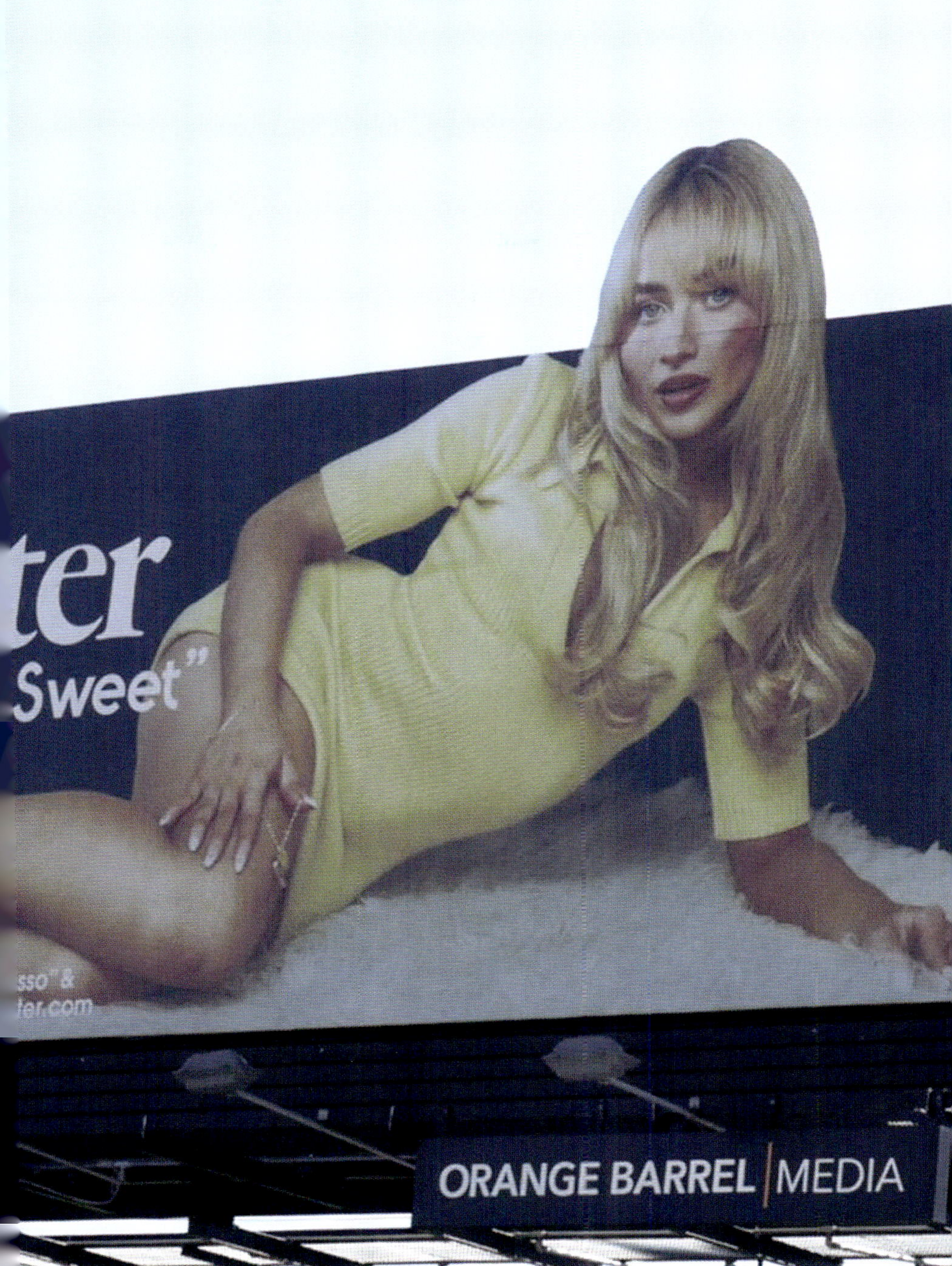
ter
Sweet"
sso" &
ter.com
ORANGE BARREL | MEDIA

On 23 August, as promised, Sabrina Carpenter officially released her sixth album. She gave the album the title *Short n' Sweet*, not because she's 'vertically challenged', as she told Zane Lowe, but also because many of the songs focused on how some of her shortest relationships had the biggest impact. She shared a carousel of videos and never-before-seen photos on Instagram on release day, writing 'i feel extremely lucky that each time i write a new record i learn a little bit more about myself, and can create from that place', adding 'the making of short n' sweet was one of the most special, honest, up and down, stupid and fun experiences of my life'.

> *'I think the series of* ***unfortunate events*** *I've encountered in* ***relationships*** *are* ***no secret.'***

On the same day, Sabrina shared 'Taste', the album's third single. The song, a combination of steady, '80s glittering beat and vibrating rock guitars, centres on an ex and the on-again, off-again girlfriend they always return to. The lyrics are tongue-in-cheek, as Sabrina reminds the girlfriend, 'you'll just have to taste me when he's kissing you'. At one point, she shines a light on the public speculation around her relationships, singing, 'I've been known to share.' When asked about her confidence when digging into the topic of love triangles, Sabrina joked with *PAPER*, 'I will write any song. It doesn't mean I'll put it out, but I'll write it,' adding, 'I think the series of unfortunate events I've encountered in relationships are no secret to people who know me or think they know me.'

Sabrina kept mum on the specific characters she was alluding to in the track, but fans speculated that it was about her and fellow pop stars Camila Cabello and Shawn Mendes.

Cabello and Mendes called it quits in 2021, after being super public about their two-year relationship and collaborating on the hit song 'Señorita'. The pair were still believed to be dating off and on, thanks to being spotted multiple times and being seen together at Coachella in 2023. Sabrina was also spotted with Mendes multiple times in early 2023, sparking dating rumours and leading onlookers to assume that he'd been dating her before he decided to rekindle his relationship with Camila at Coachella. By June of 2023, sources were reporting that Mendes and Cabello had called it quits again.

Performing on the Short n' Sweet *tour, Madison Square Garden, New York, September 2024*

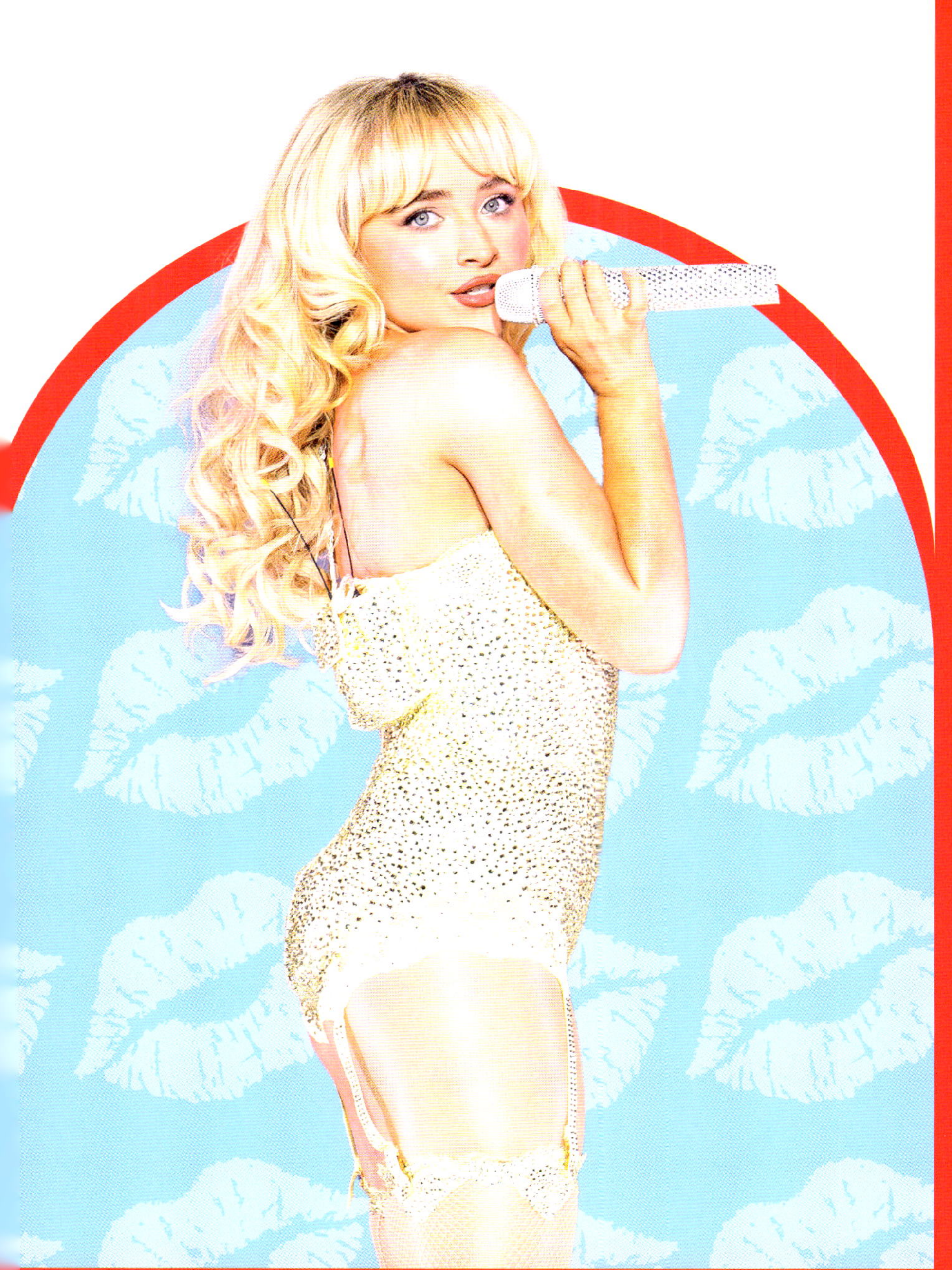

For her part, Sabrina has stayed out of any specifics, telling *W*, 'I get why people are interested, but they can listen to my album and decide for themselves what the songs are about.' Still, it didn't exactly slow the rumour mill when, during her September 2024 iHeartRadio performance of 'Señorita', Camila sang the lyrics, 'But friends don't know the way you...', leaving out the word 'taste' and covering her mouth with her finger knowingly. Mendes threw fire on the allegations when he shared on John Mayer's SiriusXM show, *How's Life*, that while he was dating someone, he reunited with his ex-girlfriend due to 'unresolved feelings'. He also said that he should've told the person he was dating 'two weeks' ahead of time about those feelings instead of 'two days' before the reconciliation.

In the video, directed by Dave Meyers, which opens with a parental advisory and viewer discretion warning, Sabrina turns the song into a delightful horror film. Inspired by the 1992 film *Death Becomes Her* and 2003's *Kill Bill Volume 1*, the video sees actress Jenna Ortega play a dark-haired vixen opposite the pop star as the two fight in a bloody battle over a love interest. The gruesome visuals show the pair sawing, fighting, shooting at each other, torturing each other's voodoo dolls, and even sharing a kiss in a gag where Sabrina body-swaps with the male love interest. After killing off the man in the middle, the two walk away from his funeral giggling, while Ortega says he's 'very insecure' and Carpenter responds 'you kill me'.

The sultry pop song was another massive success for Sabrina. It debuted at number 2 on the Billboard Hot 100, at the same time as 'Please Please Please' was at number 3 and 'Espresso' was sat at number 4, making Carpenter (again) the only act other than the Beatles, and the only solo act, to chart three top five hits simultaneously.

Performing on the Short n' Sweet *tour, Barclays Center, New York, September 2024*

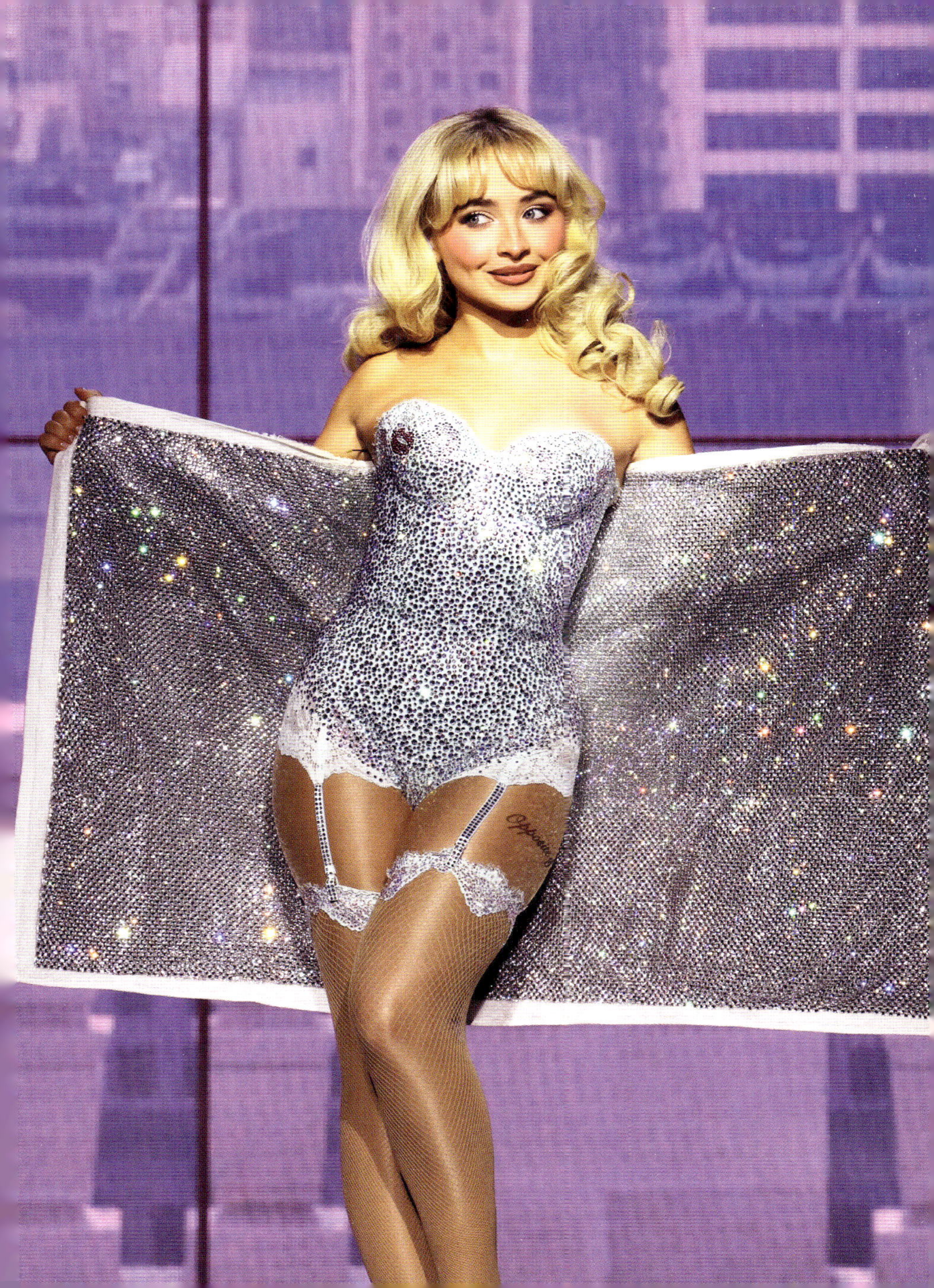

The night is spent drinking **cocktails**, *hanging out with* **friends** *and wearing an array of* **scanty outfits.**

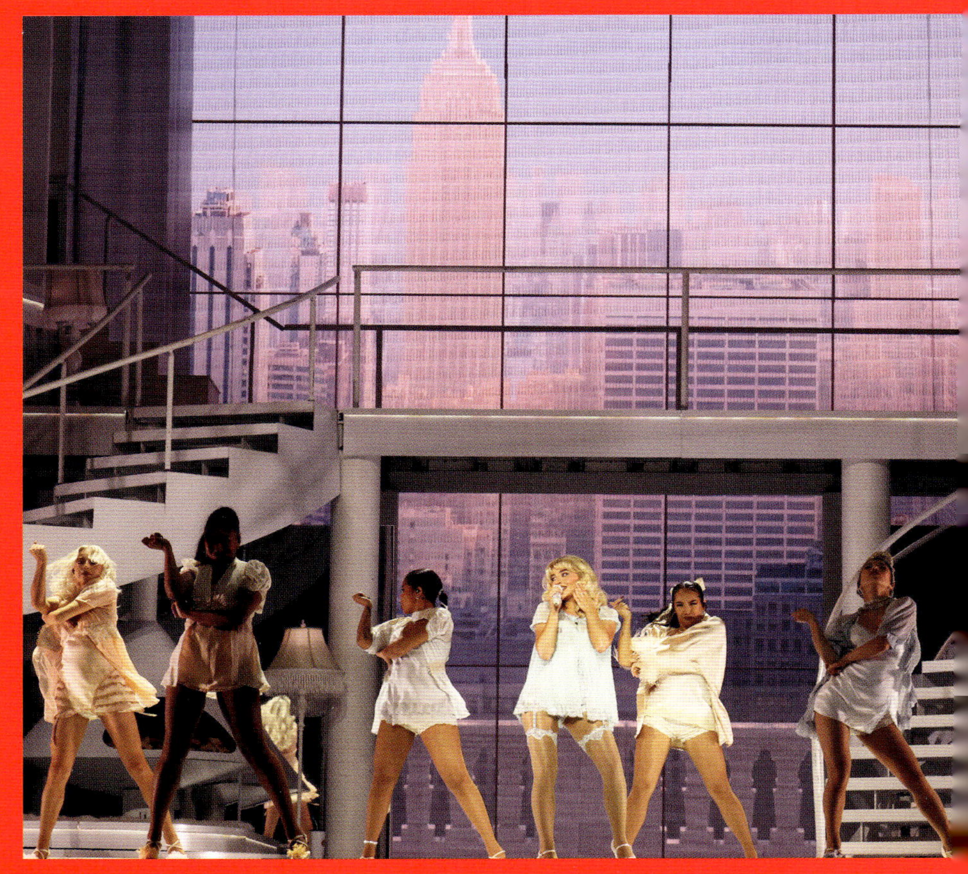

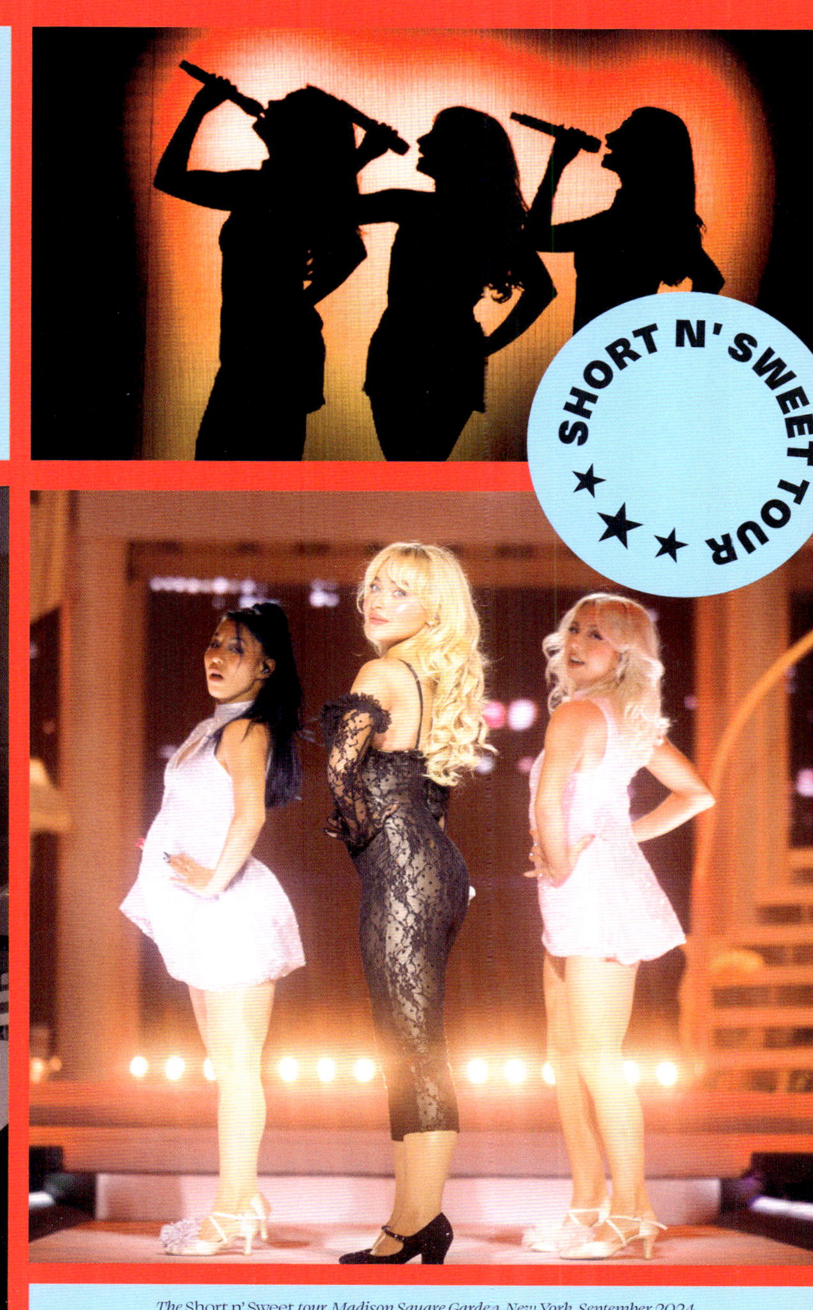

The Short n' Sweet *tour, Madison Square Garden, New York, September 2024*

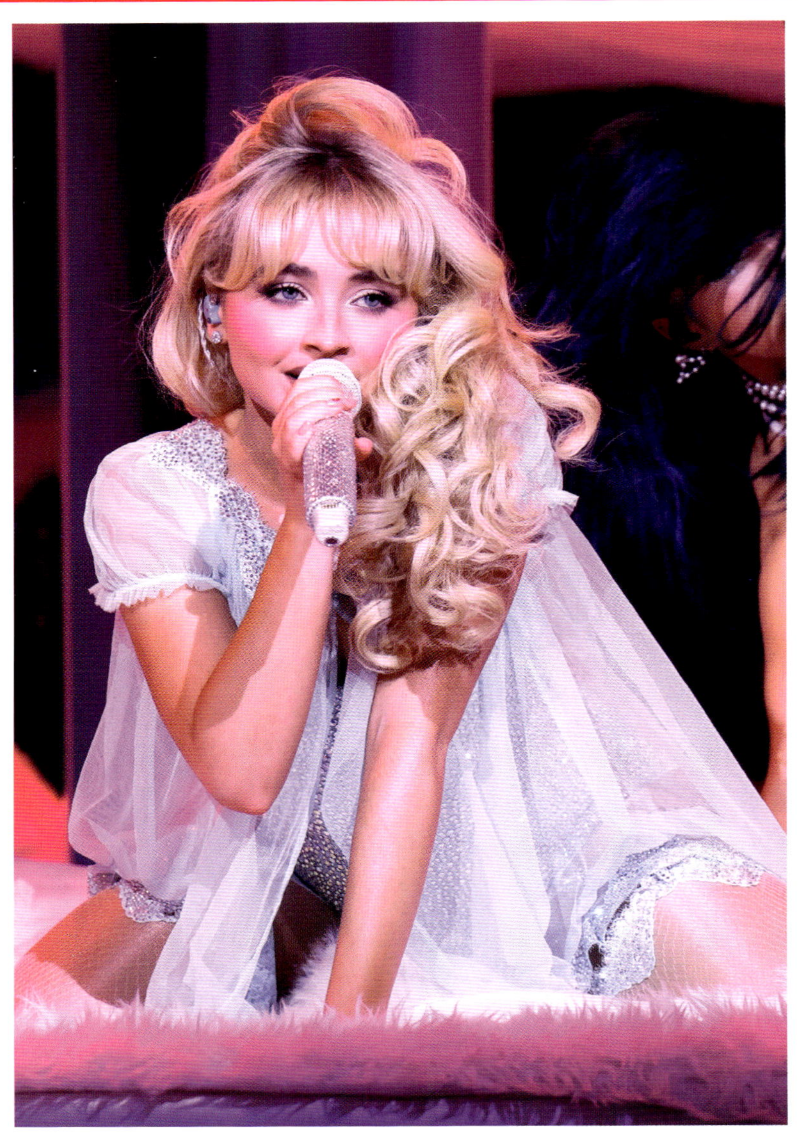

NIGHT MOVES

On 23 September 2024, Sabrina officially kicked off her *Short n' Sweet* tour in Columbus, Ohio. It was her first official arena tour. The show itself came with a new stage set, with a theme based on the *Playboy After Dark* series (she even wore the famous bunny costume at her Halloween stop in Dallas), where the night is spent drinking cocktails, hanging out with friends and wearing an array of scantily clad outfits. The set list opened with 'Taste', ended with 'Espresso', and featured songs from *Short n' Sweet* as well as *emails i can't send*. Fans noted that she had moved on from her 'Nonsense' outro (the microphone cutting off cheekily during the portion of the song where she's meant to give her typical innuendos) and away from the songs she'd shared before signing to Island Records. She did start a new viral trend, however, during her song 'Juno', a track named after the 2007 coming-of-age film about a teen who gets pregnant. The track, which also dabbles in retro disco sonics, features Sabrina singing about an intense attraction to someone, so strong that she wants them to make her Juno. In reviews, the sweet, almost ballad-like track was called the album's 'horniest' and 'raunchiest'. At one point Sabrina sings 'Wanna try out some freaky positions? Have you ever tried this one?' During live performances, Sabrina began acting out positions each night during that part of the song. Some fans found the NSFW poses inappropriate. At one point, a tweet in reaction to Sabrina's on-stage antics went viral, as one fan wrote 'i'm 17 and AFRAID of Sabrina Carpenter when she's performing'. Fans made hats and t-shirts with the phrase scribbled across them. Carpenter continued to keep her stage presence playful throughout those first dates, even changing the words in 'Juno' from 'baby' to 'Barry' when her then boyfriend came to a tour stop in Virginia.

Despite their break-up, it's thought that Barry may also be a permanent fixture in yet another *Short n' Sweet* song. In the '90s R&B-tinged track 'Bed Chem', Sabrina sings about, well, bedroom chemistry. In the opening of the song she sings about wearing a sheer dress the night she met her love interest, while he wore a white jacket and had a thick accent. Eagle-eyed fans noted that on the day the pair supposedly met, at the Givenchy show in Paris, Sabrina wore a sheer black dress, while Barry wore a white bomber jacket. Still, the song's sonic character and lyrics expand beyond their relationship, reflecting Sabrina's desire to write a song that was both 'sexy and lighthearted' and would reflect the songs she grew up listening to, with, of course, all of the innuendos and euphemisms she's become known for. She chose the song to be the album's fourth single, releasing it on 8 October; it peaked at number 14 on the Billboard Hot 100 chart.

Performing on the Short n' Sweet *tour, Barclays Center, New York, September 2024*

Elsewhere on *Short n' Sweet*, Sabrina leans into twangy vocals over acoustic guitar, her voice trembling as she sings about how 'all the good ones are taken' and complains about never having had a gay awakening in the Country song 'Slim Pickins'. 'Coincidence' plays like a classic '70s rock song, as Sabrina spins out a story of a lover who has an ex creeping back into his life. At one point, against backing vocals, she tells the story of a lover whose phone died as he drove from LA to 'her thighs' then Palm Springs (fans theorized that the song may be about Mendes going to Coachella to see Cabello, but, again, that's all speculation that hasn't been confirmed by any party involved). On 'Dumb & Poetic' Sabrina calls out a man who, well, wears being a good person as some kind of aesthetic: he meditates, reads self-help books, but all as a means of deception. With 'Lie to Girls', Sabrina explains the strange dichotomy in toxic relationships – singing sweetly that you don't have to lie to girls, because ultimately they'll lie to themselves to be with you. It was the same diary-like writing Sabrina leaned into on *emails i can't send*, combined with the confidence she first showed off on *Singular: Act II*, with a charisma and comfort in her womanhood and sexuality that only Sabrina, having gone through those previous albums, could have written. Delectable, smart and charming, *Short n' Sweet* was the album pop fans were waiting for, and Sabrina delivered.

Even without its chart-topping singles, as a collection of songs *Short n' Sweet* was a triumph for Sabrina, who for the past five albums had fought to have her own voice – humorous, horny and earnest – at the heart of her music; going with her gut paid off tremendously. Her diary-like accounts of various relationships – the good, bad, worse, and sometimes fun – are as delectable as the pristine vocals with which she delivers the antidotes. Also, her confidence in showing no allegiance to genre – hopping from '70s disco, to classic country, back to R&B and pop again – showed off her intense grasp and understanding of the history of popular music, but also an unmatched delivery and musicality.

A SURE, SWEET HIT

Short n' Sweet debuted at the top of the Billboard 200 chart, making it her first number 1 and top 10 album. In fact, all 12 of the album's tracks made their way on to the Hot 100 chart. In November of 2024, Sabrina received her first Grammy nominations, six in total. She shared multiple videos of herself hearing the news for the first time, joking about receiving a Best New Artist nomination by saying 'I don't know how that's possible. I'm the best old artist.' She wrote that she'd been dreaming about the day her whole life, and that she was filled with gratitude. She was also nominated for Album of the Year, Best Pop Vocal Album, Record of the Year and Best Pop

Solo Performance for 'Espresso', as well as Song of the Year for 'Please Please Please'.

Short n' Sweet, though it arrived six albums into Sabrina's career, will forever be a testament to what she could create when she could fully show up as her most raw and creative self. It is the album that made her more than just a pop star – a global icon.

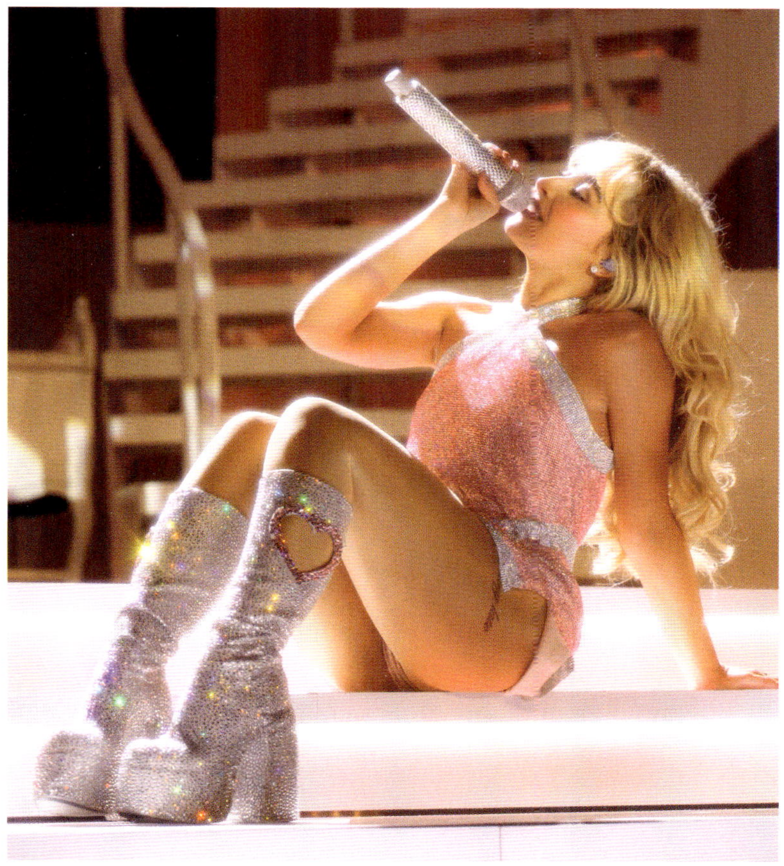

Performing on the Short n' Sweet *tour, Madison Square Garden, New York, September 2024*

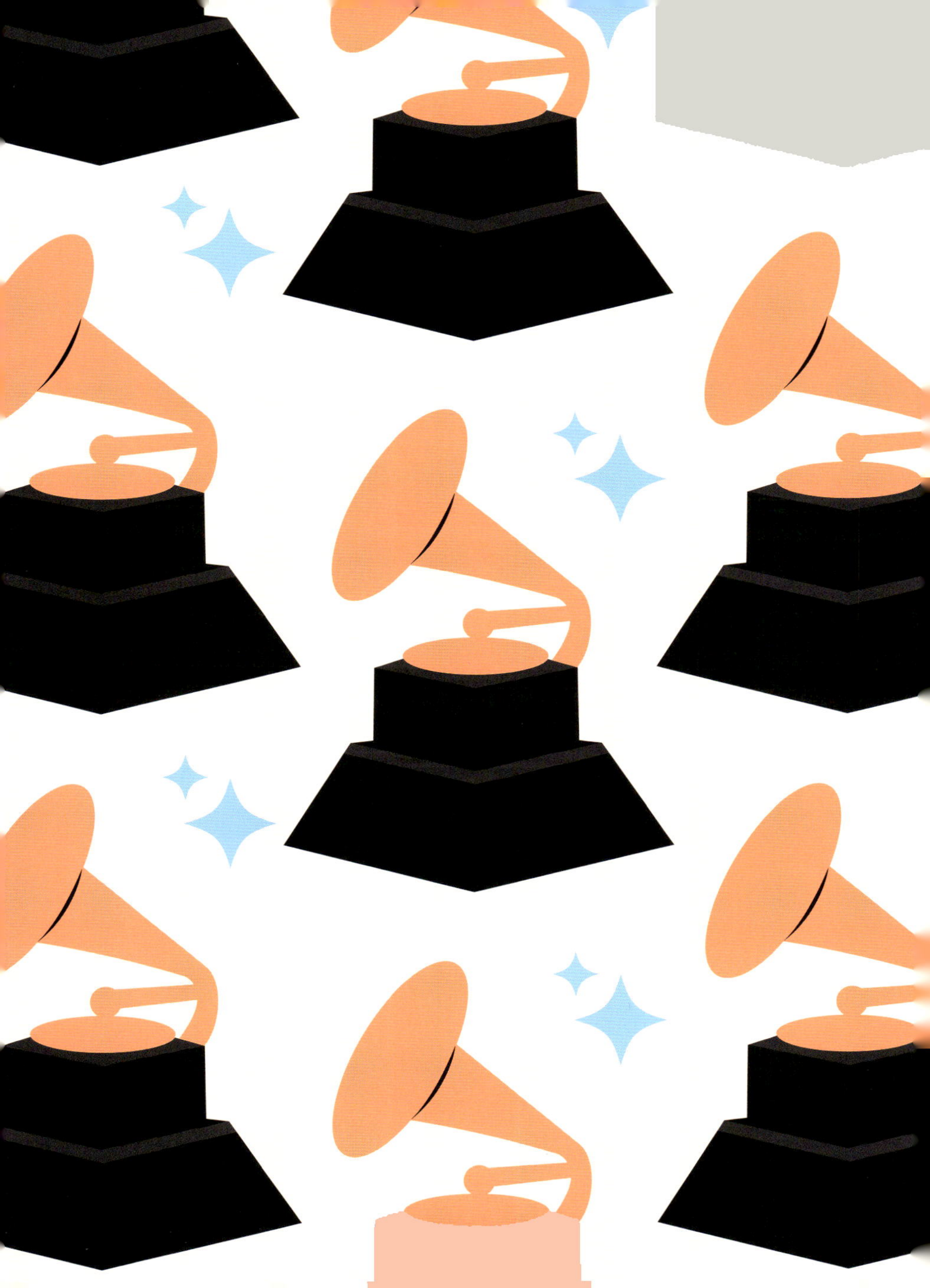

SABRINA'S GLOBAL *Impact*

Worldwide Superstar Status

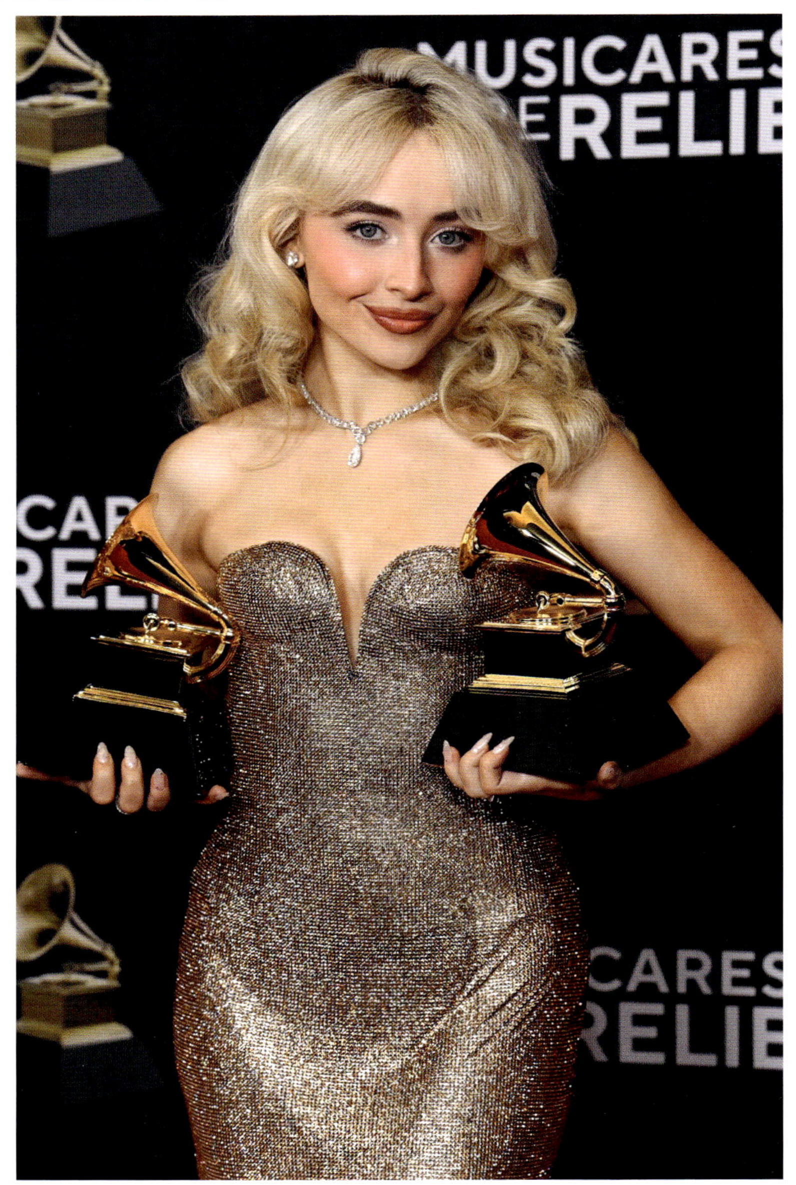
MUSICARES

In February 2025, Sabrina Carpenter attended the 67th Annual Grammy Awards in celebration of her massively successful sixth album, which had earned the singer six nominations in total.

She picked up two wins that night: one for Best Pop Solo Performance for 'Espresso' and another for Best Pop Vocal Album, for *Short n' Sweet*. She was thrilled. 'Hello! I'm still out of breath from the performance, so I really was not expecting this,' she said, after sharing a medley of 'Espresso' and 'Please Please Please'. 'All those nominees that were just on the screen are some of my favourite artists in the world, and I can't believe I'm nominated against them or even in this room right now,' she added, acknowledging Billie Eilish, Chappell Roan, Taylor Swift and Ariana Grande. She went on to thank the Recording Academy, her mum for driving her to voice lessons, her team and Island Records. Then she accidentally slipped in a few expletives because of her excitement, wondering out loud if it was ok to say 'hell'. She thanked her producers and told everyone how special *Short n' Sweet* was to her, and how it meant the world, before dropping a 'holy shit, bye!' that was edited out of the telecast. Six albums in, she was finally standing at the peak to which her slow and steady climb had led. Of course, however, she kept climbing.

Winner of Best Pop Vocal Album and Best Pop Solo Performance, 67th Annual Grammy Awards, Los Angeles, February 2025

DELUXE

On 4 February 2025, just a couple of days later, Sabrina dropped a surprise announcement for fans. 'As a thank you for giving the album 2 Grammys,' she wrote on her Instagram, captioning a photo similar to the original *Short n' Sweet* album art, but this time with wild, untamed hair and a slightly different pose. '*Short n' Sweet* deluxe is now available for pre-order ... and yes, that does say featuring Miss Dolly Parton,' she added (the second photo she posted had 17 track names scribbled on notebook paper covered with red smooch marks). She added cutely: 'She wouldn't want me to swear but holy shit!'

The extended version of the album came with five new songs. On the danceable '15 Minutes', she winks at the parties and people pretending to be nice that come with fame, as she sings sweetly over electric guitar and keys that peak at the bridge. With the slow-strumming, '70s-style ballad 'Couldn't Make It Any Harder', Sabrina lets her voice take centre stage, and 'Bad Reviews' is a country song about ignoring red flags in relationships – choosing to love someone who is bad for you. At one point, over a surging fiddle solo, she admits to wanting to force the relationship to work because she can't lose another guy, pointing to the modern dating dilemma of situationships.

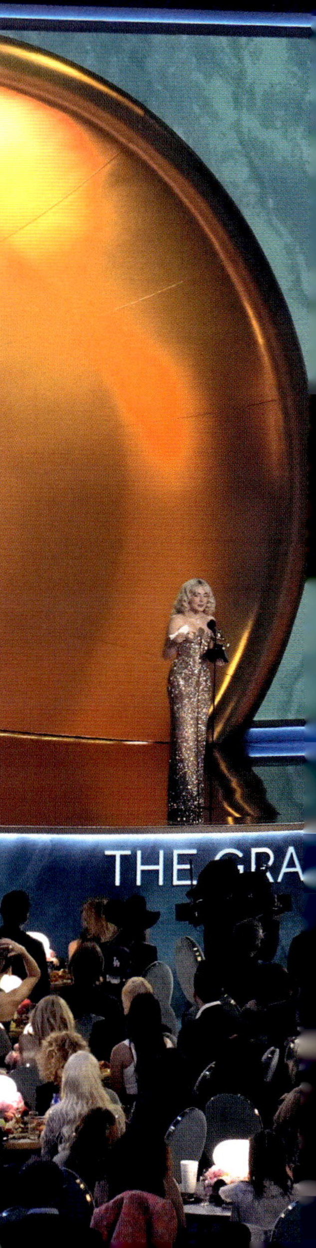

Accepting the award for Best Pop Vocal Album, 67th Annual Grammy Awards, Los Angeles, February 2025

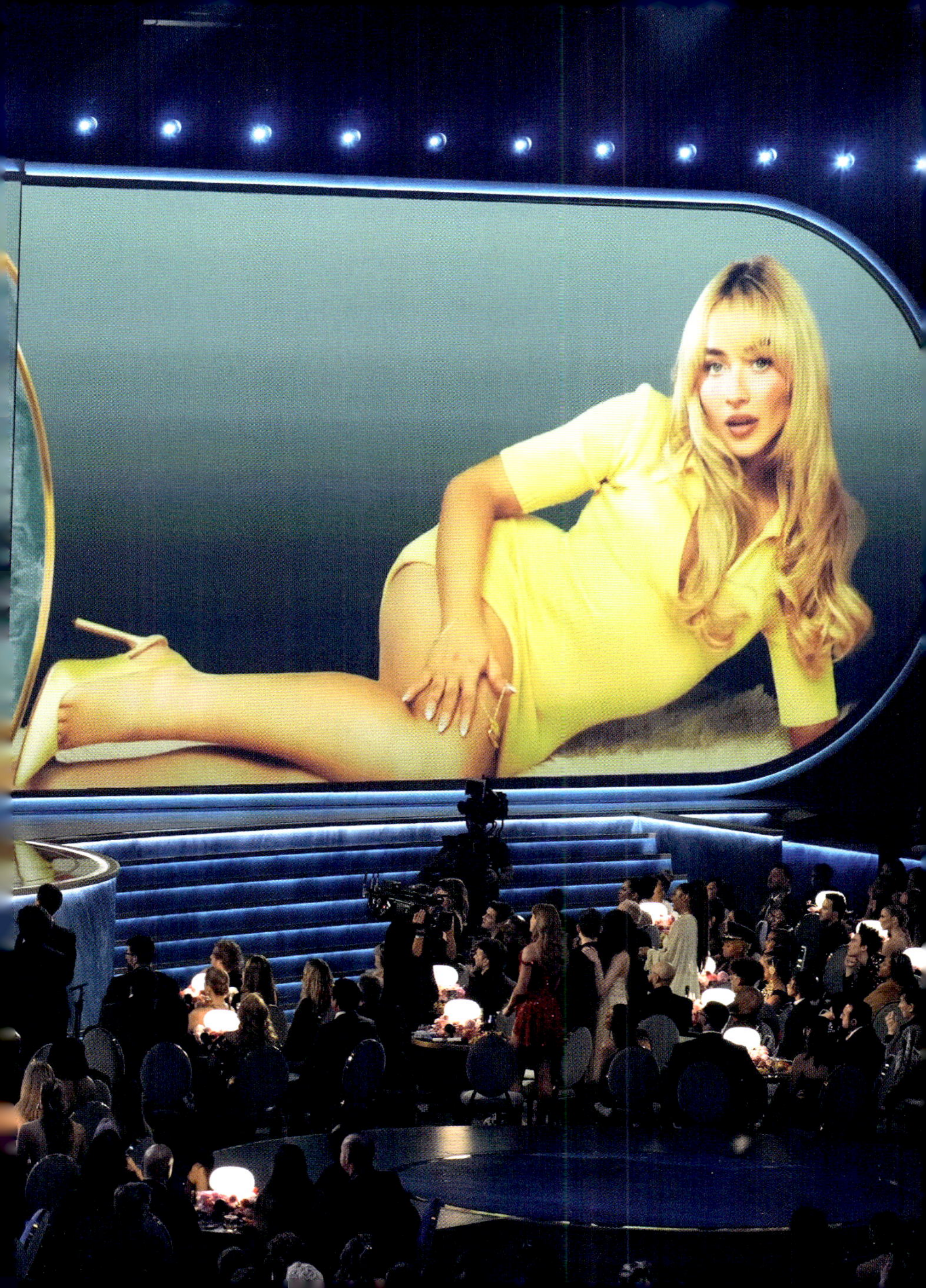

'Busy Woman', a quintessential Sabrina song, became a standout from the deluxe version of her album. Over '80s-style synths and drum machine, she takes her quippy writing to the next level, narrating a love song only she could write. In one line she sings of taking off her clothes and heading to a romantic interest's place; in the next, she sings that if he doesn't want her, she doesn't want his 'little bitch-ass anyway'. The cheek of the song is that, even when calling out the man at the centre of the track, her writing is clearly a hilarious call-out of her own inability to face rejection. At one point she even sings that if she is turned down, she'll just assume the potential lover is gay. She'd previously shared the song in August 2024, for a limited time, telling fans that she'd written the witty track with Jack Antonoff and Amy Allen after turning in *Short n' Sweet* and was 'sad I couldn't include it', writing on Instagram that it was one of her favourites. Fans were also familiar with the song, since she'd added it to her set list on tour, with *Nylon* calling that moment in her set where she played the 'punchy, thirsty and funny as hell' song the highlight of the night. The song debuted at number 11 on the global Spotify chart, making it the biggest female solo debut of 2025 at the time.

CUTE COLLABS

As she mentioned in her deluxe album announcement post, 'Please Please Please' featured none other than legendary country singer Dolly Parton. The inclusion of Dolly was a full-circle moment, since, as Antonoff shared, both he and Sabrina referenced her singing as inspiration for the initial version. Parton told *Knox News* in an interview that she had one condition for her collab with Sabrina: 'I told her, I said, "Now, I don't cuss. I don't make fun of Jesus. I don't talk bad about God, and I don't say dirty words ... on camera, but known to if I get mad enough."' In a short video on her Instagram, showing the pair meeting and comparing their similar short stature, Parton wrote 'Turns out, two things can be short and sweet.' She jokes that the two look like 'befores and afters', adding to Sabrina 'You'll be this old one day', with a giggle. Sabrina replies, while beaming, 'I know, I can't wait! I hope I look like you.'

'I ***adore you*** *to the end!'*

Sabrina does keep her word to Parton in the duet, which features more twang in the vocal delivery, as well as a country-inflected orchestration, by changing the lyrics to 'I hope you don't embarrass me like the others', and leaving out the much-quoted MF-bomb from the track. In the monochrome visuals for the song, Sabrina and Dolly play *Thelma & Louise*-like characters, driving around in a pick-up truck together. They also just so happen to have a man tied up in the trunk – one who happens to be wearing the same outfit that Sabrina's ex, Barry Keoghan, wore in the original 'Please Please Please' video, making this new version a bit of a revenge sequel.

Speaking of working with her idols, Sabrina also made another dream come true, singing with her long-time hero Christina Aguilera in September 2024. Sabrina took part in Aguilera's Spotify Anniversary Project, put together in honour of the 25th anniversary of the singer's self-titled debut. During the video special, Sabrina told the singer that the first time she heard her voice was when she was just eight years old, and her mum played her Aguilera singing 'A Sunday Kind of Love'. 'That was the most inspiring thing for me ever to see as a young girl that wanted to sing but just didn't know I could do it at that age,' she said. She added that it was the 'main reason' she wanted to become a singer: 'I'm just so grateful.' The pair sang a duet of Aguilera's flirty hit song 'What a Girl Wants'. But that's not where the collab ended. During Sabrina's first night in Los Angeles in November 2024, Aguilera surprised fans by coming out on stage and duetting on her track 'Ain't No Other Man', before again sharing the duet of 'What A Girl Wants'. Sabrina commemorated the moment on Instagram with a video from the night, in which Aguilera dressed in a black bodysuit, perfect for the *Short n' Sweet* tour aesthetic. In the caption, she thanked Christina 'for coming out last night, giving everyone (me included) the surprise of our lives'. She also thanked her again for being the main reason she loves and wanted to make pop music, adding 'I adore you to the end!'

When she wasn't busy picking up awards, Sabrina was busy dominating the world's charts and stages. She continued to shock fans and the internet alike with the positions she played out in 'Juno' on tour, like the Eiffel Tower-themed position she did in Paris or the London Bridge position she did while performing at the O2 Arena. She also continued a tradition of picking an attendee to receive handcuffs, right before the sexy song starts and her long, sparkling skirt falls off, revealing the shorter version underneath. In London, she said 'You're kind of, like, spicing up my life a little bit. Wow, really spicing up my life ... my clothes are falling off', before asking Spice Girl Emma Bunton to take the cuffs and 'do the honour of being mine forever?' Other recipients of the furry handcuffs include actresses Millie Bobby Brown, Margaret Qualley and Salma Hayek, and *SNL*'s Marcello Hernandez. But one of the funniest throwback moments in 'Juno' handcuff history was when Sabrina's two close friends Paloma Sandoval and Whitney Peak were 'arrested', while dressed and acting as the male characters they played in the 'Nonsense' video, Paul and Will.

Not everyone was pleased with Sabrina's global takeover. She made shockwaves in the UK in March 2025, when she attended the BRIT Awards in London. She officially kicked off the award show with a medley of her hits 'Espresso' and 'Bed Chem', mashed up with 'Rule Britannia!' She wore a glittery, crimson, military-style, majorette-inspired look, and was surrounded by dancers dressed as the King's Guard, before slipping into a barely-there bralette and high-waist underwear combo with a lace short skirt, fishnets and suspenders. She wore the second look while performing 'Bed Chem' on a heart-shaped oversized bed and moving in ways that some watching from home felt was inappropriate for telecast before 9 pm. That's when the headlines, grievances and social media comments started. According to the *Daily Mail*, the performance sparked almost 1,000 Ofcom complaints from viewers. For Sabrina's part, she responded to the complaints in the caption of her photos from the night, writing 'I now know what watershed is!'

Still, even beyond the antics, her music came first, and Sabrina picked up the Global Success honour that night. While accepting the prize, she told the audience that she'd first come to the UK ten years previously and nobody knew who she was, before thanking fans for allowing her to now sell out two nights at the O2. She also thanked fans in the UK for understanding her dry humour, before sharing her gratitude that they streamed 'the shit out of "Espresso"', despite living in a 'primarily tea-drinking' country. She then left the stage with a 'cheerio'.

'I now know what ***watershed*** *is!'*

Sabrina embraced her comedic, singing and acting skills in her own Christmas special, Netflix's *A Nonsense Christmas with Sabrina Carpenter*. The show features sketches, duets with the likes of fellow pop icon Chappell Roan, and, of course, Carpenter's charisma, bursting through the screen. Shania Twain, Tyla and Kali Uchis also show up to sing holiday hits during the special, with actress Quinta Brunson, model Cara Delevingne and *SNL*'s Kyle Mooney among those playing parts in the skits. Sabrina called it the 'ho-ho-ho-iest special of all' and there are (of course) jokes about 'Nick' being good in bed. It may not be a family holiday watch, but it's a must-see for Sabrina fans.

Right: A Nonsense Christmas with Sabrina Carpenter, *Netflix, December 2024*
Overleaf: Performing at the BRIT Awards, London, March 2025

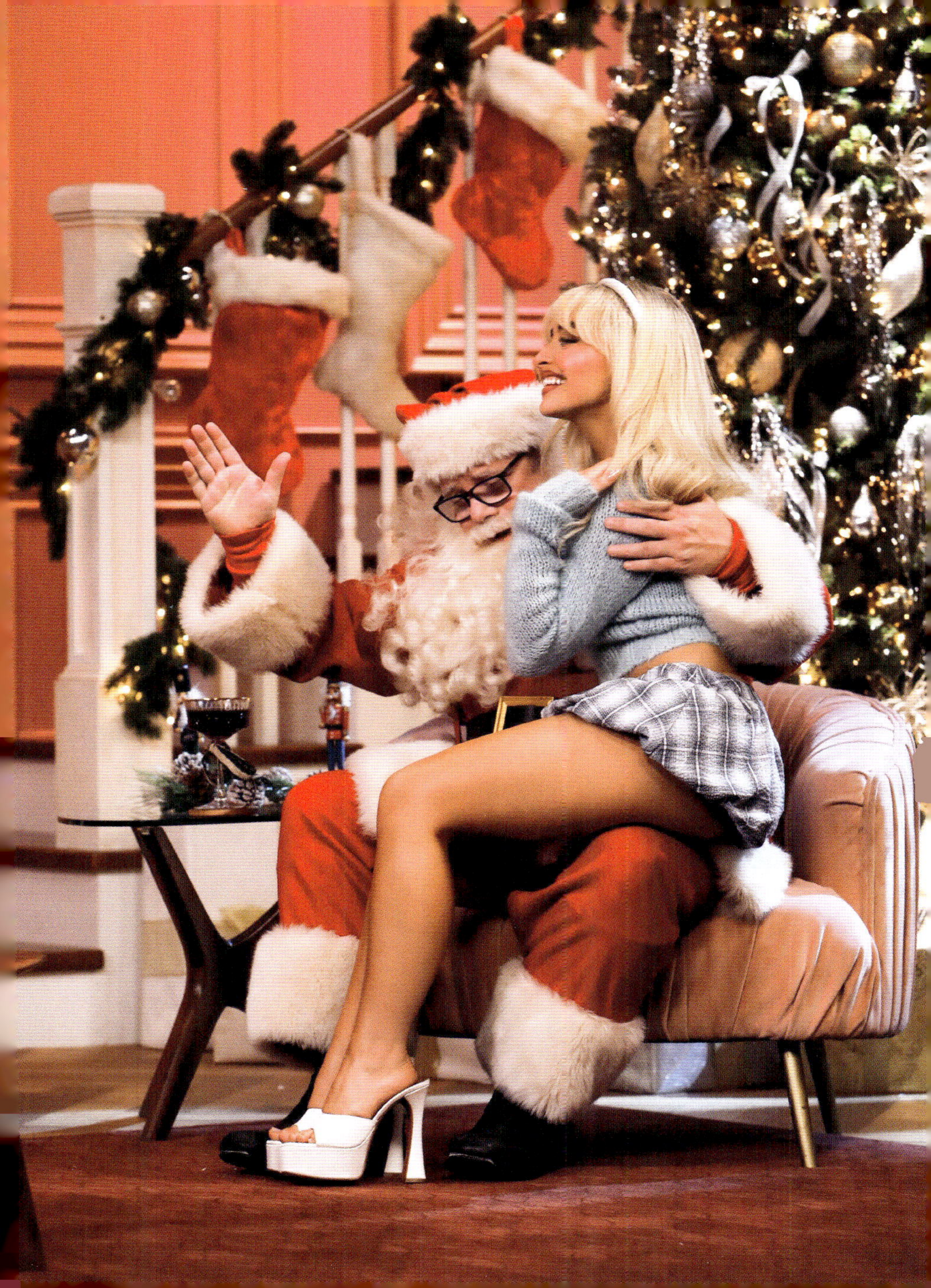

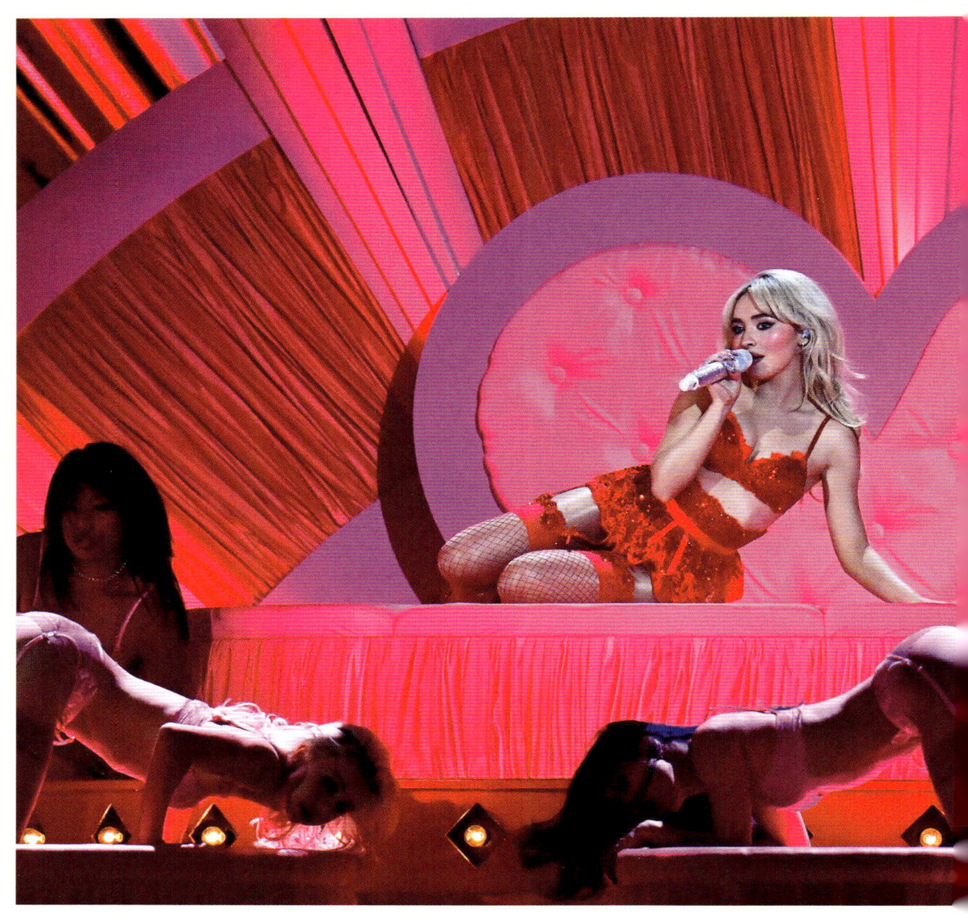

'If you ***can't handle*** *a* ***girl*** *who is* ***confident*** *in her own* ***sexuality,*** *then* ***don't come*** *to my shows.'*

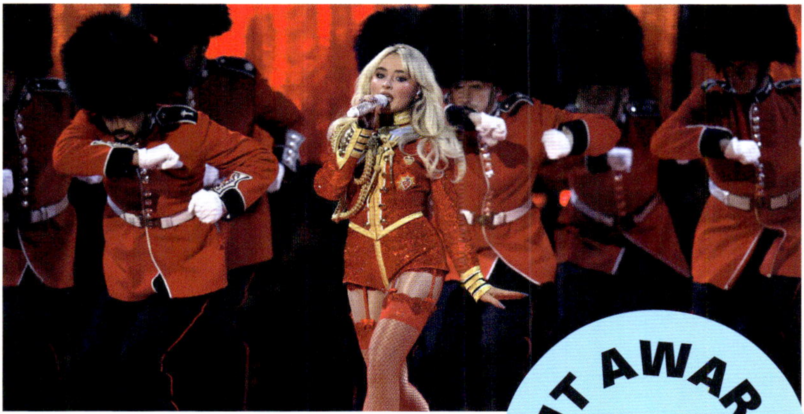

BRIT AWARDS ★ 2025

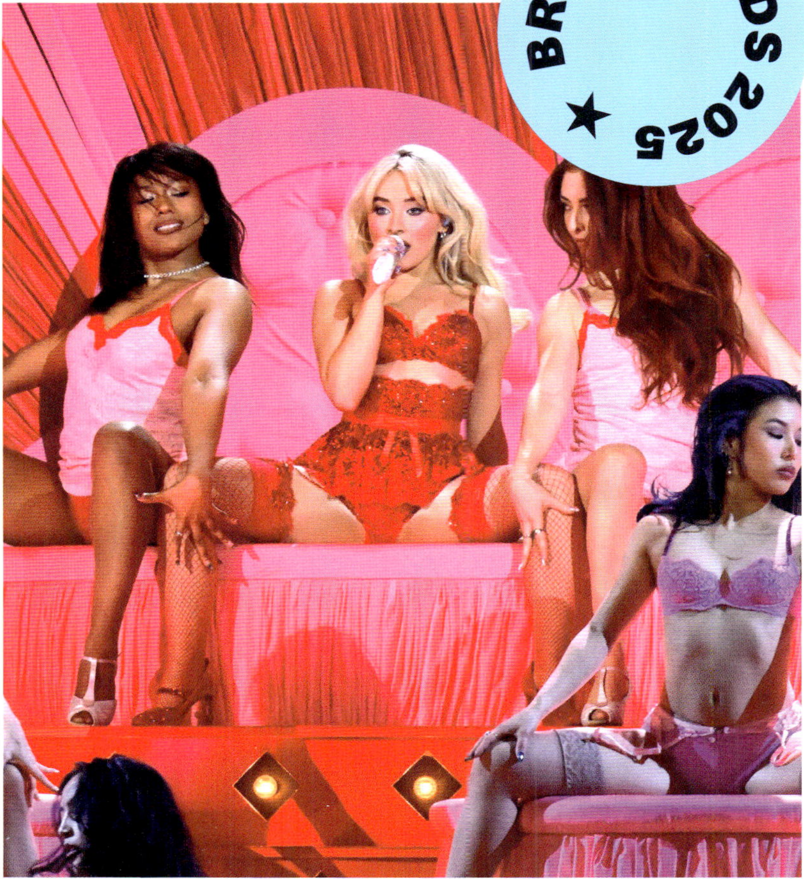

MORE, MORE, MORE

The hits keep coming for (and from) Sabrina, well after the release of her career trajectory-changing album *Short n' Sweet*. She became a skin on the popular video game Fortnite, where fans can perform 'Espresso' and 'Please Please Please' as the star's avatar. She attended the Met Gala again – cementing her status as a fashionable favourite at the event – this time in a tailored ringmaster-inspired, pantless look by Pharrell Williams at Louis Vuitton. She also let fans know that she's stretching out her *Short n' Sweet* tour dates, giving the tagline 'It's even sweeter' to new stops in New York and London, and more in the summer, autumn and winter of 2025.

In May 2025 it was announced that Sabrina had officially made it onto Spotify's Billions Club, for having four songs – 'Nonsense', 'Espresso', 'Please Please Please' and 'Taste' – all reach a billion streams or more on Spotify. As you're reading this, she's likely working on or announcing another luxury fashion campaign, tour date, brand collaboration or (another) surprise appearance on *SNL* – proving that she really is working late because she's a singer.

From the moment she uploaded that first Taylor Swift cover at just nine years old, Sabrina had already made the decision to pursue her career in music as if there was no other option – she had decided to be a star. As she continues to rise, from the girl who grew up in a small town in Pennsylvania to an artist who can't seem to get away from the top of the charts, her story will live on in her songs, her wit and her determination to move in the direction of her dreams.

Wearing Louis Vuitton to the Met Gala (Superfine: Tailoring Black Style), New York, May 2025

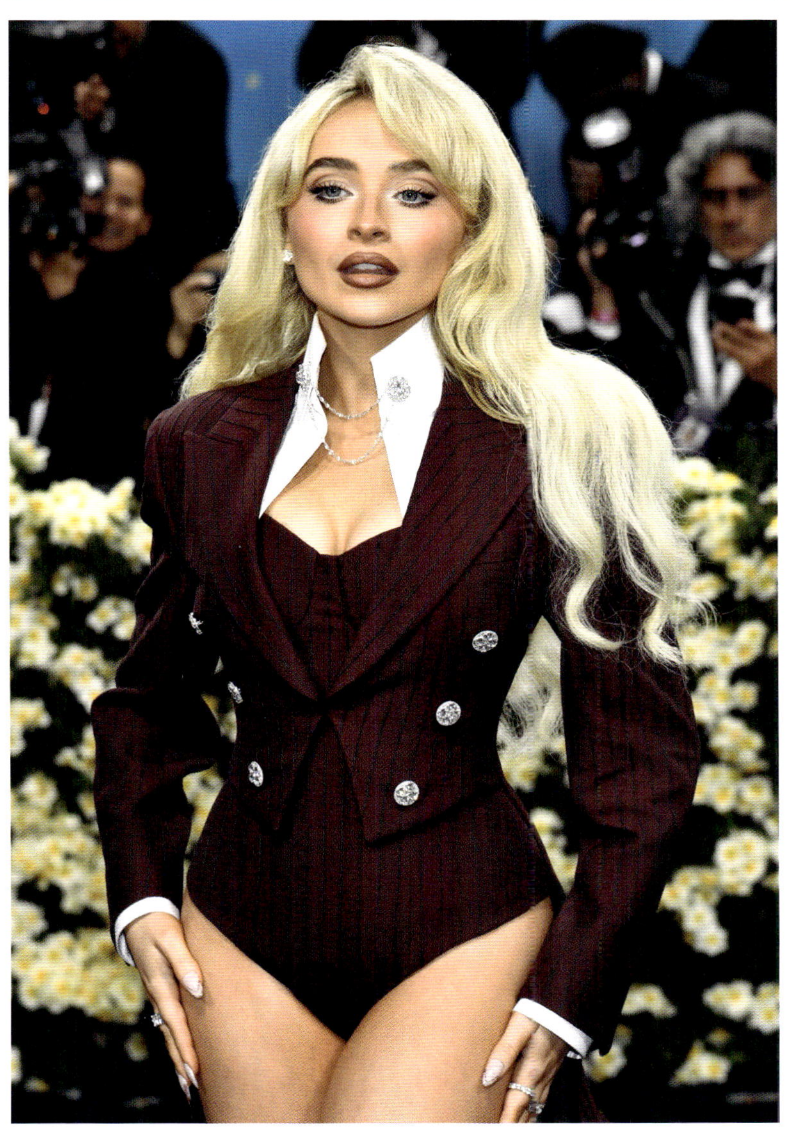

SONG CREDITS

From Disney Darling to Pop Princess

'Espresso'
Written by Amy Allen, Julian Bunetta, Steph Jones and Sabrina Carpenter
Year of release: 2024
Record label: Island Records

Sabrina the Singer

'Eyes Wide Open'
Written by Meghan Kabir, Audra Mae and Jerrod Bettis
Year of release: 2015
Record label: Hollywood Records

'Almost Love'
Written by Mikkel Storleer Eriksen, Nate Campany, Steph Jones and Sabrina Carpenter
Year of release: 2018
Record label: Hollywood Records

'Sue Me'
Written by Zaire Koalo, Trevorious, OAK, Steph Jones and Sabrina Carpenter
Year of release: 2018
Record label: Hollywood Records

'I'm Fakin''
Written by Andrés Torres, El Dandee, Katie Pearlman, Jackson Lee Morgan and Sabrina Carpenter
Year of release: 2019
Record label: Hollywood Records

'Tell Em'
Written by Dayyon Alexander, Blush, Sidney Swift and Sabrina Carpenter
Year of release: 2019
Record label: Hollywood Records

Sabrina's Internet Era

'drivers license'
Written by Dan Nigro and Olivia Rodrigo
Year of release: 2021
Record label: Geffen Records, Interscope Records

'Skin'
Written by Ryan McMahon, Tia Tia and Sabrina Carpenter
Year of release: 2021
Record label: Island Records

'emails i can't send'
Written by JP Saxe, Julia Michaels and Sabrina Carpenter
Year of release: 2022
Record label: Island Records

'skinny dipping'
Written by Leroy Clampitt, JP Saxe, Julia Michaels and Sabrina Carpenter
Year of release: 2021
Record label: Island Records

'because i liked a boy'
Written by John Ryan, JP Saxe, Julia Michaels and Sabrina Carpenter
Year of release: 2022
Record label: Island Records

'Vicious'
Written by Jason Evigan, Amy Allen and Sabrina Carpenter
Year of release: 2022
Record label: Island Records

'how many things'
Written by Ryan Marrone, JP Saxe and Sabrina Carpenter
Year of release: 2022
Record label: Island Records

'Nonsense'
Written by Steph Jones, Julian Bunetta and Sabrina Carpenter
Year of release: 2022
Record label: Island Records

Talkin' 'Nonsense'

'Nonsense'
Written by Steph Jones, Julian Bunetta and Sabrina Carpenter
Year of release: 2022
Record label: Island Records

'Nonsense (Remix)'
Written by Julian Bunetta, Steph Jones, Sabrina Carpenter, Worldwide Fresh, Coi Leray
Year of release: 2023
Record label: Island Records

A Caffeine Hit

'Espresso'
Written by Sabrina Carpenter, Julian Bunetta, Amy Allen and Steph Jones
Year of release: 2024
Record label: Island Records

Short, Sweet and Sitting at the Top

'Please Please Please'
Written by Sabrina Carpenter, Amy Allen and Jack Antonoff
Year of release: 2024
Record label: Island Records

'Taste'
Written by Sabrina Carpenter, Julia Michaels, John Ryan, Amy Allen and Ian Kirkpatrick
Year of release: 2024
Record label: Island Records

'Juno'
Written by Sabrina Carpenter, John Ryan and Amy Allen
Year of release: 2024
Record label: Island Records

'Slim Pickins'
Written by Sabrina Carpenter, Amy Allen and Jack Antonoff
Year of release: 2024
Record label: Island Records

Sabrina's Global Impact

'Busy Woman'
Written by Jack Antonoff, Sabrina Carpenter and Amy Allen
Year of release: 2024
Record label: Island Records

REFERENCES

All quotes from social-media platforms are accurate and visible online at the time of publication. They come from verified, official accounts on these platforms.

From Disney Darling to Pop Princess

p.7, 'I always knew deep down…': Erica Campbell, 'Sabrina Carpenter, Superstar', *Paper*, 21 August 2024, https://www.papermag.com/sabrina-carpenter-cover#rebelltitem22

p.8, Sabrina says David once said he was in a band…: 'Stars In Cars With Sabrina Carpenter', JJ Ryan on YouTube, 1 August 2018, https://www.youtube.com/watch?v=qizkaAwmuYY

p.11, 'After that contest ended…': Abby Aguirre, 'How the World Fell for Sabrina Carpenter', *Vogue*, 11 February 2025, https://www.vogue.com/article/sabrina-carpenter-march-cover-2025-interview

p.11, she later joked…: P. Claire Dodson, 'Sabrina Carpenter Talks New Song "Skinny Dipping," Grief & Water Under the Bridge', *Teen Vogue*, 9 September 2021, https://www.teenvogue.com/story/sabrina-carpenter-new-song-skinny-dipping-interview

p.12, 'The beauty of the show…': P. Claire Dodson, 'Sabrina Carpenter on Her Career, from "Girl Meets World" to "Work It"', *Teen Vogue*, 17 August 2020, https://www.teenvogue.com/story/sabrina-carpenter-girl-meets-world-to-work-it

p. 12, In 2023 she told *Glamour UK*…: Jabeen Waheed, 'Sabrina Carpenter on navigating her twenties, finding her voice through music and "adding to her story" with *Emails I Can't Send* deluxe edition', *Glamour*, 17 March 2023, https://www.glamourmagazine.co.uk/article/sabrina-carpenter-interview-2023

Sabrina the Singer

p.17, 'For the people who love…': Thania Garcia, 'Summer of Sabrina Carpenter: Hitting No. 1 on the Charts, Getting Advice From Best Friend Taylor Swift and What Barry Keoghan Really Thinks About Her Lyrics', *Variety*, 6 August 2024, https://variety.com/2024/music/features/sabrina-carpenter-talks-top-charts-taylor-swift-barry-keoghan-1236096003/

p.17, 'I had to fight off…': Erica Campbell, 'Sabrina Carpenter, Superstar' (see above)

p.17, She also told *Billboard* that when she first…: Connor Whittum, 'Sabrina Carpenter on Her Mature New Album and Treadmill-Ready Single "Almost Love"', *Billboard*, 20 June 2018, https://www.billboard.com/music/music-news/sabrina-carpenter-almost-love-interview-new-album-singular-8461765/

p.22, 'how it feels when they want…': varietymagazine on TikTok, https://www.tiktok.com/@varietymagazine/video/7400041724720074027?lang=en

p.22, 'epiphany': Sabrina Carpenter on X, https://x.com/SabrinaAnnLynn/status/1094704960950829056

p.22, she told *Genius* the lyrics were inspired...: 'Sabrina Carpenter "Why" Official Lyrics & Meaning | Verified', Genius on YouTube, 29 September 2017, https://www.youtube.com/watch?v=JblUpY11x40

p.24, in an interview with *Billboard*, she shared...: Katie Atkinson, 'Pop Shop Podcast: Sabrina Carpenter & Jonas Blue on Meeting Via Twitter, Exploring "Alien" Feelings for New Song', *Billboard*, 17 April 2018, https://www.billboard.com/media/podcasts/pop-shop-podcast-sabrina-carpenter-jonas-blue-alien-interview-8344372/

p.24, she told *Marie Claire* that it was her most personal album...: Rachel Epstein, 'Sabrina Carpenter Is Ready for Act II', *Marie Claire*, 28 June 2019, https://www.marieclaire.com/celebrity/a28184345/sabrina-carpenter-interview-2019/

p.24, 'playful psyche': Erica Russell, 'Sabrina Carpenter on Fan Theories...' (see above)

p.24, in an interview with PopCrush she recalls . . Sabrina spoke to *PopCrush*...: Erica Russell, 'Sabrina Carpenter on Fan Theories, ASMR and the "Vulnerable" Confidence of "Singular Act II"', *PopCrush*, 18 July 2019, https://popcrush.com/sabrina-carpenter-on-fan-theories-asmr-and-the-vulnerable-confidence-of-singular-act-ii/

Sabrina's Internet Era

p.31, 'Thank God I didn't finish...': Abby Aguirre, 'How the World Fell...' (see above)

p.31, shout-out to Darcus Beese...: Jem Aswad, 'Sabrina Carpenter Signs With Island Records', *Variety*, 26 January 2012, https://variety.com/2021/music/news/sabrina-carpenter-signs-island-records-1234891659/

p. 31, 'powerful vocals, infectious personality': Jem Aswad, 'Sabrina Carpenter Signs...' (see above)

p.34, Rodrigo told *Billboard* that...: Jason Lipshutz, 'How Olivia Rodrigo Turned a "Really Painful Moment" Into a Phenomenon', *Billboard*, 19 January 2012, https://www.billboard.com/pro/olivia-rodrigo-interview-drivers-license-geffen-feature/

p.34, She also told *Variety* that... 'I don't really subscribe...': Ellise Shafer, 'From Disney to "Drivers License": Inside Olivia Rodrigo's Musical Journey to Become the Voice of Her Generation', *Variety*, 11 August 2021, https://variety.com/2021/music/news/olivia-rodrigo-drivers-license-sour-high-school-musical-1235038112/

p.34, '[Skin] isn't calling out...': Sabrina Carpenter on Facebook, 25 January 2021, https://www.facebook.com/photo.php?fbid=10157544503346968&id=93666146967&set=a.10151892356371968

p.34, Five years later...'whirlwind': Abby Aguirre, 'How the World Fell...' (see above)

p.34, 'vent, vent, vent...': 'Sabrina Carpenter Has Hundreds of "Emails She Can't Send"', SiriusXM on YouTube, 28 August 2022, https://www.youtube.com/shorts/OLG72mHcE2o

p.36, 'first big-girl album': Abby Aguirre, 'How the World Fell...' (see above)

p.36, 'growing pains': Tomás Mier, 'Sabrina Carpenter "dealt with perceptions." Now she's making her story crystal clear', *Rolling Stone*, 14 July 2022, https://www.rollingstone.com/music/music-news/sabrina-carpenter-emails-i-cant-send-interview-1381304/

p.36, 'to feel like a random...': Sabrina Carpenter on X, https://x.com/SabrinaAnnLynn/status/1549503618184790018

p.36, 'entirely steering the ship': P. Claire Dodson, 'Sabrina Carpenter Talks...' (see above)

p.37, 'You birthed me...': Abby Aguirre, 'How the World Fell...' (see above)

p.37, She told *Teen Vogue* that...: P. Claire Dodson, 'Sabrina Carpenter Talks...' (see above)

p.38, She told *Rolling Stone* that ... She also shared that her favourite line...: Tomás Mier, 'Sabrina Carpenter "dealt with perceptions."...' (see above)

p.38, as she told *Nylon*...: Steffanee Wang, 'SABRINA CARPENTER ON "EMAILS I CAN'T SEND" & HEALING THROUGH SONGWRITING', *Nylon*, 12 August 2022, https://www.nylon.com/entertainment/sabrina-carpenter-emails-i-cant-send-fork-lyric-samsung

p.40, Speaking to *Rolling Stone* about the song...: Tomás Mier, 'Sabrina Carpenter "dealt with perceptions."...' (see above)

p.40, She told *Vogue* the image was inspired...: Abby Aguirre, 'How the World Fell...' (see above)

Talkin' 'Nonsense'

p.45, Sabrina Carpenter dropped a hint...: sabrinacarpenter on Instagram, 31 July 2022, https://www.instagram.com/sabrinacarpenter/p/Cgrv40xOdKc/?hl=en

p.45, in December of 2022, she shared another social media announcement: Sabrina Carpenter on X, https://x.com/SabrinaAnnLynn/status/1602326750825832448

p.45, 'emails I can't send is finally coming to you…': Sabrina Carpenter on X, https://x.com/SabrinaAnnLynn/status/1619991603271331840

p.46, 'The "Nonsense" outros were a happy accident…': Erica Campbell, 'Sabrina Carpenter, Superstar' (see above)

p.46, 'sabrina carpenter could write romeo…': feegle on X, https://x.com/halfmoonleslie/status/1761302631543394609

p.46, 'I think people think I'm just obnoxiously horny…': Madeleine Frank Reeves, 'I Am Pleased to Inform You That Your Massive Crush on Sabrina Carpenter Is Justified', *Cosmopolitan*, 27 March 2024, https://www.cosmopolitan.com/entertainment/celebs/a60097500/sabrina-carpenter-interview-2024/

p.46, 'I was happy that people felt they got…': Abby Aguirre, 'How the World Fell…' (see above)

p.48, 'I'm not going to lie…': 'Sabrina Carpenter discusses opening up for Taylor Swift on the Latin American leg of the Eras Tour…', Billboard on Facebook, 26 August 2023, https://www.facebook.com/watch/?v=131625899977344

p.48, 'sabrina carpenter explaining bbc…': Charli on X, https://x.com/charli_xcx/status/1630225405579001856

p.51, 'The extreme, "it's over forever,"…': Lucy Feldman, 'Sabrina Carpenter Has Waited Her Whole Life for This', *TIME*, 2 October 2024, https://time.com/7027418/sabrina-carpenter-interview-time-100-next/

p.51, 'whatever feels the most honest and connects…': 'Sabrina Carpenter Talks Nonsense While Eating Spicy Wings | Hot Ones', First We Feast on YouTube, 11 July 2024, https://www.youtube.com/watch?v=msnl0D1SDSg

The Real Sabrina

p.55, She told *Grammy.com* that she 'wanted to…': Rob Ledonne, 'Sabrina Carpenter's Big Year: The Pop Songstress Gushes On The Eras Tour, Her Christmas EP & More', Grammy Awards, 20 December 2023, https://www.grammy.com/news/sabrina-carpenter-feather-eras-tour-interview-big-year

p.56. 'We got approval in advance…': Steven J. Horowitz, 'Sabrina Carpenter on Touring with Taylor Swift, "Nonsense" Success and Scandalizing the Catholic Church: "Jesus Was a Carpenter"', *Variety*, 29 November 2023, https://variety.com/2023/music/news/sabrina-carpenter-touring-taylor-swift-nonsense-catholic-church-controversy-1235811476/

p.56, 'I literally cut my bangs…: 'Sabrina Carpenter Creates Her Self Portrait', *Vanity Fair*, 20 June 2024, https://www.vanityfair.com/video/watch/sabrina-carpenter-creates-her-self-portrait

p.58, 'One thing that experience did … It's almost like your music…': Liam Hess, 'Sabrina Carpenter on the Radical Honesty of Her New Album, *Emails I Can't Send*', *Vogue*, 3 August 2022, https://www.vogue.com/article/sabrina-carpenter-emails-i-cant-send-interview

p.58, she was thrilled when someone had listened…: Liam Hess, 'Sabrina Carpenter on the Radical Honesty…' (see above)

p.60, 'the tortoise': Steven J. Horowitz, Valerie Wu, 'Sabrina Carpenter Talks Getting Into the "Mindset of a Slow Rise": "I Am the Tortoise"', *Variety*, 2 December 2023, https://variety.com/2023/music/news/sabrina-carpenter-hitmakers-speech-1235815391

Sabrina and Taylor

p.67, she threw the phone across the room: Rob Ledonne, 'Sabrina Carpenter's Big Year…' (see above)

p.67, she wasn't going to say she peed her pants: Eliza Huber, 'Becoming a Pop Star Was Sabrina Carpenter's Destiny', *Who What Wear*, 8 January 2024, https://www.whowhatwear.com/sabrina-carpenter-interview

p.67, 'That is one of my main inspirations ever…': Rania Aniftos, 'Sabrina Carpenter Talks Opening for Taylor Swift on Eras Tour, Enjoying the "Fun" of K-Pop & More', *Billboard*, 25 August 2023, https://www.billboard.com/music/music-news/sabrina-carpenter-taylor-swift-eras-tour-k-pop-perfume-interview-1235401357/

p.68, 'art…hard to teach and hard to learn': Madeleine Frank Reeves, 'I Am Pleased…' (see above)

p.68, 'since I'm 5 feet tall…': Christian Allaire, '"It Was Magic": Sabrina Carpenter Talks Kicking Off Taylor Swift's Eras Tour', *Vogue*, 27 August 2023, https://www.vogue.com/slideshow/sabrina-carpenter-taylor-swift-eras-tour-fashion

p.68, 'I'm in my short skirt…': Christian Allaire, '"It Was Magic"… (see above)

p.68, 'I feel so lucky…': Christian Allaire, '"It Was Magic"…' (see above)

p.69, shared with followers that the show was amazing…: Sabrina Carpenter on X, https://x.com/SabrinaAnnLynn/status/10773055615?lang=en

p.69, 'This is the dreamiest dream come true': Sabrina Carpenter on X, https://x.com/SabrinaAnnLynn/status/1664678213300125698

p.70, older sisters...: Eliza Huber, 'Becoming a Pop Star...' (see above)

p.70, 'thanks blondie...being 22 is hitting differently...': Pop Base on X, https://x.com/PopBase/status/1459408442875990019?lang=en

p.70, 'I love Taylor Swift': Zak Maoui, 'Sabrina Carpenter veers into the fast lane', *GQ*, 25 February 2022, https://www.gq-magazine.co.uk/culture/article/sabrina-carpenter-interview

p.70, 'angel princess': Taylor Swift on X, https://x.com/taylorswift13/status/1664663509488074754

p.70, Sabrina later joked that after one vodka...: Waiss Aramesh, 'Sabrina Carpenter Gave Us the Song of the Summer. She's Got a Plan for All Seasons', *Rolling Stone*, 17 June 2024, https://www.rollingstone.com/music/music-features/sabrina-carpenter-espresso-short-n-sweet-taylor-swift-1235036627/

p.72, 'she's very good with words...': rollingstone on Instagram, 5 August 2023, https://www.instagram.com/reel/Cviv4siJkwB/

p.72, 'Well she nailed it': Jack Irvin, 'Taylor Swift Praises Sabrina Carpenter's Cover of "I Knew You Were Trouble": "Wow [*sic*] She Nailed It"', *People*, 19 October 2023, https://people.com/taylor-swift-praises-sabrina-carpenter-cover-of-i-knew-you-were-trouble-8363781

p.72, 'love you so so so dearly Taylor...': sabrinacarpenter on Instagram, 24 February 2024, https://www.instagram.com/p/C3tn-jYqyU1b/?hl=en

p.72, 'I don't know how you just didn't...': 'Superstar Sabrina Carpenter catches up with Today, TODAY on YouTube, 25 February 2024, https://www.youtube.com/watch?v=bUnv6x7ZIR8

p.72, 'taybrina era...': sabrinacarpenter on Instagram, 23 March 2024, https://www.instagram.com/p/C433SsWytdR/

p.73, 'the pop star of the next generation...': Sophia June, 'Sabrina Carpenter Is A '90s Bombshell In Her First SKIMS Campaign', *Nylon*, 1 April 2024, https://www.nylon.com/life/sabrina-carpenter-skims-campaign-2024

p.73 'weirdness': Waiss Aramesh, 'Sabrina Carpenter Gave Us the Song...' (see above)

p.73, 'To work with someone [who] cares...': Eliza Huber, 'Becoming a Pop Star...' (see above)

p.73, 'you can't just ask the internet': Thania Garcia, 'Summer of Sabrina Carpenter...' (see above)

p.74, Sabrina said that most of what she learned...: cbssundaymorning on TikTok, 5 October 2024, https://www.tiktok.com/@cbssundaymorning/video/7422342890958998815?lang=en

p.74, ... *Billboard* that she'd grown up taking advice from Swift's songs...: 'Sabrina Carpenter discusses opening up for Taylor...' (see above)

p.74, 'Summer of Sabrina may it continue forever...': Ingrid Vasquez, 'Taylor Swift Celebrates Sabrina Carpenter's Successful Summer: "May it Continue Forever"', *People*, 4 July 2024, https://people.com/taylor-swift-celebrates-sabrina-carpenter-successful-summer-may-it-continue-forever-8673993

p.74, 'What are you doing, why aren't you here with us?': Ashleigh Carter, 'Taylor Swift Brings Sabrina Carpenter Out for Surprise Songs at Eras Tour', *Teen Vogue*, 27 October 2024, https://www.teenvogue.com/story/taylor-swift-brings-sabrina-carpenter-on-stage

p.74, 'She's as real as they come...': taylorswift on Instagram, 29 October 2024, https://www.instagram.com/p/DBuaITCS5mL/?utm_source=ig_embed&ig_rid=e7b88469-ee02-4a51-92a6-c5023efed6f5

p.74, 'I go into it with a little...': Eliza Huber, 'Becoming a Pop Star...' (see above)

p.76, She told *Cosmopolitan* that the Eras...: Madeleine Frank Reeves, 'I Am Pleased...' (see above)

p.76, 'such a different echelon ... could never compare my life...': Waiss Aramesh, 'Sabrina Carpenter Gave Us the Song...' (see above)

p.76, 'Her stadiums make my shows...': Abby Aguirre, 'How the World Fell...' (see above)

A Caffeine Hit

p.83, 'just wanted to put out a little song...': sabrinacarpenter on Instagram, 8 April 2024, https://www.instagram.com/p/C5gaRtkR5-Z/?hl=en

p.83, 'just a blue hotel...': sabrinacarpenter on Instagram, 13 April 2024, https://www.instagram.com/p/C5t4852xGyP/

p.84, 'dtf (down town france)': sabrinacarpenter on Instagram, 16 July 2023, https://www.instagram.com/p/CuwoHjFyCyS/?img_index=10

p.84, 'creatively inspiring': Rania Aniftos, 'Sabrina Carpenter's 'Espresso' Is Here: Stream

It Now', *Billboard*, 11 April 2024, https://www.billboard.com/music/pop/sabrina-carpenter-espresso-1235654487/

p.84, 'I had my shot of espresso...': Lynn Hirschberg, 'Sabrina Carpenter Knows She Has You Hooked', *W*, 5 September 20242, https://www.wmagazine.com/culture/sabrina-carpenter-cover-interview-2024

pp.86, 'seeing femininity as your superpower': Christian Allaire, 'Sabrina Carpenter Channels Retro Beach Style in "Espresso"', *Vogue*, 12 April 2024, https://www.vogue.com/article/sabrina-carpenter-espresso-music-video-fashion

p.86, 'always been a bit delusional...': Shaad d'Souza, '"I'm a tyrant!" Pop superstar Sabrina Carpenter on freakish fame, fighting Disney and writing the song of the summer', *Guardian*, 23 August 2024, https://www.theguardian.com/music/article/2024/aug/23/im-a-tyrant-pop-superstar-sabrina-carpenter-on-freakish-fame-fighting-disney-and-writing-the-song-of-the-summer

p.87, 'I really didn't know if...':Christy Piña, 'Sabrina Carpenter "Had Literally No Idea" Anyone Would Like "Espresso" Before It Came Out', *Hollywood Reporter*, 30 December 2024, https://www.hollywoodreporter.com/news/music-news/sabrina-carpenter-dunkin-collab-espresso-new-music-1236095371/

p.87, 'I was completely alone... There was a lot of questioning...': Thania Garcia, 'Summer of Sabrina Carpenter...' (see above)

p.87, 'Since the day I heard the song, I saw a beach atmosphere': Christian Allaire, 'Sabrina Carpenter Channels Retro...' (see above)

p.88, a screenshot of shelves...: sabrinacarpenter on Instagram, 30 April 2024, https://www.instagram.com/p/C6ZCb9rRGuC/?img_index=1

p.88, 'do NOT drink that me espresso...': AJ on X, https://x.com/status/1784283354998931494

p.88, 'when we exchange our vows...': cary on X, https://x.com/brokebackstan/status/1784024596783473033

p.88, 'ppl r always scared...': Sabrina Carpenter on X, https://x.com/SabrinaAnnLynn/status/710092164340908032?lang=en

p.88, 'my married friends watching me...': mimosasandlipstick on TikTok, https://www.tiktok.com/@mimosasandlipstick/video/7408043456326602026

p.88, 'me posting like an influencer...': yourgirldiina on TikTok, https://www.tiktok.com/@yourgirldiina/video/7420705919958338848?lang=en

p.88, 'niche part of the internet ... love that for me': Tomás Mier, 'Sabrina Carpenter says she has Chappell Roan's songs on "Loopty Loop"', *Rolling Stone*, 17 June 2024, https://www.rollingstone.com/music/music-news/sabrina-carpenter-recommends-chappell-roan-1235041076/

p.90, 'What we'd like to do...': Gil Kaufman, 'Coldplay Make "Magic"...', *Billboard*, 28 May 2024, https://www.billboard.com/music/pop/coldplay-collaborate-magic-sabrina-carpenter-bbc-big-weekend-festival-espresso-1235693547/

p.90, 'I'm very drunk now': The Late Show with Stephen Colbert on YouTube, 13 December 2024, https://www.youtube.com/watch?v=QOB-s7m7KIRs

p.93, 'soft skin and i perfumed it for ya': sabrina carpenter on Instagram, 8 December 2024, https://www.instagram.com/p/DDU9Zn9x-U3P/?hl=en

p.93, 'I definitely hear it now ... Being on the radio...': Lynn Hirschberg, 'Sabrina Carpenter Knows She Has You Hooked' (see above)

p.93, You guys are the reason...': Alyssa Bailey, 'Sabrina Carpenter Thanked...', *Elle*, 11 September 2024, https://www.elle.com/culture/celebrities/a62092509/sabrina-carpenter-mtv-vmas-2024-speech/

Building a Bombshell

p.99, She told *W Magazine* in 2024: 'The First Time Sabrina Carpenter Wore High Heels', *W Magazine* on YouTube, 20 September 2024, https://www.youtube.com/watch?v=yPcW8B-dZ52c

p.99, 'styling curtain bangs to look like Sabrina Carpenter's', eggdressesup on YouTube, https://www.youtube.com/shorts/K3XUee3BLjM

p.99, Heath Owens, 'What to Wear to Sabrina Carpenter's "Short N' Sweet" Tour', *Cosmopolitan*, 21 September 2024, https://www.cosmopolitan.com/style-beauty/fashion/a62289922/what-to-wear-to-sabrina-carpenter-concert-short-n-sweet-tour/

p.101, 'a little skirt ... There's a part of me ... I felt a bit like a fairy': whowhatwear on TikTok, https://www.tiktok.com/@whowhatwear/video/7503383540949263659

pp.103, 'the epitome of glamour': Alex Kessler, 'Sabrina Carpenter Is A Gilded Goddess In Paco Rabanne At The Met Gala', *Vogue*, 3 May 2022, https://www.vogue.co.uk/fashion/article/sabrina-carpenter-met-gala-2022

p.103, 'perfect match for pop royalty... real-life pop princess': Maya Ernest, 'Sabrina Carpenter Plays Cinderella in a Blue Ball Gown at the 2024 Met Gala', *Harper's Bazaar*, 6 May 2024, https://www.harpersbazaar.com/celebrity/latest/a60705609/sabrina-carpenter-red-carpet-photos-met-gala-2024/?utm_source=chatgpt.com

p.103, 'romance and edge ... quintessential Sabrina ... romantic, fluffy, '60s vibes': 'Sabrina Carpenter & Barry Keoghan Get Ready for the Met Gala | Last Looks', *Vogue* on YouTube, 8 May 2024, https://www.youtube.com/watch?v=UeJ13WFKjEE

p.103, 'graciously allowed me to...': 'Sabrina Carpenter Plays Truth, Wear, or Dare | Truth or Wear', WhoWhatWear on YouTube, 15 November 2023, https://www.youtube.com/watch?v=2-z2MTHuz3M&pp=0gcJCU8JAYcqIYzv

p.106, 'the same vibe, the same ideas ... I just do what I feel ... When we met...': Brooke Frischer, 'Ivan Frolov is Making Onstage Outfits a Modern Spectacle', *Fashionista*, 7 June 2024, https://fashionista.com/2024/06/ivan-frolov-designer-interview

p.106, 'Brigitte is always the inspo': scottkinghair on Instagram, 31 August 2021, https://www.instagram.com/p/CTPjQ4blVLC/?hl=en

p.107, 'almost like an amped-up version...': Nikita Charuza, 'We Asked Sabrina Carpenter's Hairstylist How He Creates Her Iconic Short n' Sweet Tour Blowout – Here's What He Said', *The Quality Edit*, 25 November 2024, https://www.thequalityedit.com/articles/sabrina-carpenter-hairstylist-interview

p.108, 'times a thousand...It's inspired by *Playboy*...': 'Inside Sabrina Carpenter's 'Short n' Sweet' Tour Looks', *Vogue* on YouTube, 21 October 2024, https://www.youtube.com/watch?v=USqWI1sAuY0

p.108, 'it was an honor to wear...': sabrina carpenter on Instagram, 13 April 2024, https://www.instagram.com/p/C5t4852xGyP/?utm_source=ig_embed&ig_rid=2f521802-f421-41d3-8a89-fc6b230e2aac

p.112, 'that's that Andie Anderson Espresso': sabrinacarpenter on Instagram, 12 May 2024, https://www.instagram.com/p/C64qNnlxs-Fa/?utm_source=ig_embed

p.112, 'rash decisions... But I never wanted...': 'Sabrina Carpenter Creates Her Self Portrait', *Vanity Fair* on YouTube, 20 June 2024, https://www.youtube.com/watch?v=i6ALbJmMw_M
p.115, 'all the elements... withstand the microphone... buildable...': Catherine Santino and \ Brittany Talarico, 'Sabrina Carpenter's Glam Squad Reveals the Secrets Behind Her '60s Bombshell Beauty' Routine (Exclusive)', *People*, 23 April 2025, https://people.com/sabrina-carpenter-glam-squad-reveals-her-60s-bombshell-beauty-routine-11719099?utm_source=-chatgpt.com

p.115, 'watercolored, sensual ... a vixen eye...': Abby Aguirre, 'How the World Fell...' (see above)

pp.116, 'it's so romantic in @pacorabanne', sabrinacarpenter on Instagram, 4 July 2022, https://www.instagram.com/p/CfmDqpkuP4K/?hl=en

Short, Sweet and Sitting at the Top

p.121, 'sabrina carpenter has...': Pop Base on X, https://x.com/PopBase/status/1796591837622444512

p.121, 'when I say I hate...': Sabrina Carpenter All-News on X, https://x.com/SCANews_/status/1796752920802623635

p.121, 'this project is quite special...': sabrina carpenter on Instagram, 3 June 2024, https://www.instagram.com/p/C7wtSb1Reh1/

p.122, 'roller skating with a disco ball...': Jem Aswad, 'How Sabrina Carpenter's "Please Please Please" and Two Other Songs Were Written in One Day', *Variety*, https://variety.com/2024/music/news/how-sabrina-carpenter-please-please-please-written-in-one-day-1236235829/

p.122, 'fraction... obviously based...': Lily Ford, 'Sabrina Carpenter Makes Surprise Appearance on "BBC Maestro" to Talk Songwriting (Exclusive)', *The Hollywood Reporter*, 9 December 2024, https://www.hollywoodreporter.com/news/music-news/sabrina-carpenter-bbc-maestro-please-please-please-album-1236078533/

p.122, 'interesting and invigorating...': Madeleine Frank Reeves, 'I Am Pleased...' (see above)

p.123, He was also behind her surprise birthday...: Charlotte Phillipp and Gillian Telling, 'Sabrina Carpenter's Boyfriend Barry Keoghan Threw Her a 25th Birthday Party Featuring a Leonardo DiCaprio-Inspired Cake', *People*, 13 May 2024, https://people.com/sabrina-carpenter-boyfriend-barry-keoghan-threw-her-25th-birthday-party-8647281
p.123, she told *Variety* that Barry...: Thania Garcia, 'Summer of Sabrina Carpenter...' (see above)

p.123, 'this bitch': Sabrina Carpenter on X, https://x.com/SabrinaAnnLynn/status/1807501567245140294?lang=en

p.128, 'vertically challenged': 'Sabrina Carpenter: Short n' Sweet, Songwriting & "Espresso"', Apple

Music on YouTube, 22 August 2024, https://www.youtube.com/watch?v=enaGNnGB99I

p.128, 'I feel extremely lucky...': sabrinacarpenter on Instagram, 23 August 2024, https://www.instagram.com/sabrinacarpenter/p/C-_5PKBtz-BC/?img_index=1

p.128, 'I will write any song...': Erica Campbell, 'Sabrina Carpenter, Superstar' (see above)

p.130, 'I get why people are interested...': Lynn Hirschberg, 'Sabrina Carpenter Knows...' (see above)

p.130, 'unresolved feelings...': 'How's Life with John Mayer - Shawn Mendes FULL INTERVIEW', John Mayer France on YouTube, 16 December 2024, https://www.youtube.com/watch?v=1X-03eLKBI3U

p.135, 'horniest': Carl Wilson, 'Sabrina Carpenter, Poet Laureate of Sex', Slate, 23 August 2024, https://slate.com/culture/2024/08/sabrina-carpenter-short-n-sweet-album-review-lyrics.html

p.135, 'raunchiest': Jack Irvin, 'What Is the Meaning Behind Sabrina Carpenter's 'Juno' Positions on Her Short n' Sweet Tour? Everything to Know', *People*, 20 November 2024, https://people.com/sabrina-carpenter-juno-positions-short-n-sweet-tour-explained-8748888

p.135, 'i'm 17 and AFRAID...': ru on X, https://x.com/ruthblxney/status/1845856438-507192716?lang=en

p.135, 'sexy and lighthearted': Erica Campbell, 'Sabrina Carpenter, Superstar' (see above)

p.136, 'I don't know how that's...': sabrina carpenter on Instagram, 8 November 2024, https://www.instagram.com/p/DCIlyB-JShAU/?utm_source=ig_embed&ig_rid=-c4ee7268-ce18-4bc5-a2fa-3b692820b29f

Sabina's Global Impact

p.141, 'Hello, I'm still out of breath...': Alyssa Bailey, 'Why Sabrina Carpenter's Best Pop Vocal Album Speech Got Censored at the 2025 Grammys', *Elle*, 3 February 2025, https://www.elle.com/culture/celebrities/a63564838/sabrina-carpenter-speech-transcript-grammys-2025/
p.142, 'as a thank you ... Short n' Sweet deluxe ... She wouldn't want...': sabrinacarpenter on Instagram, 4 February 2025, https://www.instagram.com/p/DFqJHZGvT0k/?hl=en

p.144, 'sad I couldn't include it': sabrinacarpenter on Instagram, 29 August 2024, https://www.instagram.com/p/C_RE3oVy6of/

p.144, 'punchy, thirsty and funny as hell': Samantha Leach, 'Sabrina Carpenter Just Performed "Busy Woman" for the First Time', *Nylon*, 1 October 2024, https://www.nylon.com/entertainment/sabrina-carpenter-barclays-busy-woman

p.144, as Antonoff shared...: Jem Aswad, 'How Sabrina Carpenter's "Please Please Please"...' (see above)

p.144, 'I told her, I said...': Damian Jones, 'Dolly Parton laid down some rules to Sabrina Carpenter...', *NME*, 20 March 2025, https://www.nme.com/news/music/dolly-parton-laid-down-some-rules-to-sabrina-carpenter-over-please-please-please-collaboration-i-dont-say-dirty-words-on-camera-3848001

p.144, 'Turns out, two things...': dollyparton on Instagram, 14 February 2025, https://www.instagram.com/reel/DGCm49dsuMI/?hl=en

p.145, 'That was the most inspiring thing...': 'The 25th Anniversary of Christina Aguilera | Spotify Anniversaries LIVE', Christina Aguilera on YouTube, 23 September 2024, https://www.youtube.com/watch?v=mgR7n6vwwvU

p.145, 'for coming out last night... I adore you to the end!': sabrinacarpenter on Instagram, 16 November 2024, https://www.instagram.com/sabrinacarpenter/reel/DCcWxlRy5lh/?locale=it_IT&hl=af

p.145, 'You're kind of, like...': Ilana Kaplan, 'Sabrina Carpenter Arrests Spice Girls' Emma Bunton at London Concert...', *People*, 10 March 2025, https://people.com/sabrina-carpenter-arrests-spice-girls-emma-bunton-london-concert-11694382

p.146, According to the *Daily Mail*...: Laura Parkin, 'Sabrina Carpenter sparks yet MORE Ofcom complaints as BRIT Awards performance draws in almost 1,000 responses from angry viewers', *Daily Mail*, 12 March 2025, https://www.dailymail.co.uk/tvshowbiz/article-14491109/Sabrina-Carpenter-Ofcom-complaints-BRIT-Awards.html

p.146, 'I now know what...': sabrinacarpenter on Instagram, 2 March 2025, https://www.instagram.com/p/DGtGcLyPJM3/?hl=en

p.146, 'the shit out of "Espresso"...primarily tea-drinking': Flisadam Pointer, 'Sabrina Carpenter Thanked UK Fans For Understanding Her "Dry Humor" During 2025 BRIT Awards' Global Success Speech', Uproxx, 1 March 2025, https://uproxx.com/pop/sabrina-carpenter-2025-brit-awards-speech/

First published in Great Britain in 2025
by Greenfinch
An imprint of Quercus
Part of John Murray Group

A CIP catalogue record for this book is available from the British Library

HB ISBN 978-1-52944-752-1
EBOOK ISBN 978-1-52944-753-8

10 9 8 7 6 5 4 3 2 1

Design and Illustration by Beth Free,
Studio Nic + Lou

Printed and bound in Italy by L.E.G.O. S.p.A.

Papers used by Quercus are from well-managed forests and other responsible sources.

Quercus
Carmelite House
50 Victoria Embankment
London EC4Y 0DZ

John Murray Group
Part of Hodder & Stoughton Limited
An Hachette UK company

The authorised representative in the EEA is Hachette Ireland, 8 Castlecourt Centre, Dublin 15, D15 XTP3, Ireland (email: info@hbgi.ie)

THANK YOU

To my devoted parents, stunning sisters, talented nephew, Yorkie Maddox, amazing friends, the stand-up guy who helped me manage my brain while writing this book, TikTok manifestation gurus, and busy women everywhere – raising an espresso in your honor! Thank you.

Erica Campbell is an entertainment journalist and music writer with a sharp eye for pop culture and a soft spot for a good hook. She's currently the Music Editor at *PAPER* magazine and formerly the US Features Editor at *NME*. Her bylines span publications like *SPIN*, *Glamour* and *W Magazine* and her pop culture reporting focuses on spotlighting the rise of stars like Sabrina Carpenter.
She's hosted red-carpet chats and on-camera interviews with Grammy and Oscar winners, led Spotify panels, and shared her music expertise on NPR, USA Today, and SiriusXM.

PHOTOGRAPHIC CREDITS

pp.2, 124–5, 140 Jojo Korsh/BFA.com/Shutterstock; pp.4, 13 above right, 23 below, 32–3, 63 above, 63 below, 66, 94–5, 110 above, 111, 142–3, 151 Associated Press/Alamy Stock Photo; pp.8-9, 10 WENN Rights Ltd/Alamy Stock Photo; p.13 above left Jim Smeal/Shutterstock; pp.13 below, 30, 35 Everett Collection Inc./Alamy Stock Photo; pp.16, 27 The Photo Access/Alamy Stock Photo; p.19 Erik Pendzich/Shutterstock; p.20 AFF/Alamy Stock Photo; pp.23 above left, 82, 89, 100–1 ZUMA Press, Inc./Alamy Stock Photo; pp.23 above right, 86 UPI/Alamy Stock Photo; p.25 John Angelillo/UPI/Shutterstock; p.37 Bryan Bedder/Getty Images; pp.39, 117 MediaPunch Inc./Alamy Stock Photo; p.41 Jeff Kravitz/Getty Images; pp.44, 47 Steve Jennings/Getty Images; pp.48–9 Roberto Ricciuti/Getty Images; p.50 Roy Rochlin/Getty Images; p.54 Jason Kempin/Getty Images; pp.57, 60–1, 110 below Sipa US/Alamy Stock Photo; p.59 Broadimage/Shutterstock; p.62 Kristina Bumphrey/Shutterstock; p.69 Hector Vivas/TAS23/Getty Images; pp.70–1 Slaven Vlasic/Getty Images; p.73 John Shearer/Getty Images; p.75 Ashok Kumar/TAS24/Getty Images; pp.76–7, 109, 131, 132, 134 Kevin Mazur/Getty Images; pp.78, 79 below TAS2024/Getty Images; p.79 above Don Arnold/TAS24/Getty Images; pp.85, 92 PA Images/Alamy Stock Photo; p.91 C Flanigan/imageSPACE/Shutterstock; pp.98, 113 Image Press Agency/Alamy Stock Photo; p.102 NurPhoto SRL/Alamy Stock Photo; pp.104–5 Doug Peters/Alamy Stock Photo; p.107 Marc Piasecki/Getty Images; p.114 Matt Baron/BEI/Shutterstock; pp.120, 129, 133 above, 133 below, 137 Christopher Polk/Getty Images; pp.126–7 Barry King/Alamy Stock Photo; p.147 Entertainment Pictures/Alamy Stock Photo; p.148 James Veysey/Shutterstock; p.148 above NEIL HALL/EPA-EFE/Shutterstock; p.149 below Matt Crossick/Alamy Stock Photo

SABRINA
CARPENTER
SABRINA
CARPENTER
SABRINA